CONTOURS OF SOCIAL AND ECONOMIC DEVELOPMENT

About the Editor

Dr. P.V. Shenoi, IAS (Retd.) is the Director, Institute for Social and Economic Change, Bangalore, since 1993. The Institute conducts policy research and advises Government of India and State Governments. During 1990-93 he was Assistant Director-General of International Crops Research Institute for the Semi-Arid Tropics (ICRISAT) in charge of Inter-Governmental Relations, transfer of technology and administrative matters. Earlier, Dr. Shenoi was Special Secretary, Ministry of Agriculture (1985-90) with responsibilities for policy formulation for agricultural development as well as Secretary to the Government of West Bengal, 1973-85 and Commonwealth Advisor to the Government of Papua, New Guinea, (1977-80).

He has done six consultancies for the World Bank and UNDP and was recipient of Norman Borlaug Award in 1990 for "outstanding services to Indian Agriculture".

I.S.E.C. Silver Jubilee Commemoration Volume – 1972-97

CONTOURS OF SOCIAL AND ECONOMIC DEVELOPMENT
Policy Issues

Editor

DR. P.V. SHENOI, *IAS* (Retd.)

Director
Institute for Social and Economic Change
Nagarbhavi P.O., Bangalore - 560072

Published for

INSTITUTE FOR SOCIAL AND ECONOMIC CHANGE
BANGALORE

By

CONCEPT PUBLISHING COMPANY, NEW DELHI - 110059

ISBN 81-7022-630-9

First Published 1997

Dr. P.V. **Shenoi** (*b.* 1935)

Published and Printed by
Ashok Kumar Mittal
Concept Publishing Company
A/15-16, Commercial Block,
Mohan Garden,
NEW DELHI - 110059 (India)
Phones: 5554042, 5504042
Fax No. 091-11-5598898

PREFACE

A quarter of a century is an important milestone in the life of a social science research institution like the Institute for Social and Economic Change (ISEC), to pause and review its contribution to its stake holders: the policy and academic community, and eventually the economy, society and polity of India. This volume seeks to present a retrospective of ISEC's research contributions over the last twenty-five years. ISEC was brought into existence on 20 January 1972 under the signatures of eminent social scientists and policy formulators from all parts of India like Prof. Drs. V.K.R.V. Rao, Sukhamoy Chakravarty, A.M. Khusro, J.P. Naik, H. Narasimhaiah, I.G. Patel, G.V.K. Rao, M.N. Srinivas and others, with the Governor of Karnataka as its ex-officio President. ISEC Society has provided in its constitution that its membership would be restricted to 225 distinguished persons. It is privileged to count amongst its founder and life members a number of luminaries in the fields of social and natural sciences, law, education, business, public service, etc.

Professor V.K.R.V. Rao shaped the mandate and agenda of ISEC in its initial years as its Founder-Chairman-cum-Director. The name chosen by him for the Institute was itself significant. While accepting that theoretical work formed the basis of research, Prof Rao envisioned that it must also be related to the rich research potential offered by the changes taking place in the economy, polity and society in India. As he said in 1976 when ISEC's campus was inaugurated by the President of India: "The main thrust of the Institute is an attempt at integrating and understanding the social and economic changes in our country, assessing our programmes of social and economic development and evolving of its policies and programmes for increasing mass welfare and the quality of life, especially in our rural areas". Thus, in programming its activities, ISEC maintained a healthy blend of field-oriented empirical research strongly rooted in theory, in a wide range of ten disciplines: Economics, Sociology, Rural Economics, Ecology Economics, Quantitative Analysis, Monetary Economics, Agricultural Economics, Population Studies, Education and Development Administration.

Over the course of these twenty-five years, ISEC has grown to be a significant centre of policy research and education, with a faculty of over 45. Eighty-one research scholars have received doctoral degrees from six Universities on the basis of research conducted at ISEC; and 29 more are on the rolls in October 1996. Its faculty has published 194 books since 1972; and many have been appointed Members in the Planning Commission, Union and State Finance Commissions, State Planning Board and other policy making bodies.

By its constitution, ISEC is an All India Institution; and over the years, many multi-State studies have been carried out. A sizeable number of its faculty and doctoral scholars came from outside Karnataka. At the same time, ISEC has always realised that it has a special obligation to Karnataka in which it is located and from the Government of which State it has received consistent and very generous support. Because of logistical convenience, there has been a tendency for a high proportion of research studies to focus on Karnataka. ISEC has responded positively to requests from the State authorities for research support on policy issues as well as in the post-implementation and concurrent evaluation of development projects. The Union Ministries of Health and Family Welfare and of Agriculture as well as Reserve Bank of India have also supported special Units in ISEC to carry out research in their priority areas.

Fourteen papers in this volume, written by the members of ISEC faculty, sum up the bulk of socio-economic research carried out at ISEC over the quarter century. They have sought to illuminate their respective areas and highlighted the policy alternatives suggested for bringing about desirable changes in our society, economy and polity. In the following paragraphs, are highlighted the more important aspects investigated by the respective researchers and their conclusions.

Following the General Theory of John Maynard Keynes since 1936, several works have appeared dealing with various macro economic problems, like determination of the levels of aggregate income, output, employment, price, consumption, savings and their interrelationship and supply of money. During the same period, one of the important macro economic policy tools, namely fiscal policy, consisting of government revenue, expenditure and deficit financing, gained a lot of importance. Fiscal policy was recognised as critical for influencing directly the level of output, savings, investment, consumption and the general price level. In her paper *"Macro-economic Perspective: Policy Tools"* Professor Hemlata Rao highlights how these macro economic policy tools along with the analysis of national income received the attention of the researchers in ISEC. Notable among these are the works of Professor V.K.R.V. Rao on national income analysis and those of Professors G. Thimmaiah and Hemlata Rao on fiscal policies relating to taxation, expenditure, public debt and deficits and federal finance.

Prof. V.K.R.V. Rao chose to make a long term study of India's national income during the post-independence period; and he used national accounts for an economic analysis of growth and change between 1950-51 and 1979-80. Several policy conclusions were drawn regarding the growth rate, sectoral composition of income, savings behaviour and so on.

The growth pattern and distribution of national income substantially depends upon the policies of the government. In a federal country, it is the fiscal policy of not only the federal government but also of the federating units that are important. Apart from the independent policies of the different layers of governments, as Professor Hemlata Rao points out, the interdependency of the different layers of government also plays a significant role in making macro economic policies. The federal fiscal transfers, the pattern of devolution, criteria for distribution *inter se*, the institutional arrangements for federal fiscal transfers and so on are important policy tools influencing the level of central and State government expenditures. Very significant contributions were made in these areas by I.S.E.C. faculty members. The devolution formula evolved by one of the scholars, in fact, influenced the thinking of the Seventh and the subsequent Finance Commissions on the scheme of devolution. The works on measuring taxable capacity, tax effort, fiscal potential of the States and the growing State loan burden, received the attention of the policy makers both at the central and the State levels in India. The fiscal need approach to federal fiscal transfers developed by the Institute received attention not only in India but in other federal countries like Canada and the US.

Thus, apart from national income analysis the focus of the research in the field of macroeconomics in the Institute has primarily been on federal fiscal policies including tax policy, expenditure policy, fiscal stabilisation, State finances and so on. Significant contributions have also been made in the field of measurement of backwardness, regional planning, inter-State variations in fiscal capacity and tax efforts, tax reforms and tax design and public debt analysis. Professor Hemlata Rao concludes by indicating areas taken up for further research: The impact of economic reforms on various sectors and macro economic variables.

In his paper *"Development and Environment"*, Professor M.V. Nadkarni highlights the contribution of I.S.E.C. in studying the degradation to which the environment is subjected to in the course of economic development and cites a number of research studies conducted at I.S.E.C. to find solutions. Environmental degradation may manifest itself in the form of negative externalities, side effects or depletion of the stock of natural resources. I.S.E.C. studies have sought to detect the signals of their occurrence and to interpret the economic factors behind them. Secondly, these studies have sought to highlight the need for a policy and programme of eco-restoration, eco-development and pollution control taking into account its costs and benefits so as to optimise the policy outcome and also to develop effective policy instruments.

India and many other Asian countries have achieved higher growth rates in their agricultures at the cost of increased instability. High population pressure on a fragile eco-system is often the cause of the instability. Neglect of soil health has aggravated instability. Studies in Karnataka have shown that watershed development has both reduced instability and increased yield. Successful planning of soil conservation in watersheds, however, depends much on effective community organisation and cooperation.

Green revolution technologies place unduly high stress on individual efforts and market inputs to the neglect of community efforts and natural resource conservation. A study showed that there was a tendency to utilise fertilisers beyond the optimal levels in irrigated areas, and much below the optimal in dry and rainfed areas, affecting yields and profits. Wrong economic incentives to use chemical fertiliser have played an important role in contributing to unsustainable agriculture and negative side-effects in the form of chemical pollution of water resources. Similarly, supplies of free electricity for irrigation led to wastage of both water and electricity.

A study carried out in hilly terrains of Kerala showed that costs of soil conservation were high; and returns were comparatively low in hilly areas. Farmers often did not invest on soil conservation measures because they lacked title to their lands. They had encroached these lands belonging to forest department. The study showed that cultivation in encroached lands in uphill areas is unsustainable.

Professor Nadkarni cites another study to show that terrace cultivation was not economical as an alternative to *jhum* cultivation. The study advocated agro-forestry in hill regions.

The ruminants are often considered a threat to the ecology of drought-prone areas; one study brought to light that these fears were highly exaggerated. It showed that ruminant economy complements crop husbandry in a synergic way in semi-arid zones.

It is paradoxical that in a land-hungry country like India, there is considerable amount of uncultivated land. That the extent of this land is declining is not necessarily a source of consolation unless they are brought under forests and managed properly to satisfy the bio-mass needs of the people. The unfortunate fact is that much of uncultivated land is under encroachment by richer people.

Professor Nadkarni finds that the amount of uncultivated land available for conversion into forests is therefore limited. If they can be developed as common property resources under social forestry projects, the bio-mass needs of the poor can be met. This calls for an institutional arrangement to involve the poor in the management of CPRs and to provide them with equal rights.

A study showed that the benefits from raising social forests in uncultivated lands outweigh its cost. This should not tempt the government to hand over uncultivated lands to private parties. Such a course will deprive the rural poor access to CPRs and also reduce bio-diversity. Social forestry projects under community management, on the other hand, can be designed to meet local needs of bio-mass and ensure bio-diversity.

A study of industrial units has indicated that the cost of pollution control was well within affordable limits for the concerned firms and had no adverse impact on profitability and employment. The excuse given by some industries for non-compliance with Pollution Control Act is that the cost of pollution abatement is prohibitive. The study has given the lie to this kind of excuse.

In a comparative study, it was found that Karnataka was spending 0.027 per cent of its State domestic product on pollution control; this shows the State in a favourable position compared to Netherlands which spends only 0.023 per cent of its net national product for similar purpose.

Rapid growth of population in urban places has caused tremendous strains on urban infrastructure particularly in the housing sector. The result is the mushrooming of slums in the cities. Slum dwellers are found indispensable for city as they provide cheap services and inexpensive goods. Instead of trying to eradicate slums, Professor Nadkarni pleads for efforts to improve the living conditions in slums by bringing the slums within the ambit of urban planning.

Development planning in India was first launched in the early 1950's with a view to maximising national/per capita output. It was hoped that growth in output would take care of the problems of poverty, unemployment and inequality. The development experience of the next two decades belied this hope, calling for a new approach and shift in emphasis from output maximisation to spatial and social equity. In the new approach man and not output was given the centre stage in development process. Professor Abdul Aziz and Dr Madhushree Sekher highlight the need for macro and micro planning and alleviation of poverty through employment generation in their paper *"Development and Planning: The Contours that I.S.E.C. has traversed"*.

There was a search for an indigenous growth model. In this context, I.S.E.C. brought out a volume on Gandhi's relevance to contemporary India. A sequential study made a distinction between Gandhi's economic system and Gandhian economic system and commended the latter as a guide to economic planning. The merit of these contributions was that they provided theoretical justification for reducing severe unemployment in developing countries. Other studies in the same strain argued that market forces often ignored social justice and social harmony; they pleaded for special efforts to meet the basic minimum needs of every citizen.

With the Panchayat Raj Institutions becoming a *fait accompli* with the 73rd and 74th constitutional amendments, decentralised governance and decentralised planning at village panchayat, taluk panchayat and zilla panchayat levels have become inevitable. The planning must commence from grass-roots and progress upwards. Various contributions of I.S.E.C. faculty resulted in better methodologies for area planning at disaggregated levels. A supportive training system to service the needs of civil servants and elected representatives involved in managing decentralised governance, had been built in the Institute. The faculty have carried out several research studies on various aspects of decentralised governance and planning. Notable among them is the 'Tumkur Project' resulting in a number of monographs which addressed the various methodological and substantive issues relating to operationally feasible methods of delineating village clusters, blocks and regions as well as institutional innovations needed to make area plan implementation more effective. Considerable attention was also given to the efficient dovetailing of micro plans with macro plan.

Professor Aziz and Dr. Madhushree Sekher point out another area of concern—planning for the weaker sections. In these studies, the focus was on employment generation and on empowering the poor for sharing the benefits of development. Alleviation of poverty by reallocating economic resources in favour of the weaker sections as well as improving their marketable skills received attention. In this context, evaluation studies of government programmes such as IRDP, TRYSEM and RLEGP were undertaken at the Institute.

Professor Aziz and Dr. Madhushree Sekher indicate the contribution made by I.S.E.C. to planning at State level in three ways: (1) preparation of perspective plans; (2) providing critiques every now and then on plan approach, priorities and project implementation and (3) direct participation in plan formulation, with I.S.E.C. faculty members associating themselves with State Planning Department in various capacities.

Mr. M. Vivekananda in his paper on *"Policy for Agricultural Development in Karnataka"* begins with analysis of the performance of new agricultural technology and the associated inputs like irrigation, chemical fertilisers, and institutional support for credit, agricultural prices and marketing. Then he takes up the issues of farm size, productivity and development of small and marginal farmers. Since a major part of cropped area is still under rainfed agriculture, the issues pertaining to dry land agriculture are presented next. This is followed by a brief account of the recent exercise by the Planning Commission on agro-climatic regional planning. The State has varied agro-climatic regions and any attempt to plan for agriculture has to take note of these regional variations. Then he analyses the crop yields achieved in the State vis-a-vis the neighbouring States to identify the yield gaps in the State. This is followed by a discussion on the stagnation in agricultural production in Karnataka during 80's and the corrective measures initiated by the Karnataka Government. The paper concludes by highlighting the prospects for agricultural development in Karnataka.

Some of the policy thrust areas for the agricultural development of the State recommended by I.S.E.C. have been highlighted by Mr. Vivekananda.

— There is no need for the State to strive for self sufficiency in cereals at any cost. Instead, it should go all-out for the crops in which it can achieve higher productivity levels through research and extension.
— The production growth in the State would depend upon higher and stabler productivity levels in rainfed crops. This calls for serious efforts in the direction of retaining soil moisture with appropriate cost effective technology and also efforts to harness the run off water through watershed development programmes.
— To strengthen the agricultural credit system, the State Government has to infuse funds to the order of Rs. 500 crores into cooperative credit institutions. There is a need to rationalise the presently subsidised interest rates as subsidy system has led to distortions,

corruption and destruction of the rural credit market.

— The subsidies by the Government to farmers in various forms viz., supply of electricity, fertiliser and other inputs at concessional rates should be phased out over the years; and the resources saved should be used for the efficient maintenance of power system and for higher investment in agricultural infrastructure and better extension services.

Further, to achieve a sustained higher level of production, it is essential to strengthen and expand the existing marketing institutions at various levels for ensuring assured supply of agricultural inputs and for providing outlets for the produce.

Mr. Vivekananda calls for a big push for the agriculture sector in the State particularly by developing appropriate technologies for climatic zones of the State, and its adoption as well as rationalization of supporting systems.

Professor M. Prahladachar identifies five areas of research undertaken in I.S.E.C. on the strategies for industrialisation at the national and State levels in his paper on *"Industrial Policy and Development"*: public sector undertakings, regional dispersal of industries, rural industries, specific sectors, and other issues/aspects. These are reviewed in the following paragraphs.

Constraints peculiar to public enterprises which had a bearing on their performance were identified. Apart from organisational and personnel management aspects, attention was drawn to several other aspects of management like project planning, working capital and inventory management, sales promotion, marketing management and quality control.

In order to reach expected or desired level of regional dispersal of industries, promotion of rural industries was advocated as a good strategy. For this to happen, infrastructural facilities which act as a catalyst, had to be strengthened and improved across the regions. It was heartening to know that conscious efforts and initiative by the government were forthcoming to build up, nurse and tap the potential entrepreneurship, more so of a local origin and that the entrepreneurial base had become diversified in its composition.

A necessary condition for the existence and growth of rural industries as well as other small scale industries is the efficiency factor. This is all the more imperative when a strategic role is assigned to the rural industries in the development process. It is in this background that a study on relative efficiency of small scale industries was envisaged.

This study indicated that, in general, at all-India level, the small scale industries used less capital per worker than the large scale industries. Relative labour productivity was less than one in almost all the industry groups at all-India level implying that the output per worker was less in small scale industries than in large scale industries. The capital productivity of small scale industries was greater than that of their large scale counterparts. In general, small scale industries were less efficient than large scale industries.

A study was undertaken to examine the growth, structure and organisation of food processing industries in the Punjab. These industries seemed to have helped the rural sector by providing a market for their produce and certain other linkages like employment and investment opportunities in transport, trade and other sectors. However, the growth of food processing industries did not reflect adequate involvement of the rural community in it. Further, the integration of agricultural trade with processing led to no improvement in the share of the producer in the consumer's rupee, which perhaps could be attributed to the form of organisation of food processing units. Therefore, if the food processing industry were to play the role of a catalyst for rural development, it had to be organised in such a manner that rural community could participate in investment, if not in jobs.

The study on electronics industry sought to understand the constraints and problems faced by the Electronics Industry in the country in general and in Karnataka in particular. It is no gainsaying that among all the sub-sectors of the Electronics industry, the components sub-sector constitutes the vital link; and therefore, the nature of development in this sub-sector determines the development of other sub-sectors. Indigenous manufacture of components (which are presently being imported) may help bring down the cost of manufacturing and also the price of the final product, thus rendering our industry competitive in the world market. Access to components is often determining the location, pace and direction of manufacturing in the other sub-sectors.

An attempt was also made to analyse the growth characteristics of employment in the manufacturing sector in Karnataka across industries and across districts. It is crucial to recognise that the objective of employment generation *per-se* will not be realised, more so on a sustainable basis, unless it is backed up by optimal policies and facilities in several areas : factor prices, market, finance, etc. which make the industrial units economically and technologically viable.

A study was undertaken on industrial potential in Karnataka, to understand and analyse the State's industrial growth pattern across industries and regions as well as to examine various parameters: finance, resources, infrastructure and policy that contributed towards the process. The study came out with several recommendations to help improve the industrial status of Karnataka in the near future.

To sum up, the studies in the areas of industrial policy and development undertaken so far in the Institute mostly relate to Karnataka and to the scenario prior to the new economic reforms. The new economic reforms have imparted different focus, thrust, approach and policy prescriptions. The Institute is undertaking studies examining the impact of new economic reforms on industrial development to ensure the goals of growth, efficiency and equity.

In the paper *"Educational Policy and Developmental Research"*, Professor A.S. Seetharamu reviews the fifty-three studies made at ISEC including research projects, evaluation studies, consultancy reports and doctoral theses. With the exception of 5 studies, all other contributions came from the Education Unit.

There are two types of studies. One type of studies are related to policies, plann ng, strategies, issues and problems at various levels of education. Most of these studies are in the areas of primary education as well as adult and non-formal education/literacy programmes. There are also contributions in the areas of pre-primary education, secondary education, teacher education, higher education and special education.

Another type of studies have looked at the relationship between Education as both a determinant and an intervening variable in the overall development process. The abiding concerns reflected in these studies are: education for all; issues of non-enumeration, non-enrolment, drop-out behaviour, low attainment levels and quality of primary education; promotion of equity and social justice through education; reduction of regional disparities; relation between social stratification and education; gender disparities; performance of education sector in the context of development strategies; etc.

According to Professor Seetharamu, the studies in education at ISEC show that education easily integrates with other symbols of power, wealth and status in the given inegalitarian Indian society, thereby impressing upon the need for the spread, access and entitlement of education in the interests of equality, social justice and human freedom.

In his paper *"Health and Development in India: Trends and Prospects"* Dr Ramesh Kanbargi underlines the fact that improvements in health is a major instrument for overall social and economic development.

ISEC studies have revealed that India has made rapid strides in controlling mortality. Life expectancy and survival chances for children have improved considerably. As a result, incidence of widowhood and destitution of children have declined. The children of today have better opportunities for social mobility than the children of earlier decades. But a daunting challenge to health providers in the coming decades would be in the area of providing geriatric health care for an ageing population and in combating the sexually transmitted diseases more specifically AIDS.

Big gains in longevity have come from eradication and control of infectious diseases like small pox, plague and malaria and to some extent from breakthrough made in curative medicines. There is not much evidence to suggest that the general health of the people has improved. People may live longer yet suffer from ill-health. Health is intrinsically linked with nutrition, environmental sanitation, availability of safe drinking water and the condition of health care delivery system.

Research studies of health programmes have shown that much of the resources allocated for health sector went to meet the salaries of health personnel and very little is left for buying drugs or for keeping the medical equipments in good repair. The poor particularly those living in villages who depend on government sector for their health care needs are very much disillusioned. One of the ISEC studies therefore addressed itself to find the feasibility of health insurance scheme for rural population in Karnataka. Another study looked into the question of financing and pricing of health services in India.

The Government is now contemplating the expansion of the scope of 'Maternal and Child Health' programmes under a new package of 'Reproductive and Child Health Services'. ISEC faculty foresaw such development and carried out studies which went beyond the narrow confines of 'Maternal and Child Health Programme'. For example, a few studies were conducted on issues surrounding abortion. Abortion was legalised in the country in 1971; and since then abortion services are provided on demand in select hospitals. Studies show that women from upper classes were able to take advantage these facilities to a much greater extent than those from lower classes. Requests from poor and illiterate women for abortion services were often turned down on grounds that were inconsistent with the provisions of the 'Medical Termination of Pregnancy Act'.

The nutritional status of the people will improve only when there is adequate production and equitable distribution of food. Cereal consumption has improved thanks to substantial increase in foodgrain production that the country has achieved. The author finds that there is virtual stagnation in the production of pulses and oil seeds in the country and the per capita availability of pulses and oil has deteriorated over the years, causing much concern. As early as in 1980s, Prof. V.K.R.V. Rao noticed sectoral imbalance in the production structure of Indian agriculture and pleaded for reorientation of agricultural policy. He was against allowing the market forces to determine cropping pattern. He wanted priority to be given to crops which will meet the nutritional requirements of a balanced diet for Indian people. The public distribution system was established in the country to help the poor to improve their food consumption; and an ISEC study showed that the public distribution was plagued by organisational and management problems.

Improvement in environmental sanitation will reduce the incidence of diseases and make programmes of nutrition more effective. Diseases like cholera, typhoid and diarrhoea afflict millions of people every year because water is not available in sufficient quantity or quality. An ISEC study estimated that potable water supply is available in only 15 to 38 per cent of the habitations in Karnataka. It would cause a big strain on the economic resources of the State government, to provide safe drinking water to the remaining habitations.

Dr. Kanbargi concludes by highlighting that life expectancy of the people had improved and certain infectious diseases which used to take a heavy toll of human lives, are on the retreat. All the same, it is difficult to say that Indian people enjoy better health now. Much remains to be done in the area of nutrition and environmental sanitation.

Dr. M. Venkata Reddy, in his paper on "*Irrigation and Development*" points out that I.S.E.C. studies tended to treat the irrigation project as parts of a social system affecting and in turn being affected by people and not as an autonomous technocratic system. If technological options are carefully evaluated and skilfully crafted on to the social system, it would accelerate and sustain economic development. Of necessity, the focus of the studies was always on contemporary problems.

Individuals, communities and nations have tried to increase agricultural output by developing irrigation systems suited to their particular environment, needs and resources. The differential impact of canal, well and tank irrigation has been assessed in one of the I.S.E.C. studies.

I.S.E.C. has carried out Bench Mark Surveys covering almost all irrigation projects in Cauvery and Krishna basins. The data collected through these surveys provide baseline for measuring changes in the socio-economic conditions of the people, consequent to introduction of irrigation in the project area. The survey helped in identifying potential growth centres and delineating their service areas and laid the foundations for area planning of the river basins.

Concurrent evaluation studies carried out in command areas of the irrigation dams helped in identifying social, economic and technical barriers to optimising irrigation benefits. There is invariably a gap between potential created and potential utilised. I.S.E.C. studies have pointed out that under-utilisation is due to the following reasons: (1) delay in taking up land development work particularly in the tail end area of the canal before the release of water in the canal, (2) short supply of bulldozers and tractors to carry out earth digging and levelling operations; (3) lack of timely supply of institutional credit; and (4) failure to update land records. These findings have helped in formulating remedial measures.

Action research studies have brought to light the mismatch between theoretically well-conceived and designed irrigation distribution strategies and ground realities. Farmers at the head-works area go for water intensive crops depriving the farmers at tail end areas of water for their crops. As a solution, farmers participation in irrigation management has been advocated.

Problem specific studies have documented adverse effect of irrigation on the environment in the form of water logging, salination of the soil, higher incidence of water borne diseases etc. These studies have noted that most farmers are ignorant about sound water management practices. Lack of scientific on-farm development programmes, absence of drainage, poor maintenance of existing drainage canals have all added to environmental problems in irrigated areas. The studies have offered guidelines for rehabilitating the affected areas, and designing eco-friendly irrigation technologies.

Dr. Reddy concludes that I.S.E.C. studies have sought to optimise the benefits from irrigation projects in Karnataka.

Prof. H.G. Hanumappa in his paper on *"Issues in Rural Development"* deals with ISEC studies which have shed a great deal of light on living conditions in rural areas. Studies focused on rural housing revealed that a majority of rural houses have only mud walls and thatch roofs. Even houses built with brick and mortar lack essential amenities like separate toilets, kitchen and so on; thus they are no better than the mud houses. This apart, there is sizeable houseless population. This is baffling when there is a surfeit of vacant houses in villages. It appears that the houseless families are so steeped in poverty that they cannot pay the price of housing as determined by market forces. Another area of concern is drinking water. Bore-well pumps often breakdown and the authorities take their own time to fix them. It is suggested that the responsibility of maintaining bore-well pumps must rest with the local community. Rural energy demand outstrips the supply resulting in denudation of forests and exhaustion of non-renewable resources. One study suggested some alternative resources which can be harnessed to bridge the gap between demand and supply of energy.

Prof. Hanumappa cites studies on regional variations in the impact of land reform measures undertaken in the State of Karnataka. To help the landless rural poor, the studies suggested that they should be given preferential access to common property resources.

The Agro -Climatic Regional Planning (ACRP) approach is a landmark in the planning for agricultural development at sub-national level. The whole country has been divided into fifteen agro-climatic zones which have been further categorised on the basis of homogeneity in climate, soil, water and other resource endowments. At the instance of the Planning Commission, the Institute has prepared an inventory of resources for one of the agro-climatic zones. The main task is to institutionalise agro-climatic regional planning in tune with the existing administrative framework. The Institute is presently engaged in preparing district level agricultural plans.

A large scale survey carried out by the Institute in Tumkur district brought to light glaring inter-village disparities in the levels of development and persistent inequality among different social groups within the village itself. Prof. Hanumappa points out that the structural rigidities imposed by existing institutions resulted in the failure of trickle-down process.

Rural development programmes and anti-poverty programmes have been critically evaluated in many of the studies. By and large, the programmes have succeeded in providing relief and creating economic opportunities to the target groups. But the programme impact on the existing structure and production relationship leaves much to be desired. One perceptive observation emerging from these studies is that as long as there is growth at macro level, the rural elite would not mind accommodating the aspirations of the poor. But any attempt for change at village level, in the absence of economic growth at macro level would only sharpen the conflict between factions and groups within the village.

Prof. Hanumappa observes that the I.R.D.P. schemes, in particular, do not have much to offer for the agricultural labourers. They have mostly benefited the non-poor groups; and the traditional bureaucracy is incapable of delivering the goods. New strategies have got to be hammered out. There is a need to evolve a regulatory system of administration and decentralised system of NGOs and to ensure better coordination between the two.

Dr. M. Johnson Samuel in his paper on *"Urbanisation and Urban Development"* observes that the growth rate of urban population during the census decade 1981-91 has slowed down as compared to earlier decades. Given the large size of the base upon which such growth rates are calculated, the actual numbers involved in urban growth are still extremely large. The number of metropolitan cities (population size, million plus) in the country have increased from 12 in 1981 to 23 in 1991. The percentage share of class I cities (population size, 1 lakh plus) to total urban population has increased from 60 per cent in 1981 to 65 per cent in 1991. On the other hand, the smaller towns pertaining to class IV, V and VI (population size 20 thousand or less) are on the decline. Schemes such as 'Integrated Development of Small and Medium Towns' have not borne much results. This must cause concern as the smaller towns have an important role to play as 'market towns' sending growth impulses into India's vast countryside.

The rapid growth of larger cities has resulted in a number of serious problems. These include extreme pressure on urban infrastructure and civic services, persistence of poverty, congestion, pollution as well as other forms of environmental degradation and significant shortfalls in the provision of housing for urban residents. Various schemes are implemented such as ban on location of new industries within city limits, increasing the size of housing stock, infrastructure development and so on. According to Dr. Samuel, these schemes have not been able to stem the rot. The studies underline the need to reorient the development programmes in such a way to ensure balanced growth of different size categories of urban places and to improve the living conditions in cities.

In his paper *"Research on Employment and Labour"*, Prof. Hanumantha Rayappa highlights the central role played by the labour force in the growth of an economy as the supplier of the most important input in production. One of the ISEC studies was concerned with the methodology of estimating employment potential of individual plan schemes in Karnataka. The study demonstrated that there are considerable variations among individual schemes in creating new jobs both on site and off-site. Even a single scheme varies in its employment potential from phase to phase. The volume and type of labour required during construction phase is vastly different from what is required during operation and maintenance phase of the same scheme. While planning for employment generation, the study argued, that these variations must be kept in mind.

Other studies focused on the deployment of labour in different sectors of the economy. Agricultural sector, particularly its labour absorbing capacity was tested in different situations. The consensus emerging from the studies was that even a successful agricultural development strategy can only partially absorb the growing rural labour force; and jobs for the redundant labour would have to be found outside agriculture. In the short run, expansion of area under cultivation, increasing the intensity of cropping, shift in cropping patterns, adoption of labour intensive technologies such as seed - water - fertilizer technology, linking agriculture with allied activities like dairying, speedy implementation of land reforms can generate some additional employment in agricultural sector, the studies pointed out.

According to one study, forests can become a source of livelihood and employment for the local people only after the local people are allowed to have a stake in forest development and management. Another study came to the conclusion that land devoted to sericulture generate more employment and higher income in comparison with land devoted to any other crops.

Prof. Hanumantha Rayappa proceeds to analyse studies on the special characteristics of the labour force. It is usually believed that people have more children because children contribute to family kitty from a very young age. A survey done in rural areas of Karnataka exploded this myth. There was no significant relationship between children's participation in work and their parent's fertility. Child labour, however, affected school attendance in the study area. A characteristic feature of child labour is its concentration in a few select industries. In Karnataka, sericulture is such an industry. Here children constitute more than 25 per cent of the labour force. Most parents send their children to work because of the compulsions of poverty.

Child workers are often deployed for doing dull and repetitive operations in the work place. This has a debilitating effect on their physical and mental development. Above all, children are deprived of joys of childhood and opportunities for education. The study pleaded for stricter enforcement of laws regulating child labour particularly, in hazardous occupations.

Workers among the elderly were found to be more common in rural than in urban areas. One reason would be that the old people in urban areas have some savings or pension to eke out a living. But the more important reason is that urban labour market, is very restrictive of the elderly. In rural areas, the elderly often look to their children for support in the evening of their lives. The skills and experience of the senior citizens can be used productively and the Government should address this issue in a serious manner.

Professor Hanumantha Rayappa cites studies focusing on women which found that women workers suffered more frequent and longer spells of unemployment. Mechanisation of agriculture has displaced mostly women from labour force. The study stressed that every new project, before it is cleared for implementation, must be critically assessed for its possible pernicious effect on female work opportunities.

There was also a need for organising the rural labour in order to secure a better deal for them. It was difficult to organise agricultural labourers along conventional Trade Union lines. The conventional trade unions are preoccupied with struggle for better wages and neglect creation of employment opportunities. As an alternative, it was argued, that Rural Labour Co-operatives can be set up by mobilising the agricultural workers. The co-operatives cannot only bargain with employer farmers for higher wages and better working conditions but also help generate new work opportunities for themselves. Rural labour badly need a comprehensive social security legislation, the study pointed out.

Evaluation studies of RLEGP and TRYSEM programmes have identified the deficiencies in programme implementation and offered useful solutions to overcome them. The studies recommended that these two employment oriented schemes must continue until the economy is geared to provide sufflcient income or full employment to the rural households.

Professor N. Baskara Rao and Dr. K.N.M. Raju in their paper on "*Population, Health and Family Planning*" cites ISEC studies that have striven continually for new insights in the field of population policy and programmes. The studies have used a large body of data both secondary (census) and primary (sample surveys) to present existing situation succinctly and to lay out priority areas of action for the coming years. The studies that focused on Karnataka have discerned encouraging trends: decline in mortality and child deaths, rise in age at marriage, increase in contraceptive use and in recent years slow but steady decline in fertility as well. The studies have also highlighted several areas of concern—the wide gap between desired family size and actual family size implying considerable amount of unwanted fertility, the increase in couple protection rate without commensurate decline in fertility. The reasons behind these inconsistencies are complex—unfavourable socio-economic factors and organisational and motivational deficiencies in the official family planning programme.

The studies have provided many significant insights. There is still a large unmet need for family planning particularly for spacing methods. This calls for diversification of contraceptive services in order to attract young and low parity couples. If the unmet need is satisfied, as a study estimates, the current level of contraceptive use in Karnataka can go up from 49 to 67 per cent among couples in the reproductive age group. A woman's natal family bears the brunt of providing maternal and child health care, at least for the first two births. Natal family, therefore, influences a woman's fertility decision to a greater extent than her conjugal family.

Prof. Baskara Rao and Dr. Raju see certain hopeful signs emerging from the studies: despite persistent poverty, illiteracy and malnutrition, a perceptible decline in fertility has occurred in several regions of the country including Karnataka. The credit for this is given to National Family Planning Programme—the manner in which it was administered in certain regions. This prompted the ISEC's Population Research Centre to take up a region-specific study in an effort to identify factors that facilitated programme implementation. A study conducted in Mandya district—a success story in Karnataka—suggested that social homogeneity of the population, extreme population pressure on agricultural lands and better transport facilities have all contributed to the success of birth control measures in the district, despite relatively low literacy level obtaining in the district.

A number of health schemes have been devised and implemented; and a substantive part of PRC's research efforts have gone into evaluating these schemes—Integrated Child Development Scheme, Village Health Guide Scheme, Multipurpose Health Worker Scheme, Universal Immunisation programme to name a few. Poor training of grass-root workers, apathy of community leaders, short supply of drugs are often found to be the bane of the schemes. The need to integrate these schemes with population control programmes has often been felt. The studies have come up with new ideas on how to produce synergism between health and family planning.

The population projections for Karnataka prepared by the Institute are extensively used in planning exercises of the State Government. Methodological studies have sought to improve the accuracy in estimating life expectancy, mortality levels, incidence of widowhood, magnitude of widow remarriages, mean age at marriage etc. in the face of inadequacies in the available data. Another study evolved a simple procedure which can be used as a rule of thumb by local officials for setting target for family planning for smaller administrative units.

One study estimated that the cost of preventing one birth varied between Rs. 50 and Rs. 100 at 1961-62 prices. In a related study, the unit cost of performing a sterilisation operation in hospitals was compared with the unit cost of performing it in mass camps. Though mass camp provides sterilisation relatively cheaply, it entails loss of quality in terms of pre and post operative care.

National Family Health Survey (1992-93) has generated a large volume of demographic data for the first time, urban and rural areas separately for 25 States and union territories in the country. The PRC has helped in gathering a wealth of data on nuptiality, fertility, family size preferences, knowledge and practice of family planning, potential demand for contraception, unwanted fertility, utilisation of antenatal services, breast feeding and weaning practices, child nutrition, immunisation, child health, infant and child mortality and so forth.

Prof. M.R. Narayana in his paper on *"Economic Modelling for Policy Decisions"* has provided a coherent review of the research studies in which economic modelling/ theorisation has been explicit for supporting policy decisions. In particular, he has focused on technical details in regard to (i) the formulation of the models and their main analytical results; and (ii) the nature and extent of applied/ empirical research which have been based on these models and their policy implications. An overview of nature and types of economic modelling and economic modelling for empirical and policy purposes have been given as the background material.

Prof. Narayana has identified five important areas of economic modelling for policy decisions (i) modelling India's macroeconomic development; (ii) modelling India's inter-regional allocation of resources; (iii) modelling India's foreign trade; (iv) modelling India's economic fertility; and (v) modelling India's economic reforms. In order to make the review comprehensive he has covered all the studies which are available in the form of research reports (i.e. in published and unpublished forms) and journal articles up to April 1996.

Prof. Narayana's review shows the diversity of the models for different empirical applications and policy uses. Further, it underlines that there exists a vast scope and potential for empirical and policy studies in future based on economic modelling.

As an applied social science research institution, ISEC has to make a judicious combination of theory and application in all systematic research. This was the vision of Professor V.K.R.V. Rao as well. Professor Narayana shows that the vision of Professor Rao has been a guiding spirit behind economic modelling for policy decisions in the Institute.

Prof. G.S. Aurora and Dr. T.V. Sekher in their paper on "*Voluntary Organisation and Social Science Research*" highlight the processes whereby applied social science research helps to assess the role and potential of the voluntary organisations in socio-economic development. They cite the studies conducted in the Institute in this area.

Their introductory section gives a brief account of the dominant patterns of organisation and articulation of concerns of the voluntary sector institutions in the context of the relationship between research and grassroots action. For the Voluntary Organisation (VO) sector, the level of idealism has remained fairly high and this has made most VOs to seek policy level reflections from the academic community. There is a greater interaction between the VOs and the research institution now than ever before. At the same time, the VOs are also becoming increasingly involved in research activities.

First, their paper refers to Dr. V.K.R.V. Rao's paper of 1973 where he discussed the importance of the role of voluntary sector in development as well as to Srinivas and Aurora's paper "From Structural Adjustment to Structural Change". The authors systematically discuss the studies conducted by the Institute on rural development, greening India, common property land resources, group lending in NGO credit programmes, self-employment programme for rural youth, reproductive health, and on sericulture and finally on the major on-going study funded by HIVOS—a Dutch organisation.

All these studies indicate the evolving pattern of the ISEC's involvement in the applied area of social concern. These studies not only have close linkages with the action agencies but also serve as a focal point for policy level thinking and assist in training grassroot functionaries.

Prof. Aurora and Dr. Sekher consider it a positive development that a large number of students of Ph D have chosen to work on the broad area of NGOs and Development.

Twenty-five years is a short period in the life of science, but a long one in the lives of people. The world, and along with it India, and Karnataka, have witnessed mammoth changes in this quarter century. The basic philosophy relating to the roles of the State and private enterprises in socio-economic development has undergone a tremendous metamorphosis, with the demise of the Soviet empire and with the rise of

China and Eastern "tigers". Dr Mahbub ul-Haq has established that human welfare can very well be the centre of socio-economic development, with 'right roles' assigned to the State and the private enterprise.

India took a U-turn to economic liberalisation in 1991 and joined a number of other developing countries in downgrading the role of the State as an entrepreneur, though a couple of decades too late according to some scholars. GATT agreement signed in 1993 has accelerated the globalization of developing economies. India and Karnataka are in the process of coping with these mammoth changes in the socio-economic philosophy and in the ground roles flowing therefrom. ISEC has undertaken a study on "Policy Research and Voluntary Action" to read the socio-economic changes of 4000 families in twenty villages. The seventy-third and seventy-fourth amendments to the Constitution seek to transfer much power from the State to the local bodies for grass-root development. ISEC is involved in training the Panchayat Members and in making a concurrent evaluation of their contributions to local development.

ISEC faculty is thus involved in the exciting mission of analysing the implications of the new paradigm shifts, holding field investigations on its impact and developing policy alternatives for the future. There is a welcome realization in the policy and academic community that research Institutes like ISEC can contribute more than ever before to accelerate socio-economic changes towards a more equitable and prosperous life for every one.

P.V. SHENOI

ACKNOWLEDGEMENT

While preparing this volume on *"Contours of Social and Economic Development — Policy Issues"* of research contributions by the Institute during nearly a quarter of century, I recall our debt of gratitude to several individuals and organisations.

In the first place, I must recall with gratitude our indebtedness to the Founder Chairman and Founder-Director of the Institute, Professor V.K.R.V. Rao, who envisioned the thrust areas of research activity for the Institute. The successor chairmen of Board of Governors and the Directors have pursued these guidelines. The present Chairman, Mr. Justice E.S. Venkataramaiah has been a constant source of help and encouragement in all of our academic activities in the Institute. Of course, the Board of Governors have always supported various research efforts of the Institute since its inception. To all of them, I owe a debt of gratitude.

There are several organisations which have provided the required financial and other support in order to carry out the research activities to their logical end. In particular, the Government of Karnataka, Indian Council of Social Science Research (ICSSR), New Delhi, Union Ministry of Agriculture, Union Ministry of Health and Family Welfare and Reserve Bank of India (RBI) have continuously supported our research efforts by providing regular grants to the Institute. In addition, several national and international organisations have come forward to sponsor research projects through which additional studies were undertaken. I thank them all for generously sponsoring research projects in the Institute.

It is the faculty of the Institute who have contributed to research activities on a continuous basis on various themes of local, national and international importance. The variety of research themes that have been addressed in this volume bears testimony to this fact. In particular, I must thank all the contributors to this volume who undertook the onerous responsibility of distilling the material contained in several publications and manuscripts and of presenting them in an organised manner. I acknowledge their labours with appreciation and gratitude.

The earlier drafts of the papers were carefully edited for their content, language and style of presentation. In this effort, Professor P. Hanumantha Rayappa made valuable contributions, supported by Dr. M. Johnson Samuel and Mr. V.S. Parthasarathy who went through the earlier drafts carefully and made the necessary changes before sending it to the press. The typing burden of the manuscript was shared by Mr. M.K. Mohan Kumar, Mr. N. Boopathi and Mr. T. Amarnath who laboured hard to put together the volume in its present form. In addition, the members of the library staff, technical staff of the Institute and some of the administrative staff have all co-operated in different ways in putting together this volume. I place on record my appreciation for their efforts.

Finally, I owe a special thanks to M/s Concept Publishing Company, New Delhi, for bringing out this volume at extremely short time.

P.V. SHENOI

CONTENTS

LIST OF CONTRIBUTORS*

ABDUL AZIZ, Professor, Economics Unit.

A.S. SEETHARAMU, Professor, Education Unit.

G.S. AURORA, Formerly Professor, Sociology Unit.

HEMLATA RAO, Professor, Economics Unit.

H.G. HANUMAPPA, Professor, Agricultural Development and Rural Transformation Unit.

K.N.M. RAJU, Associate Professor, Population Research Centre.

MADHUSHREE SEKHER, Assistant Director, Decentralisation: Training and Research Project.

M. JOHNSON SAMUEL, Associate Professor, Population Research Centre.

M. PRAHLADACHAR, Professor, Rural Economics Unit.

M.R. NARAYANA, Professor, Quantitative Economics Unit.

M. VENKATA REDDY, Associate Professor, Ecology Economics Unit.

M. VIVEKANANDA, Assistant Professor, Agricultural Development and Rural Transformation Unit.

M.V. NADKARNI, Professor, Ecology Economics Unit.

N. BASKARA RAO, Formerly Professor, Population Research Centre.

P. HANUMANTHA RAYAPPA, Professor, Population Research Centre.

RAMESH KANBARGI, Associate Professor, Population Research Centre.

T.V. SEKHER, Research Officer, Policy Research and Voluntary Action Project.

---

* The Contributors are drawn from the constituent Units of the Institute for Social and Economic Change, Bangalore-560 072

PART ONE

MACRO-POLICY ISSUES

1

MACRO-ECONOMIC PERSPECTIVE
Policy Tools

HEMLATA RAO

Introduction

Macro-economics received great impetus from the publication of John Maynard Keynes's *The General Theory of Employment, Interest and Money* in 1936. Following General Theory, several works appeared dealing with various macro-economic problems, like determination of the levels of aggregate income, output, employment, price, consumption, savings and their interrelationship, and supply of money. The study of national Income, its determinants, trend, growth and distribution received lot of importance in the literature on macro economics. The two important macro-economic policy tools are the monetary and the fiscal policies. Between the two, the fiscal policy consisting of government revenue, expenditure and deficit financing policies was recognised as important for influencing directly the level of output, savings, investment, consumption and the general price level. These macro-economic policy tools, along with the national income, received the attention of the researchers in ISEC.

National Income Analysis

Compared with the other branches of economics, the study of national income is comparatively new. From a practical viewpoint, it dates from the publication in 1936 of John Maynard Keynes's book on General Theory. However, the subject had received the attention of Professor V.K.R.V. Rao as early as in 1925-29 itself, when he published his book on *Essays in India's National Income*. In this book, he dealt with the history of previous estimates of India's national income. After a gap of forty years, Professor Rao chose to make a long term study of India's national income during the post-independence period and he used the national accounts for an economic analysis of growth and change between 1950-51 and 1979-80.

Based on a comparison of the four cost of living indices, Professor Rao concluded that, taking the period as a whole, they all have a similar upward trend, but there are variations in their comparative degree of rise. It has brought out that:

(i) the national cost of living index was uniformly higher than that of urban non-manual workers, indicating that the price effect of inflationary development was more unfavourable to the upper and upper middle classes than to the lower middle classes;

(ii) it was also uniformly higher than the cost of living index of industrial workers during the earlier part of the period (1960-61 to 1969-70). This trend was reversed during the latter half of the period, indicating that the better-off sections of society suffered a larger price effect during the second half of the period than industrial workers; but they fared better than the agricultural labourers throughout the period;

(iii) within the three specified classes, urban non-manual workers who were identified with the lower middle class experienced a lower measure of the price effect than industrial workers and a much lower effect than agricultural labourers; and

(iv) the most affected were the agricultural labourers whose cost of living index was uniformly higher than that of either industrial workers or non-manual urban workers or the national cost of living index, except during the last two years of the period.

Broadly speaking, therefore, it was the working classes, both rural and urban, who suffered most from the price effect on their cost of living.

The changes in the structure of the Indian economy during the thirty-year period have been many. There has been a significant change in the structure of the economy, with the primary sector's share in the Net Domestic Product (NDP) at constant prices falling in each of the three sub-periods covered by the years 1950-51 to 1979-80, while that of the tertiary sector has risen during all the sub-periods, and that of the secondary sector has fallen marginally in the first sub-period and risen in the second and third sub-periods.

Over the period as a whole, the Indian economy became less geared to the primary sector and its dominant component—agriculture—and more attuned to the secondary and tertiary sectors. This may be regarded from the developmental point of view as a progressive change in the structure of the Indian economy during this period. If this becomes a trend that continues over the coming decades, India may reach a more balanced occupational structure between agriculture and non-agriculture by the end of the century. It may also lead to a narrowing of the difference in the income per worker in agriculture that would be more in line with the rise in the NDP.

In spite of the rapid growth of organised sector, the unorganised sector still continues to dominate the Indian economy with two-thirds of the NDP, which is not entirely due to the agricultural sector. The public sector has nearly doubled its share of the NDP at constant prices during this period, and now accounts for one-fifth of the economy. It may be added that a major portion of the increase in the NDP share of the public sector is due to government enterprises, both departmental and non-departmental, which represent commodity production and marketed services. However, the private sector still continues to dominate the Indian economy, claiming nearly 80 per cent of the NDP at the end of the period, and this is not wholly due to the role of agriculture.

Aggregate savings are drawn from three sources—the public sector, the private corporate sector, and the household sector. Of the total savings, household savings accounts for 76.26 per cent. The public sector accounts for 19.31 per cent of the total savings during the period and has declined marginally. The corporate sector's share is relatively small. As a proportion of the NDP, however, both household and public sector savings have shown a more or less steady increase over the different quinquennial periods. The performance of the corporate sector has been disappointing as far as its contribution to raising the Indian savings rate is concerned.

The largest contributor tc savings has been the household sector. The savings behaviour of the household sector seems to suggest several explanations in addition to that of a savings income lag. It is possible that the period has seen a redistribution of money income in favour of savers. Money redistribution is also in favour of the high income groups whose marginal propensity to save is much higher irrespective of whether they regard the increase in income permanent or transitory. Financial assets are mostly held by the affluent and an increase in household savings in the form of financial assets may be another indication of the increase in money income favouring this class. All these possible explanations seem consistent with the observed phenomena, and can give a reasonable explanation of the secular increase that has taken place in the average rate of household savings along with the existence of a large proportion of the population below the poverty line in both rural and urban areas.

Capital is considered to be the crucial factor in determining economic growth, even though it is recognised that income generation also depends on natural resources, human skills and organisational efficiency. There is an increasing difference in the rates of growth of the Gross Domestic Capital Formation (GDCF) over successive five-year periods at current and constant prices. The ever increasing expenditure which the economy has been incurring and the continuous rise in the rate of growth of the GDCF over successive five-year periods in the last two decades has been accompanied by a progressively smaller increase in real capital formation. Inflation has brought down the rate of growth in the country's real capital formation. Altogether, the progress in capital formation has not produced satisfactory results for either economic or human welfare.

There has not been much improvement in the operational management of the Indian economy or any considerable increase in national productivity in terms of either land, labour, capital or management, which could have been expected from the investments made or the resources created; or the scientific, technological, or managerial, or other relevant developmental skills built over the last thirty years of planning; or the significant increase in the role of government and the public sector after independence in the country's economic development. It is held that the major problem areas in the Indian economy are productivity and economic management. It is not simply an increase in output that affects national development but also the cost that accompanies the growth in output and the extent to which the potential created is converted into output.

Creating productivity consciousness and working for an increase in productivity, (whether of land, labour, capital or management), or of individual enterprises, (whether public or private, incorporated or household), are major factors affecting economic growth with minimum costs and maximum returns, and the conversion of production potential into actual output. It is the establishment of this mutually reinforcing link between growth and productivity that makes for an increase in the rate of growth or the achievement of a high rate of economic growth.

Economic Policy

The growth pattern and distribution of National income in fact, depends upon the policies of the government. In a federal country, it is not only the fiscal policy of the federal government but also the fiscal policies of the federating units that are important. Apart from the independent policies of the different layers of government, the interdependency of the different layers of government also plays a significant role in making macro-economic policies. The federal fiscal transfers, the pattern of devolution, criteria for distribution *inter se*, the institutional arrangements for federal fiscal transfers and so on are important policy tools influencing the level of central and State government expenditure.

Issues pertaining to Federal[1] Fiscal Transfers are of perennial interest. The issues assume special importance in India, where we have multiple channels of federal fiscal transfers, such as, the Finance Commission, the Planning Commission and the various ministries. In recent years, the issue of fiscal adjustments has become highly politicised with the States mounting a joint attack on the centre for its dominant financial position and demanding a rearrangement of the Centre-State financial relations that will free them from their current dependence on the Centre. Thus, the magnitude of federal fiscal transfers, the manner in which they are determined and the channels through which these resources are transferred are very important issues pertaining to vertical fiscal imbalance which figure in the current national debate. Equally important are the problems pertaining to the relative magnitude of the federal fiscal transfers to individual States, which are based on the recommendations of both the Finance Commission and the Planning Commission. The principles, criteria and their application, thus, form another important set of issues pertaining to horizontal imbalances.

Fiscal Relations and Economic Growth in General

There are four main factors that influence directly the performance of an economy (Gandhi, 1985). They are:

(i) resource allocation and its micro-economic efficiency;
(ii) the degree of macro-economic stability that is achieved;
(iii) the equitable nature and fairness of the fiscal system of an economy; and
(iv) the degree to which the growth potential, conditioned by these

first-three factors, is actually achieved.

Fiscal interrelations can negatively affect growth through each of the following four factors. First, the differential tax rates, the scope of the tax and various incentives and exemptions offered by different federating States as well as the federal government can encourage a significant migration of the resources of either labour or capital between States and local areas. This, in turn, may arise if the fiscal system resulted in wide differentials in the taxable capacities of different locations, as well as in their access to grants, subsidies, and other transfers (Narayana, 1991) from higher levels of government (Rao, 1981). The same problem may also be associated with a situation in which provinces and localities were assigned expenditure responsibilities, the benefits of which spilled over beyond their own geographical jurisdictions to result in expenditure levels considerably in excess of available revenues (Thimmaiah, 1968).

Second, the achievement of macro-economic stability can be problematic if the central government is not given the responsibility for those categories of public expenditures that can be adjusted reasonably quickly through the course of the business cycle. Similarly, the Central Government's responsibility for macro-economic stability might be more difficult to achieve if the provincial and local governments were given the right to borrow on their own account or to run up large arrears. This is not to say that such borrowing should not be permitted—only that the possible consequences and the need for some controls should be well understood.

Third, the equity in the fiscal system may be greatly impaired if redistributive taxes (the personal income tax, wealth and inheritance taxes) and redistributive expenditures (social welfare expenditures) are assigned too heavily to sub-national governments rather than to the central government.

Fourthly, growth prospects may be impaired if provincial and local governments are assigned the responsibility for taxes on those essential raw materials and natural resources that happened to be located in their geographical locations, and if they also seek to levy excessively high tax rates on such resources. The burden of these rates would then be exported to manufacturing industries in other regions (Gandhi, 1985).

These problems give rise to, first, Vertical Fiscal Imbalances resulting from the lack of clarity about the matching up of the expenditure responsibilities of the different levels of government with their corresponding tax assignments plus shared taxes, and second, "horizontal imbalances" — imbalances between the fiscal positions of different governments at the same level (for example, local or provincial) .

Third, the important price subsidies for foodgrains, cooking oil, meat, and other essential consumer goods continue to be administered and controlled by the governments at the sub-national level, may give rise to budgetary problems for at least some sub-national governments.

Finally, a more serious problem that is felt is the absence of any real scientific basis for assessing the expenditure needs of the local administrations[2]. This assessment is done at present by incremental adjustment to a base-year allocation, which itself was not scientifically established.

A related issue of concern is that some of the tax revenue sharing arrangements, including the new arrangements for VAT sharing, which are *ad hoc* and that very little serious effort has been made to link these sharing arrangements to any assessment of the taxable capacity of different provincial and local governments, or to their expenditure responsibilities (Rao, 1993).

The distribution of a given level of public resources between different levels of government can affect an economy's performance for lack of a good fiscal policy. Several studies were undertaken by Thimmaiah and Hemlata Rao to suggest the ways in which intergovernmental fiscal relations can influence:

(i) the efficiency with which public resources can be mobilised and utilised;
(ii) the degree to which macro-economic stabilisation can be attained;
(iii) the extent to which fiscal equity can be achieved; and
(iv) the feasibility that a high level of overall performance of the economy can be continued.

Intergovernmental fiscal arrangements are a necessary requirement of decentralised government administration, particularly in a large country. At least, five, generally interrelated parameters define these arrangements.

1. *Expenditure Responsibilities*
   What level of government (central, provincial, or local) will be responsible for which public expenditures and which public services? The answer is often the result of historical, constitutional, and social developments in the country (Rao, 1994).

2. *Tax Assignments*
   What level of government (central, provincial, or local) will have

the right to levy, collect, and retain which categories of taxes, and what will the method of their collections and administration be? This, too, is frequently the consequence of historical, constitutional, and other factors (Rao, 1994).

3. *Fiscal Imbalances, if any*
Given their established expenditure responsibilities and tax assignments, and varying cost structures of public services (due to demographic factors and urbanisation) and taxable capacities (due to resource endowments and degree of industrial development), different levels of government can end up with either fiscal surpluses or fiscal deficits, implying "vertical" and/or "horizontal" imbalances of varying degrees. How serious these imbalances are, can define the relative stability of intergovernmental fiscal arrangements (Thimmaiah and Rao, 1984).

4. *Availability of Financing Alternatives*
A State with fiscal deficits may have alternative sources of external finance. Among others, these can include transfers from other (usually higher) levels of government in the form of revenue sharing (fixed proportions of revenue yields of certain taxes), grants (specific purpose or general grants, tied or untied grants, matching or non-matching grants, conditional or unconditional grants, open-ended or closed grants), or subsidies (Thimmaiah and Rao, 1984). Financing their deficits through borrowing from banks, other financial institutions, the public at large, and even higher level governments are other alternatives, and these, too, may be subject to preconditions (Thimmaiah, 1977; 1985). Where none of these financing alternatives is available, the levels of government with fiscal deficits must either curtail their public expenditures and lower the levels of public services or raise additional revenues from their "own" tax bases and other non-tax sources.

5. *Institutional Parameters*
Finally, intergovernmental fiscal arrangements everywhere contain some elements that are strictly institutional. Examples of these include the degree of autonomy and independence that governments enjoy in planning for and administering the public expenditure responsibilities given to them, or levying or raising

taxes assigned to them without interference from or support of other levels of government; freedom to grant tax reliefs or expenditure subsidies with "own" resources to entice enterprises and business from other jurisdictions; rules of contracting and purchasing for the provision of public services from "own" revenues; and so on (Thimmaiah, 1981).

The various studies undertaken by Thimmaiah and Rao during the past twenty-five years in the field of Federal Finance illustrate how the allocation of functions, resources and the magnitude and pattern of federal fiscal transfers affect the efficient working of the federal system in India.

Federal State Financial Relations in India

There are various tools of federal fiscal transfers adopted in India. Some of the important tools are : revenue sharing by way of sharing of the net proceeds of income tax and union excise duties, tax-rental arrangement in the form of additional excise duties, assigned taxes, grants-in-aid of revenue to needy States and for specific purposes, unconditional block grants for plan purposes, matching grants, specific and conditional grants. Obviously, these various tools have different theoretical bases and economic rationale, their genesis is different and hence, the principles and criteria also vary. However, some of the tools have some similarities such as 'revenue sharing through income tax and union excise duties' (Rao, 1994). Here, except for some minor change in the wordings of the respective articles in the constitution, there is no difference in the nature, theoretical basis, economic rationale and objectives of these two types of taxes of "revenue sharing" nature. Similarly, unconditional block grants also become very close to "revenue sharing" or unconditional block grants. If the entire devolution scheme is guided by the principle of "fiscal need" perhaps, with slight modification, even the revenue-gap-grants may be made to aim at the objectives of 'unconditional grants' or revenue sharing.

Presently, the criteria adopted by different Finance Commissions and the Planning Commission vary from one type of transfer to the other even though some of the tools have common basis and common ends to achieve. On the contrary, in some cases though the nature and purpose of a particular tool are different, the criteria adopted are similar.

In the scheme of federal fiscal transfers much emphasis is given to the objective of equalization. While implementing the scheme of equalization special care is needed about the size of the States, their levels of prosperity/development and need. If large States happen to be the rich States and small States happen to be the poor States, inter-governmental transfers from rich to the poor, on the one hand, will be capable of satisfying the revenue requirement of the poorer States without putting undue strain on the richer States. On the other hand, the cost of being in a federation may be less than the gains of federation to larger States. At the same time, the smaller States may find it profitable to remain in the federation. On the contrary, if large States happen to be poor and backward while small States happen to be rich, adequate fiscal adjustments cannot take place. The small rich States will not have enough surplus to finance the large deficits of large poor States. In fact, any amount of resources transferred from the small State would be inadequate to meet the growing needs of the large poor States. Thus, the federal fiscal transfer mechanism may fail to satisfy the small rich States as well as the large poor States. Therefore, while effecting the principle of equalization the size factor has to be kept in mind (Rao, 1994).

Principles and Criteria and their Application

The basic question, which arises with respect to federal fiscal transfers, relates to the principles or basis of such transfers. The objectives of fiscal transfers depend upon the tools that are adopted to effect fiscal adjustments as these various tools differ in their nature and implications, and they have varied economic rationale.

One of the important problems with respect to tax sharing pertains to working out a generally accepted sharing formula and the determination of the criteria upon which the revenue shall be distributed among the subordinated units.

A Critical Appraisal of the Criteria of Devolution

Population Criterion

In any programme of devolution, it is important to take into account the differences in the needs of the States of various public services. The Finance Commissions have taken 'population' as a measure of 'general need'. Surprisingly, so far, no reference is made to the significance of population by any of the Finance Commissions. They did not even try to justify 'population' as a measure of general need. Besides, the population of 1971 is taken as a measure of need by all the Finance commissions. The logic put forth for this is, "we consider that promoting family welfare measures, including planned parenthood and small family norms, is a matter of paramount national importance. We are of the view that this desirable national objective should be accorded due recognitions and encouragement" (GOI, 1988). This, in fact, ignores the requirement of developing States where due to the expansion of economic activities and better conditions people migrate from other States and put heavy demand for socio-economic infrastructure. Population may also increase due to low mortality rate.

It does not mean that population should not appear at all in the distribution scheme. Population is also one of the determinants of State level expenditure and hence, has some relevance in assessing the programme needs of the States. There are certain items of expenditure which are directly related to the number of people residing in a region e.g., housing, sanitation, drinking water, health facilities, number of public transport vehicles providing police protection and others. Some weightage to population is desirable or at least population can be taken as a scale factor and all the determination of expenditure can be expressed in relation to population. Thus, implicitly but in a great way, population factor can be brought into the distribution formula. An alternative criteria has been suggested by Narayana (1992). He has developed a concept of Migration Adjusted Population Size (MAPS) .

Socio-Economic Backwardness

Inclusion of this criterion in the scheme of devolution by various Finance Commissions is a step in the right direction. However, an important issue that emerges in this respect relates to the question, how should socio-economic backwardness be measured or what should be the indicators of backwardness? The success of 'this criterion' depends solely upon the selection of indicators and measures adopted by the Finance Commission. Arbitrary indicators based on political consideration, biased views and irrational selection, could give a 'measure' which may defeat the very purpose of introducing the criterion of 'relative levels of development'. Unfortunately, in India this is what has happened. For example, there is no economic rationale in taking the SC/ST population or agricultural labourer as a measure of development. First of all, there is very high correlation between SC population and agricultural labourers. A large number of agricultural labourers belongs to SC/ST community. Secondly, the list of

SC communities may be shortened or lengthened by any Commission dealing with the question of scheduled castes and tribes.

To take SC/ST population and agricultural labourer as the sole index of backwardness is to accept that the State's expenditure responsibility is restricted only to the upliftment of these communities and nothing else. This is not true.

Apart from the above, some other criteria are also adopted such as per capita income, poverty ratio, income adjusted total population, distance of the average per capita income, revenue equalization and so on. But these also suffer, from various shortcomings (Rao, 1994).

Alternative Approach

The principle of "equalisation" is endorsed by a large number of economists and accepted by most of the federations. Even in India, various Finance Commissions have stressed upon the objective of "equalisation" in their scheme of devolution and grants-in-aid. Once we accept that the basic objective of federal fiscal transfers is "equalisation" and "incentive", then all the means of federal transfers, either in the form of revenue sharing or unconditional grants given either by the Finance Commission or the Planning Commission, should subserve the same goal. In fact, the various Finance Commissions and also the Planning Commissions have been imbued with the same objective. Under such circumstances, there should have been an integrated approach governing federal fiscal transfers in India (Rao, 1981). Quite contrary to this, there has been a host of heterogeneous criteria amounting to a different treatment of the federal problems by different commissions. A uniform approach adopted by different commissions would help bring certainty in the federal fiscal system besides help coordinate the various agencies handling federal fiscal transfers. The fiscal transfers should be guided by the criterion of fiscal need and incentives for tax efforts and economy in expenditure. Fiscal need can be assessed on the basis of the development levels (Rao, 1974 - see Ch. 4) and the relative fiscal capacity of the States. And, for providing incentive tax effort and relative expenditure can be arrived at (Rao, 1993). The three criteria together determine the eligibility of a State to receive federal grants and a share in the divisible pool.

Burden of Union Loans on the States

In India, the public debt has been growing enormously. Public authorities are no doubt realising the economic implications of the problems created by such a phenomenal growth of public debt—both internal and external. These problems have also roused the interest of economists as is evident from some studies made on the public debt of India.

It is generally believed that intergovernmental borrowing should also be used as a tool of federal fiscal policy for achieving certain objectives like raising public revenue, promoting economic development, reducing wide inter-State disparities in income, maintaining economic stability, etc. Though intergovernmental debt operations can be used to promote these objectives, they are inadequate when taken in isolation. However, in the context of the universal presence of vertical federal fiscal imbalance, intergovernmental debt operations become useful supporting tools when used along with other more effective federal fiscal transfers such as tax sharing and grants for achieving these multiple objectives.

The first consideration which should be examined in any theory of intergovernmental debt operations is: when should the State governments borrow from the national government and for what purpose?

In a developing country, the government can play two important roles in the field of economic development. First, by providing social and economic infrastructure facilities for rapid development of the country such as health, education, transport communications, banking, etc., and second, by acting as an entrepreneur by undertaking investment programmes in various fields of economic activity mostly in production activities. It would be ideal if the State governments borrow from the market for the purpose of undertaking investments in production activities which yield direct monetary returns. However, it may not be possible for the State governments, particularly the backward States, to obtain adequate funds from the market and therefore, they may have to depend upon Union loans. For the purpose of undertaking investments in social and economic infrastructure facilities which are essential for promoting socio-economic development, the State governments' dependence on Union loans becomes inevitable as they may not be able to undertake these investments with their own normal budgetary revenues. In such cases the State governments can resort to borrowing from the Union government on easy terms. These two specific justifications for the Union loans to the States are consistent with the general theory of public debt.

The next consideration is to examine the source from which the Union government should lend loans to the State governments. Supposing the Union government experiences enormous revenue surplus from its own normal revenues, then it should not use it for giving loans to the State governments as that would amount to commercial nature of relation between two layers of governments which are intended to serve the same country and people. When the Union government is unable to meet its own legitimate expenditure obligations with the receipts from its own non-loan revenue sources, but still is required to financially assist the States, then the Union government should borrow from either the public or from the financial institutions for assisting the State governments in the form of loans. This method would also create a healthy psychological condition in the minds of the State governments so that they will be able to repay the loans borrowed. Otherwise, if the revenue surplus of the Union government is used to give loans to the States, they may think that the amount is their rightful share in a cooperative federalism and consequently they may become complacent not only in regard to the use of the loan money but also they may become indifferent in regard to servicing and repayment of such loans.

The magnitude of States' borrowing from the Union government has increased phenomenally during the last 23 years. It may be noted that the magnitude of States' borrowing increased only after the introduction of economic planning under which the States have been assisted by the Union government, largely in the form of loans for the plan purposes. Thus, the gross as well as net loans have been increasing in absolute terms whereas their relative importance has been gradually declining both in the capital budgets of States and in the total resources transferred from the Union government to the States.

Major conclusions on the burden of union loans on the States are given below:

1. the income effect of the financial burden of interest charges is not significant and also it is declining;
2. the income effect of the financial burden of repayments is not only significant but also increasing;
3. the total income effect of the financial burden is increasing;
4. the substitution effect of the financial burden of Union loans has been unfavourable to the financial independence and stability of the State governments;
5. the allocation of economic burden of Union loans has been severe, particularly on the less developed and newly created States;
6. the economic development burden of Union loans has been increasing on less developed and newly created States; and
7. the distribution of burden of Union loans is also showing a

similar trend.

These conclusions suggest that any attempt to find solutions to the mounting burden of Union loans on the States should aim at reducing both financial and economic burden of Union loans.

Institutional Set-up

In India, federal fiscal transfers take place through statutory and non-statutory sources. While all transfers through the Finance Commission are statutory in nature, Plan transfers and grants through ministries are non-statutory. The multiplicity of grant giving agencies and the operation of economic planning within the framework of democratic federal fiscal set-up has created certain problems which have confronted not only the planners and the Planning Commission but also the Finance Commission. First of all, as in any other older federations, the functions of the States in India have been expanding thereby leading to the expansion of their expenditure as against a relatively slower expansion of expenditures of the central government. A major factor which has been responsible for this trend of State governments' expenditure in India has been economic planning which has been implemented mostly at the State level. Secondly, as against this expansion of State governments' expenditure, the revenues constitutionally assigned to them have proved inadequate. Though the problem of non-correspondence between the functions and revenues assigned to the States is common to all federations, it has been accentuated in India owing to certain reasons, (in addition to the impact of economic planning). An important reason has been the financial superiority of the central government which possesses many elastic sources of revenue.

Even the State governments have been assigned some elastic sources of revenue such as sales tax, State excise duties on liquors and motor vehicles tax. But, in many of these fields, there is overlapping of taxing powers of the centre and the States, particularly in the field of commodity taxation. The State governments' ability to exploit their elastic sources of revenue has been limited by the central government's superior position in administration and priority of taxation. Another reason for the inadequacy of State governments' revenues is that even after the introduction of the constitution in which both political and financial balances were tilted in favour of the central government, there has been a perceptible tendency towards centralization of States' taxing powers such as sales tax on mill made cotton textiles, woollen fabrics, rayon and artificial silk fabrics, sugar and tobacco and tax on railway fares. The operation of all these processes simultaneously has reduced the revenue potentiality of the States' sources of revenue, though their inability to tap the agricultural sector has also been responsible to some extent, for their inadequate revenues.

No doubt, the balancing federal fiscal transfers have been provided in the constitution in the form of tax shares and grants-in-aid to reduce any possible vertical federal fiscal imbalance. However, these balancing federal fiscal transfers have not been able to reduce the ever widening vertical federal fiscal imbalance. A fundamental reason for this tendency is that the framers of the constitution, though aware of the need for economic planning, did not specifically integrate it into the constitution and arrange the functions and sources of revenue between the centre and the States as also the balancing federal fiscal transfers in accordance with the requirements of economic planning. This major failure of the framers of the constitution compelled the leaders who initiated economic planning to adapt the federal fiscal set-up created in the constitution for the requirements of economic planning. But the extent of vertical federal fiscal imbalance, which was expected in the original constitution without reference to economic planning, widened enormously when economic planning was actually imposed on the superstructure of fiscal federalism. Hence, the original balancing federal fiscal transfers which were meant to reduce normal vertical federal fiscal imbalance that would ordinarily emerge in any federation, have become inadequate in the context of economic planning. The resultant additional vertical federal fiscal imbalance that has arisen on account of economic planning has come to be reduced by developing another balancing financial transfer in the form of plan grants under Article 282. But, these transfers are made at the discretion of the Parliament and on the advice of the Planning Commission, which has also been created outside the constitution. A major part of these plan grants has been made in the form of central loans creating interest burden as well as the burden of repayment. This entails further burden on the revenue as well as capital budgets of the States a part of which becomes the responsibility of the Finance Commission to take care of. It would be relevant to note here that had the financial provisions of the constitution been framed taking into account the requirements of economic planning, perhaps the extent of the vertical federal fiscal imbalance would have been less than what it is.

In the absence of any integration of economic planning and the financial provisions of the federal fiscal set-up, the implementation of economic planning and the accompanying economic policies during the last twenty-two years have not only accentuated the problems of vertical federal fiscal imbalance but also have changed the *de facto* nature of the original federal set-up of the country in its operation. This *de facto* change has come to be resented by the States and the *Report of the Rajamannar Committee* (appointed by the Tamil Nadu Government). The process of economic planning and the process of federal fiscal transfers, leaving aside other policies, have not only not been able to reduce the originally existed inter-State economic disparities and inter-State disparities in certain essential social services, but also, to an extent, have further widened them. This has been partly on account of the negligence of the Planning Commission and partly on account of the failure of the Finance Commission to formulate relevant approach and principles to discharge its responsibility.

In the theory of fiscal federalism, an independent expert body becomes necessary to reduce the vertical as well as horizontal federal fiscal imbalances, by estimating the net fiscal needs of the States. In India, no Finance Commission ever raised this point and the Fifth Finance Commission which mentioned the broad fiscal need of each State never recommended the financial devolution on the basis of 'net fiscal need' approach.

The consequences of the failure of the Finance Commissions to formulate a rational approach, in keeping with the theory and practice of federal fiscal transfers, have come to be wrongly attributed to the parallel operation of the Planning Commission in India. This method of scapegoating was started by the Finance Commissions and has been taken up by the antagonists of economic planning who have been advocating radical change in the structure and powers of the Planning Commission to convert the economy into an anarchy of *laissez faire* capitalism (Thimmaiah, 1973). The Planning Commission was no doubt created by a Government of India Resolution in 1950 to formulate economic planning for the entire country, to assess the available resources and to allocate them according to the priorities of the plan. Though the Planning Commission started functioning in 1951, it did not come in the way of the first Finance Commission in regard to the distribution of central assistance (both plan and non-plan) among the States.

Thus, the failure, on the part of the framers of the constitution, to integrate planning into federation compelled the planners to adapt the constitution to the needs of planning without destroying the federal structure. This led to the operation of two dissimilar institutional bodies to distribute resources among the States. This situation at one stage gave rise to the conflict of interests and overlapping of functions.

Tax Design and Tax Reforms

Apart from the federal fiscal policies, the tax policies and tax reforms also received the attention of the researchers. It is rightly felt that in spite of the fact that the practice of tax design and tax reform being several century old, they have not been properly conceptualized by experts in public finance. Even the recent attempts to suggest normative economic criteria for 'optimal' taxation have ignored the close logical as well as practical relation between tax design and tax reform (Thimmaiah, 1984). In these recent attempts, while the economists have gone on theorising on optimal tax design, tax laywers have concentrated their efforts mostly on tax reform. But, any useful exercise on tax reform should take into account both the theory and practice of tax design. Since both tax design and tax reform are concerned with practical aspect of the operation of the tax structure, they should be based on both theoretical foundations as well as on practical aspects involved in their actual operation.

Tax design is concerned with designing a tax or a tax structure *de novo*, whereas tax reform is concerned with adjusting an already existing tax or a tax structure to changed circumstances. Tax design includes:

(a) imposition of an altogether new tax;
(b) replacing an already existing tax by a new tax;
(c) abolishing an already existing tax to give a new appearance to the tax structure; and
(d) introducing a new tax base and/or new rate structure to the existing tax.

Tax reform includes introduction of changes in the existing tax base, tax rates, exemptions, concessions and the administrative procedures.

The merits and demerits of a tax/tax structure are examined and identified with reference to the major objectives which the tax/tax structure is supposed to achieve. These objectives are invariably the economic policy objectives or plan objectives of the government which are attempted to be achieved through the budget. While considering the rationality of tax design and tax reform, we examine them with reference to certain economic policy objectives of the government. These objective functions are with reference to the tax collecting social agent which is the government. Generally accepted objectives include promoting higher growth rate of national output, reducing wide inequalities of income and wealth, maintaining stability of the growth of output, prices and balance of payments which are supporting objectives for the first-two objectives. If, in the course of operation, a tax/tax structure is not found to be serving these objectives, then introducing required corrections into the tax design becomes necessary. This is the core of tax reform.

Tax reform may also be necessitated by: (a) changed socio-economic and political situations; and (b) changed objectives. Changes in the economic structure may call for certain changes in the tax structure to achieve the same objectives. Change in the government may require change in the priority of different objectives and/or addition of new objectives and hence, necessary required changes in tax structure become inevitable. Thus, tax design refers to creation of a tax structure, and tax reform refers to changes in the tax structure to adapt it to the changed situations and objectives.

It has been maintained by the economists that the following characteristics should be obtained in a tax structure as a whole in order to make it more effective for the purpose of achieving the economic policy objectives mentioned in the previous section. First, built-in-elasticity of revenue yield is to meet the evergrowing revenue needs of the government. Second, progressivity in rate structure so as to make the distribution of the tax share of individuals more equitable as also to reduce inequalities of income created by the market forces. Third, planned non-neutrality in the sense that absence of haphazard and random distortion of resource allocation including consumption, investment, saving, leisure, etc. And fourth, simplicity in administering the taxes so as to minimise both the cost of collection and the cost of tax compliance. These characteristics should be injected into each and every tax, if possible.

It may be observed that the average effective rates of only income tax have been progressive. Even in this, case the average effective rates had been distorted at the highest two slabs. Such distortion is found at all levels of income in the case of marginal effective rates of income tax. In the case of wealth tax, gifts tax, estate duty and capital gain tax, the progressivity is not consistent over the entire range of tax slabs. What is more the average effective rates become regressive at the highest two slabs of wealth tax. In the case of gift tax, there were no assessees in the slabs above Rs ˉ0,00,000. In the case of capital gains tax, both average and marginal tax rates have been distorted at many levels of tax slab. These distortions in the effective tax rates, particularly at higher tax slabs, imply that evasion of direct taxes has been high at higher levels of income and wealth. This suggests that even in terms of average-marginal effective rate progressivity the direct taxes have been either proportional or regressive in their incidence. Thus, both the summary measure of progressivity and the average-marginal effective rate progressivity indicate that except income tax, all other direct taxes in India have not been progressive enough to reduce inequalities of income and wealth.

After establishing the negligible equalising effect of direct-taxes in India, it is necessary to search for the reasons for inadequacy of progressivity. Three reasons may be given to explain this phenomenon:

(a) though the legal tax rates have been steeply progressive, the effective tax rates have been made lower owing to various exemptions, allowances and deductions. In other words, 'tax-expenditure' measures which are built-into the direct tax system have distorted the legal rate structure and made them either proportional or regressive in their actual operation;

(b) tax evasion seems to be evident as the average and marginal effective tax rates become lower at the higher levels of income and wealth; and

(c) the extent of tax avoidance under legal protection, and the ever increasing arrears of assessment and of collection do indicate that at the higher levels of income and wealth, people resort to legal remedies because of defective assessment and as a result, the actual tax liability becomes far less than the expected legal liability. Consequently, the originally designed tax loses its progressivity element over time, apart from the government losing the revenue. Thus, a combination of these factors have been operating in India which have made the direct taxes ineffective in their equalising effect.

Tax reform is supposed to set right any inconsistency between the prevailing design of tax structure and the policy objective of the government. Such inconsistency may be the result of the failure to design the tax structure appropriately or the result of changed circumstances which make old design of the tax structure out-of-date. Periodically, reforms are, therefore, necessary to adapt the tax structure designed in the past to the same objective in a changed socio-economic situation, or to serve changed objectives with the same socio-economic situation or both. For this purpose, recommendations for tax reform should be based on empirical findings of the actual effects of the existing tax structure and a thorough examination of the sources of inconsistency between the policy objectives and tax levers.

Indian tax structure which was designed by the British rulers mainly for raising revenue and remotely for reducing inequality of income, was found inadequate for meeting the challenges of planned development which was ushered in by the government sponsored Five-Year Plans.

Soon after, it was found that there was large scale evasion of income tax and as a result the objective of reducing inequalities of income and wealth required certain reforms in the direct tax structure. The Government of India invited Nicholas Kaldor to suggest ways and means of redesigning and adapting the direct tax structure for achieving the objective of reducing inequalities of income and wealth. He suggested an 'integrated direct tax structure', consisting of income tax (at a moderate rate), wealth tax, gifts tax, and expenditure tax. The Government of India accepted his recommendations and implemented them with a difference, i.e., as against the suggested moderate rates of income tax, the Government of India introduced high marginal rates of income tax, and also levied other direct taxes suggested by Kaldor.

Subsequently, the economic structure of the country changed so fast and became so much sophisticated that the other policies of the government started offsetting the effects of direct taxation in reducing inequalities of income. Further, there was a plethora of hurdles in tax laws and procedures. The Government of India, therefore, appointed a one-man Committee to examine these complications and to recommend measures for rationalisation and simplification of the structure of direct as well as indirect taxes. The Committee suggested bringing down of marginal rates to encourage honesty in reporting income for taxation which was implemented in 1975. But, the tax laws and procedures continued to grow further complicated. Therefore, the Direct Tax Laws Committee was appointed in June 1977 to suggest ways and means of simplifying direct tax laws and procedures, improving the administration of direct taxes and suggest a uniform Act by consolidating all the separate Acts relating to direct taxes. This Committee submitted its Interim Report in December 1977 and the Final Report in September 1978. But, the Government of India has not yet acted on the recommendations of this Committee except adopting some suggested procedures in an *ad hoc* manner.

However, by this time the relative importance of indirect taxes had increased and as a consequence, their adverse economic effects were felt all over the economy. The economic distortions created by indirect taxes were recognised only towards the end of Fifth Plan period.

Because of the multiplicity of tax rates, exemptions and administrative complications arising from the operation of the States' sales tax along with the union excise duty in India, a plea has been made for taking over the States' sales tax completely by the Central Government and replacing it by Union taxes. This suggestion has been dismissed not merely by the State governments as constitutionally untenable but also by the economists. There is also a suggestion to replace both union excise duties and sales tax by one value-added tax all over the country. This suggestion has been thoroughly examined by D.T. Lakadawala, who has come to the conclusion that it is not possible to achieve all the objectives which have been achieved through union excise duties and sales tax, by a single system of value-added tax all over the country. Therefore, India will have to live with the combined operation of union excise duties and sales tax.

To conclude, the focus of research in the field of macro-economics in the Institute has been mainly on federal fiscal issues. However, other macro-policy issues have also received good deal of attention. Significant contributions have been made in the field of National Income analysis, Criteria of Federal Fiscal transfers, Measurement of Backwardness, Inter-State variations in Fiscal capacity and Tax efforts, Tax reforms and Tax design, and Public Expenditure Analysis. The impact of economic reforms on various sectors and macro-economic variables are being taken up for further research.

NOTES

1. The terms federal, central, union, dominion and upper level government are used interchangeably and as synonymous. Similarly, federating, states, provinces and lower level government are also used interchangeably.
2. See, in this connection, Rao 1994 and various other research papers by her.

REFERENCES

Gandhi, V.P. (1985) Inter-governmental Fiscal Relations and Economic Performance. In Jasanta Roy (ed.), *Macro-economic Management and Fiscal Decentralisation*, EDI Seminar Series. Washington D.C.: The World Bank.

Government of India (GOI) (1988) *Ninth Finance Commission Report*. New Delhi: Govt. of India.

Narayana, M.R. (1991) Federal Interregional Fiscal Transfers Policies and Population Redistribution in Space. *Manpower Journal*, XXVII (2): 1-24.

Narayana, M.R. (1992) Criteria for Federal Interregional Fiscal Transfers in India : A New Base for Population factor in the Tenth Finance Commission. *Margin*, 25(1): 104-15.

Rao, Hemlata (1974) *Centre-State Financial Relations and the Problems of Financing*

Regional Development in India. Delhi: University of Delhi. Mimeo.

Rao, Hemlata (1981) *Centre-State Financial Relations in India*. New Delhi : Allied.

Rao, Hemlata (1993) *Measuring Taxable Capacity and Tax Efforts of Indian States*. A report submitted to the Tenth Finance Commission. Bangalore : ISEC. Mimeo.

Rao, Hemlata (1994) *Federal State Financial Relations in India*. New Delhi: Ashish.

Rao, V.K.R.V. (1983) *India's National Income 1950-80*. New Delhi: Sage.

Thimmaiah, G. (1968) *Centre State Financial Relations*. Mysore: Ganga Taranga.

Thimmaiah, G. (1973) *Studies in Federal Finance*. Bangalore: Padma Prakashan.

Thimmaiah, G. (1977) *Burden of Union Loans on the States*. New Delhi: Sterling.

Thimmaiah, G. (1981) *A Critique of the Finance Commission*. Allahabad: Wheeler Publication.

Thimmaiah, G. (1984) *Perspectives on Tax Design and Tax Reform*. New Delhi: Ashish.

Thimmaiah, G. (1985) *Burning Issues in Centre State Financial Relations*. New Delhi: Ashish.

Thimmaiah, G. and Hemlata Rao (1984) *Finance Commission and Centre State Financial Relations*. New Delhi: Ashish.

2

DEVELOPMENT AND ENVIRONMENT[1]

M.V. NADKARNI

Introduction

Development is a process that improves the quality of life of the bulk of people over a period of time. It has to be distinguished from the process of economic growth which refers mainly to an increase in the production of commodities and services in a market framework. Development includes economic growth but is a broader process that also encompasses social and institutional changes that normally accompany growth. Development can even make us less vulnerable to environmental hazards, as borne out by the fact that differences in the quality of life between droughtprone and nondroughtprone areas have declined in the process of development.[2] Developed countries in Europe and America are able to carry on and prosper in spite of harsh weather.

At the same time, environment and its natural resources can impose serious constraints on our quality of life. Development cannot be allowed to destroy the source and sustenance of life. The process of economic development, left to itself, has tended to ignore environmental concerns. Such indifference to environment has had adverse impact on development itself. A process of development that has ignored environmental costs is not sustainable in the long run. Quite often, one does not have to wait too long to feel the adverse impacts of these costs on the quality of life of people, particularly of the poor. The poor depend on the natural environment directly in many ways for their very survival. A greater awareness of this has given rise to the concept of 'sustainable development' which takes into account the interests of the present as well as future generations by incorporating environmental and equity concerns into economic development. This concept tries to reconcile the needs of economic development with the needs of environmental conservation, and avoids the extremes of reckless growth on the one hand and preservation of environment at any cost on the other.

The concern about environment is as relevant to developing countries as to developed countries, probably even more. The developing countries have a much higher proportion of people directly dependent on natural resources for earning their livelihood. The concern about environment in these countries is not mainly on the grounds of health and aesthetics as in developed countries, but on the ground that environment is a source of livelihood for millions. Environmental degradation affects the poor most and deprives them of their means of survival. Developing countries cannot, therefore, afford to say that it is only for rich countries to care for environment, though the latter have even greater responsibility in taking care of the environment as they are significant consumers of global commons like the atmosphere.

The necessity to take into account environmental concerns also means that economics cannot ignore them any longer. If economic analysis has to be relevant and meaningful, it has to attend to the environmental problems. On the other hand, in solving environmental problems economic analysis is needed too. Just as economics cannot afford to ignore environmental damage caused by externalities such as pollution, environmental policy too cannot afford to ignore economics. Two propositions can be advanced in this regard : First, the process of economic growth, in so far as it is ecologically unsound, becomes unsustainable sooner or later and gives recognisable and even quantifiable economic signals to this effect, which are germane to economics. Second, a policy or programme of eco-restoration, eco-development or pollution control needs to take into account its costs and benefits so as to optimise the policy outcome and also to develop effective policy instruments including economic instruments. While the first proposition explains why environmental concern is necessary for economics, the second explains why economics is necessary for environmental concern.[3]

In incorporating environmental concerns, however, the major obstacle is not one of difficulty in quantifying environmental costs and benefits. There can be no unique valuation of costs and benefits, as it differs between interest groups. The conflicts between different valuations cannot be always settled through market processes, it is more often settled through struggles between different groups in the arena of political economy.[4] The problems of political economy of environment can be said to arise wherever more than one interest group is involved in using a natural resource. When the concerned natural resource is a free or public good, as is usually the case, there can be many claims over its use. The process of economic development induces the entry of additional interest groups in claiming the rights over resource use, making the struggle between the interest groups more intense and often unequal. These problems arise not only when ecological problems of depletion and pollution are faced: such as in the use of forests, fisheries, air and water, but also when ecological improvements are planned the gains from which have to be shared equitably. The political economy problems arise at different levels—local, regional or national, and global. Principles of sustainability and equity in the use of natural resources are useful in resolving such problems. The moral backing to these principles is so strong now that interest groups dare not oppose them. The most heartening development of recent years is the emergence of popular movements and NGOs in favour of environment which act as countervailing forces against forces of commercialization, and help to achieve a balance between environment and development.[5] At the same time, we cannot leave matters entirely to the popular movements to be resolved. There have to be in-built mechanisms in a legal and institutional framework and through economic incentives (disincentives) to prevent or at least contain negative externalities. Political consensus and backing are a necessary condition for sustainable development, though environmentalists as well as environmental economists can also help to achieve this by throwing more light on the social costs of not achieving sustainable development.

In what follows, the above issues in more specific contexts are presented, drawing from research at the Institute for Social and Economic Change (ISEC). The specific contexts in which environmental dimension are analysed below in a socio-economic perspective are agricultural development, use and management of uncultivated lands such as forests and village common property resources (CPRs), industrial development, and urbanisation.

Agricultural Development and Environment

Agricultural development, if carelessly pursued, can generate serious environmental problems. Problems such as salinity and waterlogging arising in the context of irrigation development are dealt with in another paper in this volume, and are not addressed in the present paper. But, there are other problems too—increasing instability in agricultural output, increasing real costs of cultivation following heavy dependence on market inputs like fertilisers, pesticides and fossil fuels; narrowing genetic base of increased output, making agriculture vulnerable; soil erosion etc.

The problem of droughtproneness and instability in agriculture has been studied in depth at ISEC in several studies, particularly with reference to Karnataka and also India and Asia in general. An early district-wise and crop-wise study of Karnataka for the period from 1955-56 to 1975-76 showed an increase in instability in yields in the green revolution period (1966-67 to 1975-76) in almost every crop (Nadkarni and Deshpande, 1982 and 1983). S.R. Sen had earlier raised the question of instability as associated with extension of cultivation to marginal lands. Now we have a case of extension of productivity push to less endowed areas and crops, in the wake of spreading HYVs to rainfed crops and regions. Yet, our studies also showed that instability need not be an inevitable price to be paid for growth, as there were crops and districts which combined high growth with low instability. Much depended on the efficiency with which land-use and irrigation are managed, and on timely crop protection measures. On the whole, however, India and even Asia achieved higher growth rates in agriculture at the cost of increased instability (Nadkarni, 1984; Ninan and Chandrashekar, 1992 and 1994). Incidentally, during the Green Revolution period, India recorded lower growth but higher instability in yields as compared to China in the case of rice. In the case of wheat, India had lower growth and also lower instability than China. (Ninan & Chandrashekar, 1994, p. 309). On the whole, instability in coarse cereals was higher than in the case of rice and wheat. Regions which depended more on coarse cereals also had higher instability.

A part of the problem also lies in the fact that the semi-arid tracts of India, including particularly Karnataka, have a high pressure of population and cultivated lands here cannot meet the food needs of population (Ramachandran, 1989). The resulting high pressure on the fragile eco-system is a source of instability. Neglect of soil health also seems to have contributed to increased instability. No doubt, the government has significantly stepped up soil conservation programmes particularly in watershed development in semi-arid areas. Watershed development has both reduced instability and increased yields. (Ninan and Chandrashekar, 1992; Lakshmikanthamma, 1994; Ninan and Lakshmikanthamma, 1995). A successful planning of soil conservation in watersheds, however, depends much on effective community organisation and co-operation.

The Green Revolution and its technology, however, stressed too much on individual efforts and market inputs to the neglect of community efforts and natural resource conservation. Short term gains took precedence over considerations of sustainable agriculture. This seems to have contributed both to increase in instability and costs of cultivation per unit of output at least up to the early 1980s both in the country as a whole and in Karnataka (Nadkarni, 1988). M. V. Nadkarni's study showed a significant decline in output-input ratios in agriculture in real terms, and called for more attention to maintaining soil health and reducing real costs. Based on the experience of an enterprising farmer, Narayan Reddy, near Bangalore, who gave up the use of chemical inputs and opted for organic farming, the paper suggested that efforts be directed for more research in and implementation of such an approach. The approach required looking at the farm holding as a whole, instead of individual crops, taking advantages of complementarities between crops in increasing yields and checking pests. It also made use of all organic matter generated on the farm, including crop residues, for enhancing soil health and improving water conservation, reducing the dependence on costly market inputs.

One need not take the extreme stand of rejecting all use of chemical inputs, particularly before organic substitutes are developed. But, an indiscriminate use of costly inputs is certainly to be rejected, particularly as they have side-effects of getting into water resources and contaminating them. A study showed that there was a tendency to use fertilisers beyond the optimal point in irrigated areas, and much below the optimal in dry and rainfed areas, which adversely affected farmers' yields and profits (Raj, 1990).

Wrong economic incentives play an important role in contributing to unsustainable agriculture and negative side-effects. A subsidy on chemical fertilisers distorts the choice between them and organic manure. Similarly, a supply of free electricity for irrigation at nominal rates induces wastage of both water and electricity, both being scarce resources (Nadkarni, 1987 and 1993). If a subsidy is considered desirable for agriculture, it could be more in areas vital for sustainable agriculture but where individual investments are not forthcoming. For example, they could be in the form of public expenditure on desilting tanks, regeneration of common property resources to enhance the supply of bio-mass, improvement of village infrastructure, and on soil conservation.

Investment in soil conservation by individual farmer: in their holdings is affected by institutional and economic constraints. This was particularly vident in encroached lands. An ISEC study of hilly terrains of Idukki district in Kerala showed that while some encroachments into public forests were regularised in the past, there remained many encroached-upon lands for which title deeds were not given so as to discourage further encroachment (Govindaru, 1994). Though soil conservation was of critical importance there, farmers did not invest in it on lands for which they had no title deeds. Also, costs of soil conservation were high and returns were comparatively low in uphill areas in deforested lands. Soil conservation was economical mainly in downhill areas. This also suggested that encroachments in uphill areas meant very unsustainable agriculture. (Nadkarni and Govindaru, 1995).

Shifting or *jhum* cultivation in hilly forest areas has been causing severe ecological problems, particularly after the rotational cycles have declined in length from the previous 10-15 years to the present 2-3 years. There have been attempts to settle the cultivators permanently through terracing. K.N. Ninan's study, based on the data from several areas in India showed, however, that terrace cultivation is not economical as an alternative to *jhum* cultivation. The study advocated different strategies based on agro-forestry and diversification of the economy of hill regions (Ninan, 1988 and 1992).

Diversification of the economy is a useful strategy in semi-arid droughtprone regions too, both in promoting their development and reducing their vulnerability. Instead of relying on strategies that require huge amounts of water, promoting small ruminants could play an important role. In semi-arid regions, goats and sheep have supported the livelihoods of the rural oommunities including the poor. A Ph.D. thesis at ISEC by Pasha showed that small ruminant economy complements crop husbandry in a synergic way, and that the fears of the so-called harm done by these ruminants to the ecology of the region are highly exaggerated. The availability of CPRs can stimulate the small ruminant economy of particularly the rural poor (Pasha, 1991 and 1992a).

Uncultivated Lands, CPRs and Forests

The importance of good land management has since long been emphasised in the context of cultivated part of rural lands and in Reserve Forests. However, till about the end of 1970s, attention was hardly given to land resources whose use and maintenance rested with village communities. Their magnitude and role in the rural economy, their use and misuse had remained unresearched issues. It was in early 1979 that we, at ISEC, published a pioneering paper on the magnitude of uncultivated but cultivable lands and possible factors behind their variation (Nadkarni and Deshpande, 1979). The paper drew attention to lands which were neither under forests nor under crop cultivation, and represented a largely underutilised resource. It was not the lack of rainfall alone, but lack of attention for their development and rational management which was responsible for the underutilisation and degradation of these lands. Jeff Romm's paper on the theme came out in 1981 (Romm, 1981) and Jodha's work on Common Property Resources (CPRs) was published in 1985 (Jodha, 1985a and 1985b). Unfortunately, the work on the theme at ISEC was interrupted for some time since other projects had to be taken up, but was resumed again in mid-1980s.

The extent of uncultivated lands in India can be seen from Table 2.1 here. Forests, cultivable wastes, pastures, and fallows other than current fallows together constituted as much as 29.5 per cent of geographical area in 1955-56 and 31.7 per cent in 1989-90. If area under forests and barren lands are ignored, there were 45.6 million hectares of uncultivated lands in 1955-56 (13.9% of geographical area) and 36.2 million hectares in 1989-90 (11.3%). (We have not considered current fallows as uncultivated land available for development and regeneration.) The uncultivated lands of this magnitude could hardly have been ignored in a land hungry country like ours. That the extent of this land is declining is not necessarily a source of consolation, unless the increased area under forests is well managed, and that people are not deprived of bio-mass by this change.

It is useful to classify these lands from an institutional angle into four categories:

(a) government owned land under Reserve Forests with limited access to people;
(b) government owned land under other forests, grazing lands and other 'revenue lands' which serve as common property resources (CPRs) for local people;
(c) privately owned land, with conferred title deeds; and
(d) privately occupied[6]/encroached lands but owned by the government.

No statistics are available on the distribution of these lands into these categories. But our field experience suggests that in most areas, the bulk of the uncultivated land is under government ownership and the extent of privately owned uncultivated land is rather small. In several areas as in Gulbarga district, uncultivated lands, other than reserve forests, are largely encroached upon by private individuals. Encroachment is found in other areas too, both by the poor and the non-poor, but more so

TABLE 2.1: **Extent of Uncultivated Lands in India**

(in thousand hectares)

	1955-56	1970-71	1989-90
1. Forests	51,343	63,917	67,157
	(15.6)	(19.4)	(20.4)
2. Cultivable Waste	21,537	17,500	15,738
	(6.6)	(5.3)	(4.8)
3. Pastures	11,473	13,262	11,934
	(3.5)	(4.0)	(3.6)
4. Fallows other than Current Fallows	12,544	8,759	9,552
	(3.8)	(2.7)	(2.9)
5. (2) + (3) + (4)	45,554	39,521	37,224
	(13.9)	(12.0)	(11.3)
6. Barren and Uncultivable Waste	34,476	28,161	20,068
	(10.5)	(8.6)	(6.1)

Source: *Indian Agriculture in Brief*, respective editions, Directorate of Economics and Statistics, Ministry of Agriculture, Govt. of India.

Note: Figures in parentheses are percentages to total geographical area.

by the non-poor. A study of four villages in forest areas of Uttara Kannada showed clearly that poor peasants and landless agricultural labour, who together accounted for 60.9 per cent of households accounted for only 24.2 per cent of encroached lands, while the non-poor households (30.1%) had 75.8 per cent of encroached lands. A further study of villages in semi-arid tracts of Karnataka also confirmed the same pattern. The existence of encroachment on a significant scale also means that the extent of uncultivated lands available for development as CPRs (say, under social forestry projects) is much less than what figures as in Table 2.1 would suggest. This could be tested only through micro-level field studies. In 14 villages studied by us in Karnataka, which had social forestry projects, while 2,834 ha were reported as government owned uncultivated lands as per village records, only 1,806 ha were actually available, the difference accounted for mostly by encroachment (Nadkarni and Pasha, 1991).

Though uncultivated, these lands meet the bio-mass needs of local people. How far they meet these needs depend both on their productivity in terms of bio-mass and also on the access of local people. How far they can be considered as CPRs depend both on access and involvement of local people in their management. Local people enjoy some, though a limited, access to Reserve Forests, but they are alienated from their management except where Joint Forest Management (JFM) has been introduced in recent years. These lands, particularly the first-two categories, play an important role in supporting the livelihood of the rural poor. Even the landless can maintain some livestock because of their access to CPRs, which makes them—to that extent—less dependent on the local elite. On the basis of a study of CPRs, Jodha (1985a and 1985b) had found that the rural poor derive a larger part of their income from CPRs both in absolute and relative terms than the non-poor. Our studies at ISEC showed, however, that in absolute terms the rural non-poor derive more income from CPRs than the poor; it is only relative to their meagre incomes that the poor derive a higher percentage of their income from CPRs than the non-poor. This was seen both from a study of forest villages in Uttara Kannada (Nadkarni, 1989: 165) and from a study of 14 villages mainly in semi-arid tracts of Karnataka (Pasha, 1992b). The benefits from CPRs to the rural poor are not automatic, they have to be ensured through proper institutional arrangements of involving them in the management of CPRs and ensuring them equal rights.

In terms of ecological health, and productivity (including environmental services), the best preserved of the above four categories of uncultivated lands are undoubtedly Reserve Forests. Public uncultivated lands under open access to local people as well as those under private possession are far more degraded, not even covered with adequate grass due to overgrazing. This was observed by us both in Uttara Kannada and elsewhere in semi-arid tracts, though there are a few honourable exceptions where local communities with conscious efforts have saved the village woodlots and a few plots under some social forestry projects. But, even in the case of these exceptions, while particular plots of trees are well preserved by local communities as show pieces, their pressures are diverted elsewhere including sometimes to Reserve forests which they exploit for grazing and firewood collection. In spite of biotic pressures on them, Reserve Forests are in a better state both because there are some controls on these pressures in their case unlike in other categories of uncultivated lands, and also because regeneration is normally undertaken there by the Forest Department. It is when both the local people and the Forest Department are utterly indifferent to the state of forests that Reserve Forests also degrade.

No regeneration attempts are made in other uncultivated lands except under social forestry projects, here and there. The extent of available uncultivable lands taken up for social forestry is quite modest. In the 14 villages selected by us for study, where social forestry projects were undertaken, only 300 ha were actually taken up for development out of 1,806 ha available (Nadkarni and Pasha, 1991). Since these villages had social forestry projects and there were many which were not covered by them, the proportion of area covered on the whole by these projects would be smaller than what was found in the villages selected by us for study. There are hardly any regeneration efforts in uncultivated areas under private possession too. Even where vast forest areas are encroached upon for cultivation (through direct and indirect support from politicians and even government), no soil conservation measures are undertaken. This is partly because no property rights are conferred in the case of such lands, and only short term crops are grown here. This was borne out from a study of a large village in Idukki district in Kerala (Govindaru, 1994; Nadkarni and Govindaru, 1995). Also, development of waste lands involves considerable investment, which private individuals find difficult to make. No loans for this are available particularly if lands are encroached upon.

It is interesting that private parties like farmers have shown increasing inclination to divert less fertile cultivated lands under millets like ragi to grow trees like casuarina and eucalyptus on a commercial footing, as they offer higher rates of return (Aziz, 1995). But this is done in owned lands rather than in encroached lands, obviously due to lack of property rights in the latter case.

It is important to note that economic viability as such is no constraint on the development of uncultivated lands. A study of 13 social forestry projects showed that they had fairly high benefit-cost ratios and internal rates of return. Even a project oriented to fodder with as low a density of trees as 222 per hectare had a positive net present value per hectare (Nadkarni, Ninan and Pasha, 1994). These results were arrived at following a rigorous sensitivity analysis, allowing for various discount rates, opportunity costs and risk factors. The economic viability analysis assumed, however, that social forestry projects would be looked after and sustainably used by the local people.

Though it may be a tempting proposition to give public uncultivated lands to private parties for growing trees, it has the effect of depriving the rural poor of whatever little benefits they gained from CPRs, and also of reducing bio-diversity in rural areas since private parties would grow only commercial species like casuarina and eucalyptus. Social forestry projects under community access and management, on the other hand, can be designed to meet the local needs of bio-mass and even ensure bio-diversity. Neither social forestry nor JFM have yet to become as widespread as necessary. We need patience and sustained efforts in involving people in planning and managing them to meet their environmental needs. Efforts so far have been sporadic and occasional. Whatever efforts have been undertaken have also been more obsessed with trees, ignoring grass and other fodder much needed by the people. A greater orientation to meeting their needs will ensure their co-operation, which, in turn, can make a more productive and environmentally beneficial use of uncultivated lands possible.

The State governments, including Karnataka, have historically been lenient to converting uncultivated lands into cultivated lands, particularly by regularising encroachments periodically. This has also the effect of depriving the rural poor of their access to grazing and firewood resources. The uncultivated lands, particularly forests, also provide environmental services. The existence of a significant amount of uncultivated lands is not necessarily a cause for concern; it is their degradation through unsustainable use which should cause concern. This problem cannot be met by converting them into cultivated lands. There is fortunately a general consensus that the area under forest cover is much less than desirable. This feeling is based on a conventionally fixed norm of one-third of geographical area to be under forests. It is also possible to show, in terms of productivity including environmental services, that the extent of uncultivated land in India has significantly cut into what should have been under forests. J.B. Lal has estimated that the total economic value of annual flow of goods and environmental services from India's forests was about Rs. 12,391 per hectare in 1987-88. On the other hand, the value of annual output per hectare from agriculture and livestock per hectare of cultivated land was about Rs. 8,117 around 1987-88 (Nadkarni, 1995). This shows there is a case for extending area under tree cover as forests, even at the expense of cultivated lands, and not *vice versa.* However, the comparatively higher productivity of forests over cultivated lands is seen when environmental services of forests are included, and not when timber alone is considered. Thus, the case for extending forest cover is mainly on environmental grounds, though, of course, there could be marginal lands of low productivity which can be profitably diverted from cultivation to tree growing. This would also be environmentally desirable.[7]

Industries and Environment

Environmental problems specially industrial pollution have acquired a great urgency in the context of rapid industrialisation in the Third World. It is obligatory for polluting units to treat pollution and bring it down to the permissible limits. India has a fairly good legislative and institutional framework to prevent and control pollution, though there seems to be quite a bit of resistance to this on the part of polluting units. One of the PhD theses at ISEC probed into the question of whether this resistance was due to an unaffordable burden imposed on the industrial units as a result of pollution control laws. It was found, however, that the cost of pollution control was well within affordable limits for the concerned firms and had no adverse impact on profitability and employment (Ravichandran, 1990).

This work was pursued later and a comparative study of industrial pollution abatement in India (Karnataka) and Netherlands was undertaken (Nadkarni *et al.*, 1995). Though the two countries are very different, India being a developing country and the Netherlands being developed, they were remarkably close in many respects. Due to rapid industrialization, India is facing many side-effects of industrial development which brings it closer to developed countries in the nature of environmental problems. Both countries have adopted appropriate legislation and institutional measures for controlling pollution and have adopted 'The Polluter pays Principle' for abating pollution. Both countries rely more on direct regulation than on economic incentives and both have laid down source-based emission standards and also ambient standards. In the Netherlands, however, individually tailored permits are negotiated which are even stricter so that firms capable of abating more can do so.

In addition to direct regulation, India is trying financial instruments like water cess, tax rebates and other tax concessions and soft loans for installing pollution control equipment. In the Netherlands, the economic instruments are more comprehensive and effective which do not substitute but complement direct regulation. They have achieved much better results after the levy of effluent charges, though, in some respects like the noise charge, they are not effective enough.

To probe into the working of pollution control in industrial units, several textile, cement and fertiliser units were taken as case studies in Karnataka and Netherlands for comparison. The cost incurred by monitoring auth rities in both Karnataka and Netherlands were also taken into account. It was interesting to find that in spite of being poorer, Karnataka was found to spend a slightly higher proportion of its income on pollution control than the Netherlands. The expenditure incurred by the Karnataka State Pollution Control Board (KSPCB) turned out to be

0.027 per cent of Karnataka's State Domestic Product, as against 0.023 per cent of the Net National Product spent as enforcement cost in the Netherlands. In Karnataka, the above percentage is an under-estimate because the cost incurred by the Central government's Ministry of Environment and Forests, and Central Pollution Control Board (CPCB) in Karnataka is not included.

The proportion of compliance cost incurred by firms in relation to their turnover was also compared. Here also, the proportions in the two countries come remarkably close to each other. The annualised cost of pollution control among the selected firms varied from 0.2 to 1.9 per cent of turnover in Karnataka and from 0.2 to 2.36 per cent in the Netherlands. The proportions are well within affordable range.

The pollution standards are more stringent in the Netherlands and enforcement is also more effective than in Karnataka. While almost all the firms complied with the standards and covenants in the Netherlands, it was only 38 per cent in Karnataka even in the highly polluting industrial types. Even the monitoring was inadequate. For example, of the 30 parameters prescribed for the pollution abatement, only 5 are monitored in the textile industries in Karnataka. In spite of a high number of non-compliance firms only a few are ordered to be closed down in Karnataka. Inadequate staff and funds available with the State Pollution Control Board (SPCB) seem to be the main factors behind this state of affairs. Though enforcement is much better in Netherlands, they have also quite some way to go in reducing emissions and pollution in general.

The future scenario may include more reliance on economic instruments in India than now. Effluent charges need particular attention. The derivation of effective charges is a complex issue. User charges for covering pollution abatement costs incurred by municipalities could at least be levied on small firms which do not abate pollution themselves. It should, of course, be compulsory to abate pollution at source in the case of large and medium firms. Collective treatment facilities are also another possibility being tried particularly for small firms. In the Netherlands, they may give more attention to tradeable permits to reduce cost of pollution control as well as making enforcement even more effective. Vehicular pollution is a difficult issue in both countries which was not within the scope of the above study.

Urban Environment

Increasing urbanisation seems inevitable with economic development.

The proportion of urban population in India increased from a mere 10.8 per cent in 1901 to 17.3 per cent in 1951 and further to 25.7 per cent in 1991. This is still lower than in developed countries, but, in absolute terms, it is quite huge (see Table 2.2). In 1991, the total urban population in India was as large as 218 million. Though the rate of growth of urban population has declined from 46.8 per cent between 1971 and 1981 to 36.3 per cent between 1981 and 1991, the absolute increase in population has continued unabated. It was by 58 million during the decade preceding 1991.

TABLE 2.2: **Urban Population in India since 1951**

Year	Urban Population		Increase over Last Decade	
	In million	As per cent of total population	In million	In per cent
1951	62	17.3	-	-
1961	79	18.0	17	27.4
1971	109	19.9	30	38.0
1981	160	23.3	51	46.8
1991	218	25.7	58	36.3

Source: *India 1993*, Publications Division, GOI, New Delhi, p. 16.

Urbanization of course has its use and some positive features. Urban areas provide higher order services and amenities, and also employment opportunities in the expanding non-agricultural sector. Art and culture are promoted through greater interaction among people. Creative persons can find opportunities for advancement. Yet, urbanisation has also serious environmental costs. There is a tremendous pressure on transport, housing, electricity, water supply and sanitation. Urban sprawl takes place at the expense of green areas, and create squalor and filth. For example, Industrial and Commercial areas of Bangalore are found to be highly polluted (Sastry, 1985).

A few studies taken up at ISEC focused on the problems of Bangalore City. The city attained the status of a million city in 1961 and has been growing rapidly ever since. Since this increase is both in area and population, the city has a comparatively low density of population compared to other metropolitan cities like Bombay, Delhi and Calcutta. However, this has not been an unmixed blessing. Unplanned extensions without proper amenities have become a significant feature of the growth of Bangalore. In a major study of Bangalore, based both on household survey and secondary data, Prakasarao and Tewari have lamented over the "new extensions becoming concrete jungles in sharp contrast to the green old city where buildings as a rule were hidden under the green canopy, with a welcome spell of flowering at different seasons" (Prakasarao and Tewari, 1979: 304) "Even hillocks which at least should have been covered with greenery have not been spared by extensions" (*Ibid*. 306). They ask, "should skyscrapers breed wherever space is available and finances are forthcoming, without a ceiling on their number and without concern over their impact on the structure and form of the emerging city?" (*Ibid*: 307). How apt and relevant are their observations even today!

Both very low density and high density of population in cities create problems. "The low density areas generally lack population thresholds to support urban functions as well as other infrastructure. High density areas, on the other hand, suffer problems associated with congestion, strain on infrastructure and so on. The residents, therefore, look for a trade off between these extremes" (Ramachandran, 1985a :270). A Ph D thesis at ISEC showed how per capita infrastructural costs sharply declined while moving from low density areas to areas with a density of 100-150 persons per acre in Bangalore. A further reduction in density brought only a marginal reduction in these costs. On the other hand, costs of congestion associated with density of public buses, room density, crime rate etc., increased particularly after a density of 150 persons per acre (Malini, 1987). It appears that congestion costs were not fully quantified and hence, were underestimated by the above study. The optimal density, therefore, may actually be very much less than 150 persons per ha.[8] The problems of Bangalore seem, however, to arise more on account of its overall size of population than on account of high density.

One of the problems of city growth is the proliferation of slums. A study of slums in Bangalore at ISEC took a positive and broader perspective about slums, rejecting the usual negative middle class perception of slums as an evil to be cleared away. The growth of slums in Bangalore, as elsewhere, was directly related to the growth of nonslum population. The skilled workforce that grows in cities requires also the services generally performed by unskilled illiterate and low income workforce which is forced to live in slums. The location of slums shows that they are interspersed with commercial and residential areas. 'If we accept the fact that slums are inevitable, we are then forced to bring them within the ambit of urban planning, and plan them as an integral part of the residential lay-out' (Ramachandran, 1985b:43) Slum improvement, rather than slum clearance, would then seem more logical apart from being humane.

Conclusion

The degradation of environment in the course of economic development may be either in the form of negative externalities or side effects or depletion of the stock of natural resources. The signals of their occurrence have to be identified and interpreted. They may not always be open and immediate. The studies at ISEC have thrown some light on the nature of environmental costs and economic factors behind them. It is hoped that they would guide policy making.

NOTES

1. Thanks are due to Dr. K.N. Ninan, Dr.G.S. Sastry and Dr. Syed Ajmal Pasha for summaries of their work.
2. This is seen from a cross-section study of South Indian districts based both on secondary data at two points of time, 1971 and 1981, and primary data (Nadkarni, 1985, especially chs. 2 and 6)
3. For a more detailed discussion, see (Nadkarni, 1991:148-52). The second proposition in the present essay is more general having wider applicability than the one presented in the 1991 paper.
4. For a discussion in the light of forest use in Karnataka, see "Local *vis-a-vis* the Larger Economy and the State", in Nadkarni, 1989: 19-20, and for a more general discussion at the local, regional/national and global levels, see Nadkarni, 1994a).
5. For a critical discussion of the role of NGOs and popular movements, see Nadkarni, 1994b.
6. There is a special category of lands such as bettas in Uttara Kannada which are in exclusive private possession for enjoying usufruct rights legally, though owned by the government (Nadkarni, 1989: 165).
7. It surely does not mean that food needs may be ignored. A smaller extent of cultivated lands than at present can meet our food needs well enough.
8. The actual density per acre was 85 persons in Bangalore Municipal Corporation Area, as against 67 persons per acre in Greater Bombay Municipal Corporation Area (MCA), 89 persons in Madras (MCA), and 96 persons in Calcutta (MCA) as per 1991 Census *(Primary Census Abstract Part II-B(i): General Population).*

REFERENCES

Aziz, Abdul (1995) The Economics of Eucalyptus Cultivation in Kolar district, Karnataka. In N.C. Saxena and Vishwa Ballabh (eds.), *Farm Forestry in South Asia.* New Delhi: Sage.

Govindaru, V. (1994) *Impact of Conversion of Natural Forests to Agriculture and Plantation Crops on Local Economy and Environment: Kerala.* A Ph.D. thesis (ISEC). Bangalore: Bangalore University.

Jodha, N.S. (1985a) Population Growth and the Decline of CPRs in Rajasthan, India. *Population and Development Review*, 11(2): 247-64.

Jodha, N.S. (1985b) Market Forces and Erosion of CPRs. *Agricultural Market in the Semi-Arid Tropics*, ICRISAT, 263-77.

Lakshmikanthamma, S. (1994) *Economics of Watershed Development Approach to Dryland Agriculture*. A Ph.D. thesis (ISEC). Bangalore: Bangalore University.

Malini, R.S. (1987) *Residential Densities and Living Conditions in a Metropolis - A Case Study*. A Ph.D. thesis (ISEC). Mysore: University of Mysore.

Nadkarni, M.V. (1984) Growth and Instability in Indian Agriculture—Another Look. In A.K. Singh *et al.* (eds.), *Economic Policy and Planning in India*. New Delhi: Sterling.

Nadkarni, M.V. (1985) *Socio-Economic Conditions in Droughtprone Areas*. New Delhi: Concept.

Nadkarni, M.V. (1987) Agricultural Development and Ecology—An Economist's View. *Indian Journal of Agricultural Economics*, 42(3): 359-75.

Nadkarni, M.V. (1988) Crisis of Increasing Costs in Indian Agriculture—Is there a Way Out?. *Economic and Political Weekly*. xxiii (39): A114-A119.

Nadkarni, M.V. (with Syed Ajmal Pasha and L.S. Prabhakar) (1989) *The Political Economy of Forest Use and Management*. New Delhi: Sage.

Nadkarni, M.V. (1991) Economics and Ecological Concern. In C.T. Kurien *et al.* (eds.), *Economy, Society and Development*. New Delhi: Sage.

Nadkarni, M.V. (1993) Agricultural Policy in India—Context, Issues and Instruments. *DRG Study* 5. Bombay: Reserve Bank of India.

Nadkarni, M.V. (1994a) Political Economy of Ecology: Comprehending the Problems. In G.K. Chadha (ed.), *Policy Perspectives in Indian Economic Development*. New Delhi: Har-Anand.

Nadkarni, M.V. (1994b) Voluntary Organisations in Greening India. In Studies in Third World Societies (USA), *Publication No. 59* on Non Government Organisations in India. March.

Nadkarni, M.V. (1995) Forests, People and Economics. *Presidential Address* at the 55th Annual Conference of the Indian Society of Agricultural Economics at IRMA, Ahmedabad.

Nadkarni, M.V. and R.S. Deshpande (1979) Underutilisation of Land—Climatic or Institutional Factors? *Indian Journal of Agricultural Economics*, 34 (2).

Nadkarni, M.V. and R.S. Deshpande (1982) Agricultural Growth, Instability in Productivity and Rainfall: Case of Karnataka. *Economic and Political Weekly* 17 (52).

Nadkarni, M.V. and R.S. Deshpande (1983) Growth and Instability in Crop Yields : A Case Study of Agriculture in Karnataka, South India. *Regional Studies* (UK), 17 (1): 29-39.

Nadkarni, M.V. and V. Govindaru (1995) Nobody's Child: The Economic and Institutional Aspects of Soil Conservation in India. *Journal of Environment and Development*, 4 (1): 171-83.

Nadkarni, M.V., K.N. Ninan and Syed Ajmal Pasha (1994) The Economic and Financial Viability of Social Forestry Projects: A Study of Selected Projects in Karnataka. *JFM Working Paper No.16*. New Delhi: SPWD and The Ford Foundation.

Nadkarni, M.V. and Syed Ajmal Pasha (1991) Developing Uncultivated Lands: Some Issues from Karnataka's Experience in Social Forestry. *Indian Journal of Agricultural Economics*, 46 (4).

Nadkarni, M.V., G.S. Sastry, O.J. Kuik and F.H. Oosterhuis (1995) *The Best of Both Worlds: A Comparative Assessment of Environmental Policy Approaches in India and the Netherlands*. Bangalore: ISEC and Amsterdam: Institute for Environmental Studies. Mimeo.

Ninan, K.N. (1988) Issues in the Development of Hill Regions in India. Bangalore: ISEC. Mimeo.

Ninan, K.N. (1992) Economics of Shifting Cultivation in India. *Economic and Political Weekly*, 28 (13).

Ninan, K.N. and H. Chandrashekar (1992) The Green Revolution, Dryland Agriculture and Sustainability—Insights from India. In G.H. Peters and B.F. Stanton (eds.), *Sustainable Agricultural Devèlopment—Role of International Co-operation*. Dartmouth, U.K: IAAE, University of Oxford.

Ninan, K.N. and H. Chandrashekar (1994) Growth and Instability in Asian Agriculture. *Productivity*, 35 (2): 307-13.

Ninan, K.N. and S. Lakshmikanthamma (1995) The Case of Watershed Development in India. *International Journal of Sustainable Development and World Ecology*, (UK), 1 (4).

Pasha, Syed Ajmal (1991) Sustainability and Viability of Small and Marginal Farmers: Animal Husbandry and CPRs. *Economic and Political Weekly* XXVI (13): 827-30.

Pasha, Syed Ajmal (1992a) *Economics of Small Ruminants in Droughtprone Areas of Karnataka*. A Ph.D. thesis (ISEC). Bangalore: Bangalore University.

Pasha, Syed Ajmal (1992b) CPRs and the Rural Poor—A Micro Level Analysis. *Economic and Political Weekly*, 27 (46).

Prakasarao V.L.S. and V.K. Tewari (1979) *The Structure of an Indian Metropolis—A Study of Bangalore*. New Delhi: Allied.

Raj, D. Sunitha Anand (1990) *An Economic Analysis of Fertiliser Use and Crop Productivity in Andhra Pradesh*. A Ph.D. thesis (ISEC). Bangalore: Bangalore University.

Ramachandran, H. (1985a) Residents' Perception of Living Conditions in Bangalore, India. *Ekistics*, 312: 266-72.

Ramachandran, H. (1985b) Slumming of a Metropolis. In Vinod Vyasulu and A.K.N. Reddy (eds.), *Essays on Bangalore*, Vol 2. Bangalore: KSCST.

Ramachandran, H. (1989) Resource Use in the Agricultural Eco-systems of Semi-arid Lands of Karnataka. In Ramachandran, H. (ed.), *Environmental Issues in Agricultural Development*. New Delhi: Concept.

Ravichandran, M. (1990) *Economics of Pollution Prevention and Control: A Study of Industrial Pollution in Karnataka*. A Ph.D. thesis (ISEC). Mysore: Mysore University.

Romm, Jeff (1981) The Uncultivated Half of India. *Indian Forester*, 17 (1 & 2).

Sastry, G.S. (1985) Metropolitan Cities' Environment: India. *Nagarlok*, 17 (3).

3

DEVELOPMENT PLANNING
The Contours that ISEC has Traversed

ABDUL AZIZ and MADHUSHREE SEKHER

Introduction

With the meteoric rise of the former Soviet Union as a world power following adoption of planning, planning as a strategy of development came to be no longer looked upon as "a road to serfdom"; rather, it was seen as a means of creating vast number of choices to people. The third world countries, which were steeped in poverty, unemployment and inequalities, and caught in the under-employment equilibrium for years, not surprisingly found planning as a panacea for all their social and economic ills. By the 50s the planning fever caught almost all the underdeveloped countries and they were found seriously engaged in planning for development. India was leading in this respect.

In India, as elsewhere, planning was understood as a process of resource allocation with a view to maximising national/per capita output. It was assumed that growth of output would take care of problems of poverty, unemployment and inequalities. But, after two decades of planning, when it was found that these problems remained unabated, some rethinking went on about the appropriateness of the planning strategy followed till then. The writings of Dandekar and Rath, Minhas and others in India and the contribution of Mahboob-ul-Huq at the international level, in particular, led to evolving a new approach to and a new goal of planning. While the macro approach to planning continued to have its sway over planners, planning at meso and micro levels assumed importance. Also, there was a shift of emphasis from output maximisation to the questions of what type of output to be produced, where and for whom to be produced. Going further, a man-centered focus of planning became the in-thing of the time. The planning goal now became the all-round development of the common man—his social, economic and political development—rather than merely maximising output at the national level.

The man-centered focus of planning shifted the emphasis hitherto given by the researchers from the planning concerns like optimisation of output, consistency in resource allocation and so on in the plan models to poverty reduction, employment generation and provision of minimum needs. Such a shift of emphasis brought into fore planning for securing spatial and sectional equity. Following this, multi-level planning and target group approach got added to the planning kit in the mid-seventies. As will be seen presently, this shift was to culminate in the years that followed in a fullfledged decentralized planning strategy to be formulated and implemented by Panchayat Raj institutions.

We have thus travelled a long way in the realm of planning starting from the centralised macro plans to decentralized micro plans. Also, the issues that attracted the attention of researchers have undergone a metamorphosis over the years. By the time ISEC researchers were in place in 1972, the euphoria about macro plans, and the issues like optimization and consistency had begun to wane; planning down the lane, focus on spatial and sectional planning and issues of planning specific development projects and implementing them effectively came to the fore. It was in this environment of changed focus that the ISEC researchers began to work on planning issues. The purpose of this chapter is to review the contributions of the ISEC faculty to the planning discipline and view them in the perspective of the demands placed on them by the country.

Planning Approach

As stated earlier, the Institute was established at a time when a debate was on with regard to the appropriate approach to be followed for development planning. The Harrod-Domar model and its variants which guided planning in India had attracted a serious criticism (not unjustifiably) that the model was not relevant to Indian situation. Therefore, there was a search for an indigenous growth model notwithstanding the development of a wage goods model by Vakil and Brahmananda in the mid-fifties. Gandhians—the followers of M.K.Gandhi's philosophy—had come out with a growth path that sought to eradicate poverty, unemployment and inequalities. In this context, the ISEC faculty brought out a volume on Gandhi's relevance to contemporary India. Among others, the articles included in this volume looked into Gandhi's ideas about development and their relevance (Das and Mishra, 1979). A follow-up paper on the same theme made a distinction between Gandhi's economic system and Gandhian economic system and commended the latter as a guide to economic planning. It was argued that since the Gandhian path of development laid emphasis on employment growth and proposed as well an appropriate rate of savings for future growth, this system could be likened to Joan Robinson's concept of "Golden Age" which envisaged a situation of capital accumulation taking place at a rate that it absorbed the growing labour force at each point of time along the time horizon. However, since in the Gandhian system, resource allocation is proposed in a manner that growth rate of employment takes place at a rate that it coincides with the desired future growth rate of the economy at different points of time along the time horizon, the Gandhian "Golden Age" was treated as a mere "Robinsonian Golden Age" *in reverse*. Thus, the Gandhian Golden Age was made to acquire a theoretical legitimacy and was commended as of great analytical importance to the developing economies which suffered from severe unemployment (Aziz, 1983a:95).

While the above attempt merely signified a token participation by the faculty in the on-going debate, a more serious attempt was made by Professor V.K.R.V. Rao (1984) to give a new direction to planning approach at the national level. After listing the reasons behind popular dissatisfaction with the plans—such as wrong priorities, non fulfilment of targets, increased poverty and unemployment, neglect of ecological concerns, widening disparities between rural and urban areas, between rich and the poor, growing consumerism culture, fall in public morals—he suggested a new approach to planning. This approach emphasised on social dimension of the development paradigm, and sought to reduce disparities of all kinds and improve quality of life by strengthening the redistributive bias of public policies and services in favour of backward spaces and weaker sections. This approach also sought the active involvement of all sections of the community in the process of development as a means to giving due importance to human factor in development. But, it should go to the credit of Professor Rao that he was one of the earliest economists in India to have recognised the role of human factor in development. However, his definition of human factor went beyond the conventional concept of human resource development. In that, he would include all the good qualities of a human being and of a human society. Thus, in an earlier paper, he had argued that a value system and code of conduct that is conducive to development and human welfare should be treated as *infrastructure for development.* In his view, such a value system has to encompass social and national commitment, social justice and social harmony, gospel of work, social concern for the backward regions and sections and special attention to meeting the basic minimum needs of all (V.K.R.V. Rao, 1980: 11). In continuation of this strain of thought process, as it were, a collection of essays brought out in honour of Professor D.M. Nanjundappa (Bharadwaj and Nadkarni, 1992), the human factor was once again emphasised. These essays highlighted the need for planning to take care of those aspects which were often ignored by the market forces so that economic development became humane and purposeful, and also reiterated that planning should not merely aim at accelerating growth rates but must work towards placing the human being at the centre of the planning process.

Planning at the State Level

Coming to planning at the State level, the role of ISEC can be seen at three levels:

(a) preparation of a perspective plan and assisting the planning department by giving some such crucial planning inputs;
(b) commenting on the State planning efforts, particularly on the plan approach, priorities and project implementation; and
(c) directly participating in the plan formulation efforts of the State Planning Department.

The attempt at looking into planning problem by the ISEC faculty began with a seminar on the social and economic development of Karnataka, the basic issues arising therefrom and the role social scientists could take up to resolve them. This seminar had facilitated a dialogue between social scientists and administrators and highlighted the need for a more active role for the former in planning for development (V.K.R.V. Rao *et al.*, 1975). As a follow-up, a perspective plan for Karnataka (V.K.R.V. Rao, 1978a) was prepared by a team of researchers drawn from different disciplines of the Institute (Two of them were, however, from the Institute of Economic Growth, New Delhi, our sister Institute). This study kept as a perspective for the next 15 years the imperatives of accelerating growth, dispersing it to spaces and accessing it to the poor, and worked out the various parameters, particularly sectoral and regional growth rates to achieve this goal. The focus on the thrust of planning for the next three Five-Year

Plans, apart as a useful input to the State Planning Department, this work, for the first time, brought together a vast amount of scattered data about the Karnataka economy and its sectors at one place, presented a vivid account of Karnataka's developmental problems, and laid down policy and programme imperatives to tackle these problems.

The other significant attempt at providing inputs to the State Planning Department was an exercise carried out on estimation of employment potential of Karnataka State plan schemes as a guide to resource allocation. As employment generation became an important goal of planning effort, the Government of Karnataka needed employment coefficients of investments in different plan schemes and approached ISEC to work these out. The study that followed (Aziz and Rayappa, 1980) looked at the employment potential of investment in the Kahn employment multiplier framework as suggested by Professor D.M. Nanjundappa. By way of operationalizing Kahn's concept, it was hypothesised that a given plan investment would generate direct on-site as also indirect off-site employment. The on-site employment would have construction, maintenance and operation components. The indirect off-site employment is generated from the raw material supplying, consumer goods providing, social and economic infrastructure affording economic activities that emerge in response to the on-site economic activities. Apart from providing the much needed employment coefficients of plan investment, this study made a significant contribution to conceptualisation and methodological aspects of employment potential.

As part of its practice of critically evaluating the policies and programmes of the Government of Karnataka, the ISEC faculty organised workshops at two points of time—one, in September 1984, and another, in 1990, when, respectively, the State Seventh and Eighth plan reports were discussed. On the Seventh Plan report the observations made were as follows:

> "It was felt that priority should be given to agriculture and allied activities, though support for industrial growth could not be ignored. The thrust of agricultural development was to be on utilising the productive potential of all types of cultivable wastelands and increasing crop intensity by providing irrigation facilities and by popularising dry land development technology.
> The focus of industrial development was to be on eliminating regional disparities and ensuring proper dispersal of industrial units. Herein, there was a felt need for labour intensive industrial

> enterprises and for setting up of rural and agro-based industries. The overall thrust of the development planning was to be on the removal of poverty in rural areas by laying emphasis on programmes such as minimum needs, rural employment for the poor and public distribution of foodgrains. In this regard, emphasis was to be on creation of economically viable and durable assets which provide continuous employment and reasonable incomes to the beneficiaries"

Direct involvement of ISEC faculty in plan formulation has taken the form of our faculty working in various capacities in the State Planning Board. In fact, Professor D.M. Nanjundappa heads the Board as deputy chairman. And some of our faculty members—P.R. Brahmananda, G. Thimmaiah and H.G. Hanumappa—have served or have been serving the Board as members. The presence of our faculty in the Board has given a high degree of analytical rigour to planning policies and programmes of the State.

Multi-level Planning

It is in regard to multi-level planning and planning for the development of weaker sections that the ISEC faculty has made significant contributions by undertaking a series of field-based studies. In this section, a review of the work done with regard to multi-level planning is reviewed to identify their specific contribution.

It may be noted that the notion of man-centered development and of people's participation in the development process had by the 70s catapulted decentralized planning into a very important position as far as the planning strategy was concerned. For effectively handling decentralized planning, a basic infrastructure is needed which is not merely establishment of a decentralized governance system but also, the availability of decentralized planning technology and skills. ISEC has been providing such technology and skills in various forms.

In the first place, persons involved in managing decentralized governance and planning have been trained by ISEC. As far back as 1973, a programme of training district level planning personnel was organised. In 1986, the Chief Secretaries of the proposed Zilla Parishads were trained. More recently, the Zilla Panchayat members, presidents and vice-presidents are being trained in the Institute since June 1995. A programme of training for the district level official and non-official members in agro-climatic regional planning has also been organised. All these programmes sought to target planning inputs to the official and non-official members of the decentralized governance bodies. This apart, the contribution of ISEC lies in providing planning inputs by undertaking research studies on various aspects of decentralised governance and planning. We may now turn to take a look at this aspect.

Decentralized planning process consists in identifying the felt needs of the people and the local resources, formulating development projects by keeping the needs and resources in view, drawing up priorities, and finally, sequencing and locating the prioritised projects on a rational basis. Prerequisites to carry out such an exercise are the methodological inputs. Many ISEC studies were targeted to providing these inputs.

The Tumkur Project, started in 1976, under the stewardship of Professor V.K.R.V. Rao collected a vast amount of village and household data from Tumkur district on the socio-economic conditions. As part of this project, a series of monographs were prepared using these data and keeping in view the perspective of planning at the block and village levels. These monographs have developed methodological framework for undertaking decentralized planning. A study by H.G.Hanumappa (1981), keeping the integrated rural development framework in view, takes stock of the human and natural resources in a block with a view to assessing the development potential of the block in question. The methodology followed for this study can be of immense use to researchers and planners. It consists in developing first, a typology of villages, and their spatial distribution pattern, production activities in different sectors, availability of rural amenities and status of politico-economic village level institutions, the development potential of the village clusters, in particular, and the block, in general. Following the lead given by the above study, a series of papers were prepared and presented in the internal seminars and brought together in a volume (Aziz, 1983b). These papers examined the various methodological and substantive issues relating to planning at the block level and addressed the issues relating to the operationally feasible methods of delineating block, regions, identification of target groups needing income and employment generating projects, criteria for identifying employment-income-oriented projects and the institutional innovations needed to make block plan implementation more effective. Two questions raised in the volume which are relevant even today are: should block plans be merely plans for employment generation to the target groups? And how should micro plans be meaningfully linked with the macro plans? Another study, which provided some methodological input to block level planning with a basic focus on regional development, was a study (Hemlata Rao, 1984) that developed criteria to be used for assessing the backwardness of block units viz., Taluks. This study, covering 175 taluks in Karnataka, and using the factor analysis technique identified a set of indicators of development/ under development which are being used by regional planners in the State for inter-taluk allocation of development resources. A study, subsequently carried out by the ISEC (Aziz and Krishna, 1996) provided methodological and substantive inputs to the Hyderabad-Karnataka Area Development Board for its development efforts.

While the Dantwala working group which prepared a report on block level planning had emphasised on planning at the block level, there was an alternative view that we should go further down perhaps to the village cluster level to meaningfully carry out grass-root level planning. One of the proponents of this view, Professor V.K.R.V. Rao (1978b) had advocated a closer integration of rural settlements by promoting contacts and amenities within a cluster of settlements. The rationale underlying this was that it would promote rapid rural growth with social justice. This idea triggered off studies by the ISEC faculty to; (a) look for an appropriate micro area for planning; (b) identification of growth centres for locating amenities; and (c) methodology of cluster formation.

One of the studies (Vivekananda, 1980) argued that the present approach of providing various amenities and services to individual villages needed to be changed in favour of providing them to individual village clusters with coextensive ranges covering all the constituent villages. This study favoured village cluster as a planning unit area for rural development. The size of the village cluster depended on the number of "functions" to be provided by it. As for the location pattern of these functions/amenities, the consideration is that it should meet the requirements of promoting horizontal integration within the clusters so that this could help promote contacts among the constituent villages. Also, certain functions could be provided at a central place within the cluster such that they may be effectively utilised by the inhabitants. V.M. Rao (1980) also favoured village cluster as a planning unit area but on a different ground. Since the Indian villages are of different sizes and homogeneous in nature, village as a unit area may not be suitable for diversifying economic activities and thereby generating growth impulses. He argued that clustering of different sizes of villages, building of rural institutions for locating amenities would by promoting interaction and exchange provide growth impulses.

On the question of cluster formation, an attempt made by

Ramachandran (1980) should be recalled here. Accepting the lateral than vertical linkage and the emerging village cluster as the best way of maximising rural growth, he went on to lay down a procedure for cluster formation. The two criteria laid down for forming a village cluster were: (i) contiguity of villages (with a distance range restricted to no more than 7 kilometers; and (ii) a viable population size—between 4 to 6 thousand—so that demand for amenities is big enough to attract locational decisions of amenities. Keeping these criteria in view, he then went on to linking one village with the other till a village cluster that met these criteria was arrived at.

Two studies which evaluated the cluster approach at a general level commended it with some reservations. M.V. Nadkarni (1992), who reviewed the Tumkur Project studies had all appreciation for the rural development approach that emerged from these studies. He held that though it could make rural development more broad-based and perhaps faster, the cluster approach by itself may not result in decisive improvement in the relative shares of the poor in the benefits from rural development unless the property relations and the power structure in the rural sector are altered. In the same strain, Aziz (1983b), who compared the theoretical bases of the cluster approach and the approach of vertical integration of human settlements advocated by D.R. Gadgil (1967) and Lalit K. Sen (1975), held that though the former was relatively more equity-oriented, it was, in fact, less growth-promoting in nature.

Notwithstanding its limitations, cluster approach to rural development seems to have stood the test of time. That the Government of Karnataka adopted this approach when they chose Mandal Panchayat in 1987 and Grama Panchayat in 1993 as the basic unit area of planning is a great tribute to the contribution made by the ISEC faculty to micro-level planning. For, these panchayats constitute what are approximately the cluster of villages which the ISEC faculty has been talking about.

Before closing this section, it may be of some relevance here to refer to two works which evaluated the decentralized planning process in Karnataka. The first study (Aziz, 1993) which examined decentralised planning at Zilla Parishad and Mandal Panchayat levels concluded that these bodies did better at implementation than at the plan formulation level. This was attributed to inadequate political and financial autonomy, and professional expertise available to them. The second study (Aziz, 1995) which evaluated the Mandal Panchayat plan process, while appreciating its impact on community and economic development was somewhat critical or the Mandal Panchayat body's inability to enthuse and involve people in the planning process.

Planning for Socio-Economic Groups

The imperative of planning for socio-economic groups arose in response to the criticism that the weaker sections of the society did not share the benefits of economic planning during the first-two and half decades of planning in India. Though the major focus was to alleviate poverty, the implied proposition was that resources have to be relocated and re-allocated in favour of weaker sections such that they are empowered to share the benefits of development in future. As part of this important goal, the planners, to begin with, made attempts to provide employment opportunities to the weaker sections on the premise that employment was an important means of empowering the poor to share the benefits of growth. Therefore, the self and wage-employment generation schemes were targeted to the poor. These two schemes respectively reached income yielding assets to the poor households and group/community assets at the village level. Both were intended to improve the household level productivity. But, the question remained as to whether the intended results were achieved at all. A major thrust of the ISEC faculty research has not only been on this question, but also on the wider issue of whether merely planning for employment generation at the household and village levels would adequately empower the poorer sections for sharing benefits of development.

P.H. Rayappa and D. Grover (1980) examined the socio-economic conditions of scheduled caste/scheduled tribe households in Karnataka and found that under conditions of economic adversity and social retardation, not only the incidence of poverty was high amongst these groups, but these households forced the marginal workers such as young, very old and women into the labour market. They felt that there was a need for improving the asset position of these groups by redistributive measures as also improving the levels of worker efficiency. They went further and suggested that any kind of employment planning for these groups has to be preceded by a clear assessment of work, their preferences, attitudes and skills so that more appropriate employment opportunities can be generated. Taking a cue from this study, Aziz (1989) evaluated the self-employment generation programme, namely IRDP, in the Karnataka situation and found that it was lacking in many respects as far as planning was concerned. He found that the IRDP was not planned properly by keeping in view the household skills and expertise and the availability of local resources and infrastructures. Intuition and informality appeared to have guided the planners in preparing the household plans. This resulted in overcrowding of assets in certain village clusters and mismatch of schemes with the local infrastructure. Therefore, it was suggested that planning for employment generation at the household level, to be more effective, ought to be consistent with the household skills and expertise and with the availability of local resources and infrastructures.

A concomitant of IRDP is the programme of TRYSEM which was supposed to provide training to the rural youth to enable them to take up self-employment. The effectiveness of this programme was examined by the ISEC faculty (Sangita and Jayalakshmi, 1986) and found that both the selection of the trainees and monitoring of what happened after the training, were not satisfactory. Also, by critically examining the administrative and organisational structures of this programme, the study suggested that there was a need for proper coordination among various departments and agencies involved in the process of planning and implementation of this programme. As for the wage employment generation programme, a study that evaluated RLEGP in Karnataka (Vivekananda, 1989) was also of the same view as that on the self-employment generation scheme; it was pointed out that this scheme had not been planned properly, and therefore, needed appropriate planning at the village level if better results were to be achieved.

While the above studies looked upon these programmes as anti-poverty programmes and evaluated them as such, two studies went beyond this and argued for planning and implementing them in a wider perspective. V.M. Rao and S. Erappa (1989) looked upon IRDP as an instrument of bringing about structural changes in the rural economy by reducing dependency on farm activities. Therefore, they saw in IRDP a potential for diversifying economic activities and argued that the programme should be given, on a priority basis, to villages that needed wider economic diversification. A. Aziz *et al.*, (1989) did not see TRYSEM in a narrow sense of preparing the rural poor for being merely linked up with IRDP after the training; but rather they wanted TRYSEM to be used as an instrument of making entrepreneurs out of poor by providing them not merely with the managerial skills but also with inputs of entrepreneurs such as innovativeness and risk-bearing abilities.

Concluding Remarks

The seventies saw a marked shift in the planning perspective: the emphasis was now on how planning should promote growth to ensure social justice rather than on maximising national income. This called for a move from planning from top to planning from below by involving people. Adopting a new strategy such as this, presupposed the availability of institutional and intellectual infrastructure. From what has been stated in the above pages, it is clear that ISEC faculty rose to the occasion and provided intellectual support system not only to the State Planning Department in the plan preparation exercises but also contributed to the stock of planning ideas. Our faculty's contribution appears to have been more on the multi-level plan process, especially, spatial and sectional plan process though its participation in the debate on national plan approach and in the preparation of State plans has in no way been insignificant.

Notwithstanding all this, there are certain areas of planning which have not received adequate attention from the ISEC faculty. These areas on which future research should be focussed are as follows:

1. In the context of the market-friendly new economic policy that is being implemented by the Government of India there is need for redefining the role of planning, its focus and strategy.
2. With almost all the States establishing decentralised, governance systems, following 73rd and 74th amendment to the constitution, decentralised planning has assumed importance as an instrument of promoting rural development and development of urban settlements. The future research effort should be not merely on evaluating the process of decentralisation but also on generating new planning paradigms, especially on urban planning which has not received the attention it deserves.
3. Finally, it is very important that, having carried out field studies on various aspects of multi-level planning it is perhaps time to put the field insights together, examine the implications of such insights to the theory of planning and, on its basis, build a theoretical base for the benefit of students of planning as a discipline.

REFERENCES

Aziz, A. (1983a), Gandhian Economic System: Its Relevance to Contemporary India. In V.T. Patil (ed.), *Studies on Gandhi*. New Delhi: Sterling Publishers.

Aziz, A. (ed.) (1983b) *Studies in Block Planning*. New Delhi: Concept.

Aziz, A. (1989) Approaches to Integrated Rural Development: Some Reflections. In K Munirathna (ed.), *Area Planning for Regional Development*. New Delhi: Inter-India Publications.

Aziz, A. (1993) *Decentralised Planning: The Karnataka Experiment*. New Delhi: Sage.

Aziz, A. (1995), *Decentralisation: Mandal Panchayat System in Karnataka*. Hyderabad: National Institute of Rural Development.

Aziz, A. and Sudhir Krishna (eds.) (1996) Regional Development: Problems and Policy Measures. New Delhi: Concept.

Aziz, A. and P.H. Rayappa (1980) *Estimation of Employment Potential of Plan Schemes. Indian Journal of Industrial Relations*: 433-46.

Aziz, A., P. Thippaiah and M. Devendra Babu (1989) Rural Industries Project: Experience in making Entrepreneurs out of the Rural Poor. In V.M. Rao and A. Aziz (eds.), *Poverty Alleviation in India*. New Delhi: Ashish Publishing House.

Bharadwaj, R. and M.V. Nadkarni (eds.) (1992) *Planning for Social and Economic Development: Essays in Honour of Professor D.M. Nanjundappa*. New Delhi: Sage.

Das, B.C. and G.P. Mishra (eds.) (1979) *Gandhi in Today's India*. New Delhi: Ashish Publishing House.

Gadgil, D.R. (1967), *District Development Planning*, Gokhale Institute of Politics and Economics, Poona.

Hanumappa, H.G.(1981) *Socio-economic Inventory for Block Level Planning*. Bangalore: Shiny Publications.

ISEC (1984) *Approaches To Karnataka Seventh Plan: Priorities and Policy Issues*. Bangalore: ISEC. Mimeo.

ISEC (1986) *Orientation Workshop on Panchayati Raj for Chief Secretaries at the proposed Zilla Parishads*. Bangalore: ISEC. Mimeo.

ISEC and Department of Planning, Government of Mysore (1973) *District Planning Officers' Training Course*. Bangalore: ISEC. Mimeo.

Nadkarni, M.V. (1992) Rural Underdevelopment and the Cluster Approach—A Review of Tumkur Studies. *Economic and Political Weekly*, XVII(26): 1346-50.

Ramachandran, H. (1980) *Village Clusters and Rural Development*. New Delhi: Concept.

Rao, Hemlata (1984) *Regional Disparities and Development in India*. New Delhi: Asish Publishing House.

Rao, V.K.R.V. (ed.) (1978a) *Planning in Perspective: Policy Choices in Planning for Karnataka (1973-74 to 1988-89)*. Bombay: Allied Publishers.

Rao, V.K.R.V. (1978b) Issues and Problems of Development of Tumkur Keynote Address at the UNAPDI - ISEC Workshop on Population Planning and Area Development for South Asia, Bangalore.

Rao, V.K.R.V. (1980) Infrastructure and Economic Development. *Commerce, Annual Number*.

Rao, V.K.R.V. (1984) *The New Approach to Indian Planning: Some Suggestions*. The first VT Krishnamachari Memorial Lecture. Delhi: Institute of Economic Growth.

Rao, V.K.R.V., H.K. Mazumdar and Amal Ray (eds.) (1975) *Planning for Change*. Delhi: Vikas.

Rao, V.M. (1980) *Rural Development and the Village: Perspectives for Planning for Development*. New Delhi: Sterling.

Rao, V.M. and S. Erappa (1989) IRDP and Rural Diversification: An Experience. In V.M. Rao and A. Aziz (eds.), *Poverty Alleviation in India*. New Delhi: Ashish.

Rayappa, P.H. and D. Grover (1980) *Employment Planning for the Rural Poor: The*

Case of Scheduled Castes and Scheduled Tribes. New Delhi: Sterling.

Sangita, S.N. and K. Jayalakshmi (1986) *Training of Rural Youth for Self-Employment—An Evaluative Study of Karnataka.* Bangalore: ISEC, Mimeo.

Sen, Lalit K. *et al*., (1975), *Growth Centers in Raichur: An Integrated Area Development Plan for a District in Karnataka*, National Institute of Community Development, Hyderabad.

Vivekananda, M. (1980) *Planning Unit Areas for Integrated Rural Development.* New Delhi: Ashish.

Vivekananda, M. (1989) Rural Landless Employment Guarantee Programme. In V.M. Rao and A. Aziz (eds.), *Poverty Alleviation in India.* New Delhi: Ashish Publishing House.

PART TWO

SECTORAL DEVELOPMENT

4

POLICY FOR AGRICULTURAL DEVELOPMENT IN KARNATAKA[1]

M. VIVEKANANDA

An attempt is made in this Chapter to bring out the policy issues emanating from the studies conducted in the area of Agricultural Development in the Institute for Social and Economic Change since 1972. The policy issues are presented in a thematic way, keeping in view the state of art evolved in the literature on agricultural development in India in theories, findings and challenges. Most of the studies have focussed on Karnataka agriculture and a few, on other States and all-India.

New Agricultural Technology

The most important factor in the substantial increase of agricultural productivity in India since late sixties has been the introduction of land-augmenting farm technology, often referred as "Green Revolution". However, the performance of high yielding varieties is spectacular only in rice and wheat crops. The growth of wheat production, primarily because of a sharp increase in yields, increased the profitability and, in turn, accelerated private investment in irrigation. In this context, a comparative analysis of the adoption of new agricultural technology in Karnataka was carried out in early seventies for the crops of paddy, jowar and cotton (ISEC, 1979b).

These studies pointed out that the new technology had not made significant impact in the State; and among the reasons for the limits to the extension of hybrid varieties in the State were local rainfall conditions, higher yields from some local varieties which were fertilizer responsive, and the comparatively better prices obtained for local varieties. It was also found that wherever these constraints were not operative, inadequate credit facilities and non-timely application of fertilizers stood in the way of the extension of hybrid varieties. Further, the local improved varieties had an edge over hybrid varieties because of their suitability to local agro-climatic conditions, lesser fluctuation in their yield and prices, lower costs and marketing. In Karnataka, wheat is not a significant crop and rice continues to share only about 10 per cent of the gross cropped area. The growth in the production of rice was higher in the pre-green revolution period than during the green revolution or post- green revolution periods (Vivekananda and Satyapriya, 1994a).

Nature of Irrigation

The major complementary inputs to the new seeds are irrigation and fertilizers. In Karnataka, irrigation is provided by three major sources viz., canals, wells and tanks, and these sources present five typical situations, each suggesting a different perspective on how irrigation may be harnessed to promote agricultural development (Rao, 1979). Among these five, two may be identified as having the attributes of 'farming-with-irrigation' situation. These are tank irrigation and a sub-type of canal irrigation-canal (W) where canal water is available only during the main crop-season of the area. Areas of well irrigation and areas receiving perennial irrigation from canal-(P) provide the two situations at the other extreme, resembling the "irrigated farming" situation. Canal irrigation has yet another sub-type called the dry-cum-wet irrigation-canal (DCW), which offers some scope to the farmer to grow a wet crop in addition to the customary dry crop.

The field studies conducted under the different sources of irrigation showed that the benefits of irrigation to the farming households varied with the nature of irrigation (ISEC, 1979a). Various policy options came out of these studies. Where perennial irrigation did not give rise to problems of depletion of water resources, deterioration in land and conflicting claims of regions, the choice was in favour of well irrigation. On the other hand, if perennial irrigation led only to an enclave-like development, the choice would be in favour of the dispersed light irrigation with investment on major irrigation projects which are controlled and managed by the command area authorities. However, it should be recognised that the suggested cropping pattern is not followed in many command areas.

A study, conducted in Lower Bhavani area where irrigation is protective in nature, showed that more and more rice crop was cultivated over the years in the area. The water use efficiency for light irrigated crops was much less than for heavy irrigated crops. Rationalising water rates may seem beneficial to control water supply to the entire area (Giriappa, 1983).

The ultimate irrigation potential of the State by tapping all sources of irrigation is estimated around 40 per cent of the cropped area. Hence, there is a need to augment the facility by utilisation of sewage/sullage water that is thrown up by metropolitan cities as a waste. Care has to be taken to use the water for irrigation after proper treatment. This waste source has the potential to increase crop yields. The underground drainage projects of the local bodies may become more viable if the irrigation aspect is also taken into consideration (Govindaraju, 1981).

Irrigation has a dual role in bringing growth and stability in yield levels. In a study of yield uncertainty in Karnataka agriculture, it was found that not only across districts in respect of foodgrains as a whole, but even across individual crops at the State level, irrigation was not significantly correlated with stability in yields. The coefficient of variation in yields of foodgrains during the period 1955-56 to 1975-76 in 19 districts of Karnataka as the dependent variable, only instability in rainfall emerged as a significant explanatory variable, but not the proportion of irrigated area. Across crops, highly irrigated crops like maize and summer rice were found to have highly unstable yields, whereas relatively rainfed crops like jowar and tur showed less instability (Nadkarni and Deshpande 1980). But the analysis carried out for three different periods viz., 1955-56 to 1970-71, 1970-71 to 1980-81 and 1980-81 to 1990-91 had shown lower instability in crop yields in the last period compared to the earlier two periods (Vivekananda and Satyapriya, 1994a). This could be due to the use of pest resistance seeds or awareness brought in farmers to combat the pests in the latter period. These results show that irrigation by itself may not bring instability in yields if proper steps are taken to combat the pests either by using pest resistant seeds or better pest management.

Though irrigation plays a pivotal role in the development of agriculture, it can be viewed only as part of an overall strategy for rural development and cannot be wholly identified with it. Irrigation has not led to industrial development in some regions (Nadkarni, 1984). However the success stories of industrial development in some parts of the country like Punjab and coastal Andhra in recent times are associated with the surpluses generated from agriculture based on irrigation. Irrigation is a resource which can be translated to industrial development through entrepreneurship of the people.

Chemical Fertilizers

Increased use of fertilizer has been the single most important indicator of technological change in agriculture. The yield response to fertilizer varies across soils, climatic conditions, crops, and use of different technological and management options. These resulted in spatial disparities in the use of chemical fertilizers. About 80 per cent of Nitrogen and Phosphorus had been consumed in less than one-third of districts in India which had well developed irrigation sources. The studies on fertilizer consumption in Karnataka showed that the fertilizer use in the State was about 51 kgs per hectare compared to 100 kgs in Tamil Nadu and 75 kgs in Andhra Pradesh (Govindaraju, 1989). In respect of the use of fertilizers by seasons, kharif season had higher share in fertilizer consumption in South and West Zones of India compared to North and East zones. Among the southern States, Karnataka had higher share in fertilizer consumption in kharif season which was about 62 per cent in the year 1984-85. In the State, the medium and high rainfall regions, and canal irrigated regions have larger share in fertilizer consumption and also higher level of fertilizer use per hectare of gross cropped area. The crops—paddy, sugarcane, cotton, groundnut—account for about 70 per cent of the irrigated area and these crops account for about 86 per cent of the total fertilizer consumption. Though the fertilizer consumption per unit area was more in small holdings, the percentage of farmers using fertilizers were lower in small holdings (Vivekananda and Venkataramanan, 1986). Fertilizer being the important input in crop production, the price hike of fertilizers may adversely affect its consumption resulting in lower yields. A primary survey conducted in three villages in the State showed that the price hike had insignificant impact on HYVs of rice and cotton, and on richer segments of rural population. However, the price rise had adversely affected consumption of fertilizers in the case of dry crops and poor farmers (Hanumappa and Rajasekhar, 1994). The higher subsidy on nitrogen has led to indiscriminate use of nitrogen and brought imbalance in the proper use of NPK to obtain better yields.

Agricultural Labour

The other major input in agriculture is labour. In the context of development planning aimed at the elimination of poverty and unemployment in a society where two-thirds of the population depend on agriculture for their employment and income with no sign of any significant reduction in the percentage of population dependent on agriculture in the near future, the development strategy of agriculture should be labour-intensive. Can the impact of irrigation and new technology on high productivity facilitate absorption of the growing labour force is an interesting question with implications for policy. In addition, in low rainfall areas, the potential for surface or ground water irrigation is limited raising doubts about the labour absorption capacity in these areas. In Karnataka, there is a positive relation between agricultural labour-land ratio and value output per hectare in the northern and southern *maidan* regions. A rate of growth of 4 per cent in the value of agricultural output would bring in 2 per cent growth in labour employment. Since the rate of growth of the supply of agricultural labour will be greater, even a successful agricultural production development strategy can only partially absorb the growing agricultural labour force (Venkataramanan, 1985). If agriculture has to absorb the increase in the rural labour force, the output has to grow at the rate of 4.9 per cent per annum (Vivekananda, 1992). The factors that have a positive and significant impact on use levels of human labour are material inputs, bullock labour, value of output and the level of irrigation (Satyapriya, 1992). A study conducted in Tumkur district of Karnataka showed that the use of new technology in unirrigated areas led to increased crop production and to an increase of employment by 18 per cent in the seven-year period 1970-71 to 1977-78 (Satyapriya, 1981). These findings show that a big thrust is needed in agriculture in the State not only to boost agricultural production but also to absorb the growing labour force.

Agricultural Credit

A strong institutional credit system is a basic requirement for agricultural development. The felt need is met with the expansion of rural banking in India. The rapid expansion in rural credit is impaired by poor loan recovery. The poor loan recovery cannot be solely attributed to the bad years of agriculture. A study on agricultural credit and droughts pointed out that there was not much of difference in the loan recovery performance during drought and non-drought years (Hanumappa and Shylendra, 1990). Efforts are, therefore, necessary to strengthen the credit delivery system. One such effort is the initiation of a pilot project at the district level in thirteen districts in India to strengthen the credit delivery system. An evaluation study of the project brought out that the pilot project contributed positively towards strengthening the credit delivery system (Vyasulu *et al.*, 1990).

The flow of agricultural credit is not adequate to the agricultural sector in Karnataka (Shenoi and Vivekananda, 1995). The farm credit system in Karnataka could serve only 20.3 per cent of the operational farm holders in 1986-87 (according to the State Agricultural Input Survey 1986-87). From the cooperative credit institutions, only 13 per cent of marginal and 21 per cent of small farmers could get credit in 1986-87. The requirement of crop production credit is of the order of Rs. 1,800 crores a year (assuming that 75 per cent of small and marginal farmers and 40 per cent of other farmers would need production credit of Rs. 3,000 per hectare) while the actual credit provided was of the order of Rs. 300 crores in 1991-92. The annual medium and long term credit requirement to strengthen the assets and step up production was of the order of Rs. 800 crores while the actual was Rs. 259 crores in 1991-92. Thus, there is a wide gap between agricultural credit requirement and its actual availability in the State.

Agricultural Prices

The important policy measures, generally accepted to accelerate agricultural production, are stepping up the capital formation in agriculture and provide price incentives to farm produce. As far as capital formation is concerned there is no second opinion about the need for investment in agriculture, particularly on infrastructure. Coming to price incentives, there is an opinion that the initial gains to agriculture are cancelled to a large extent as a result of inflation. Agricultural prices have not been deliberately depressed in India considering the cost of production, terms of trade and world prices. The main crisis in agriculture is not one of unremunerative prices but of unviable holdings (Nadkarni, 1987). Changes in the relative prices bring in changes in the cropping pattern. The change in the relative prices are responsible for increase in the area under rice and groundnut and decrease in bajra and ragi in Andhra Pradesh (Venkataramanan and Prahladachar, 1978). The change in the cropping pattern in Karnataka, particularly after the 80s has been a shift in favour of high value crops of maize, oilseeds and pulses from bajra, jowar and ragi, and from rice to sugarcane and garden crops though there is no productivity gain in many of these crops (Vivekananda and Satyapriya, 1994a). Though in the 80s there was general decline in per hectare total costs, yields and total returns, the net returns recorded an improvement for many of the crops, particularly for commercial crops, due to favourable relative prices (Rao, Hanumappa and Shylendra, 1993). The deliberate change of relative prices of agricultural produce may not really prove to be advantageous in the long run. The changes in the relative prices of commodities may bring in a cobweb type cropping pattern which may not benefit all sections of farmers equally (Satyapriya and Vivekananda, 1996).

Marketable Surplus and Marketing

The generation of a marketable surplus and its transfer from the agricultural to the nonagricultural sector are crucial to the achievement of self-sustaining economic growth. In addition, the behaviour of marketable surplus of foodgrains help in designing a system of procurement and public distribution. The marketed surplus in foodgrains has increased in areas exposed to the new technology. The availability of marketing facilities also increased market orientation and marketable surplus (Nadkarni, 1977). A study on arecanut marketing showed that the location of the market had a considerable influence on the extent of its utilisation by the producer-sellers. Distantly located markets from the producing areas acted as a hindrance to the producer in taking advantage of such organised markets. The structure and functioning of the marketing organisation has a considerable impact on the pattern of arrivals and sales in the regulated markets (Satyapriya, 1984). Development of market areas may not bring in their utilisation unless physical facilities are provided (Satyapriya, 1986).

Farm Size and Productivity

The empirical relationship between farm size and productivity has important policy implication for agricultural development strategy, land reforms, and agricultural taxation. Studies based on "Farm Management Data", collected in the 1950s from selected districts in India, showed that farm size and productivity were inversely related in traditional agriculture. This relationship has important implications for policies affecting land reform and farm organisation, as it implies that output could be increased simply by dividing large farms into small ones. In other words, it implies that implementation of land reform not only improves equity but also efficiency. But most of the studies which verify the inverse relationship used data from the 1950s; at that time, Indian agriculture was characterised as traditional agriculture with the absence of technological change and use of modern inputs.

In modern agriculture, the role of purchased farm inputs becomes crucial, with limited possibilities for substitution between labour and purchased farm inputs. In such a situation, the small farmers, as compared to large farmers, have relatively limited access to credit and purchased inputs. As a result, the small farmers may not be able to apply optimal amounts of purchased modern farm inputs and this may lead to the change in the relationship between farm size and productivity that existed in traditional agriculture. The Farm Management Studies conducted in Karnataka after the introduction of green revolution showed a mixed pattern ranging from inverse relationship to direct relationship (Rajapurohit, 1984).

In the case of inverse relationship, it was observed that small farmers achieved higher crop yields at higher cost of production per unit of land by using relatively more labour and animal power. This resulted in lower economic efficiency of small farms compared to large farms if market wage rates were used in the imputed costs for family labour. In the absence of gainful employment the opportunity cost for family labour was lower than the market wage rate for hired labour. Using market wage rates for family labour resulted in the overestimate of labour cost and hence, production costs (Satyapriya, 1990). Considering net income per unit of land, the relationship is direct in case of dry holdings and inverted 'U' in the case of irrigated holdings (Vivekananda, 1992). These results showed that small holders were not economically efficient compared to the big farmers. To revive and rejuvenate Karnataka's agriculture there is a need to create economically viable land holdings. It is possible to make size of the farm economically viable by allowing leasing of land (Nadkarni, 1993; Thimmaiah, 1996). This requires changes in the Land Reforms Act 1971 of Karnataka.

Development of Small and Marginal Farmers

Several programmes were initiated to make small and marginal farmers economically viable. The recently conceived Small Farmers Agri-Business Consortium (SFAC) by the Government of India is among such attempts. The SFAC envisages active participation of the farm families in decision-making and implementation of various strategies through integration of production processing and marketing functions in order to carry the benefits of modern agri-business to resource poor small and marginal farmers. Dharwad is one of the 12 districts selected for SFAC to identify projects which are technically feasible and financially viable and generate employment. The Dharwad study (Hanumappa and Bhende, 1994) identified three projects—(1) Spice Oleoresin, using chillies as raw material,

(2) Cotton Ginning and Pressing, and (3) Manufacture of Particle Boards, using Cotton Stalk as input. The study also proposed an administrative system to carry out these projects.

It is not out of context to mention here that sericulture in the State has brought in economic viability to many small and marginal farmers. It generates income not only through additional employment but also through diversification (This is well documented in the edited volume of Hanumappa, 1993b).

Dry Land Agriculture

Substantial breakthrough in dry land agriculture is a key component in the agricultural strategy proposed for the Eighth Plan. This is important not only for sustaining agricultural growth in the coming decades but, even more, to stimulate agricultural growth processes in vast areas which have remained largely stagnant so far. The increase in land productivity under rainfed conditions has to be achieved by conserving soil and moisture, and by choosing crop varieties having the potential for higher productivity. The dry land agriculture cannot depend only on miracle seeds or crops, but also requires comprehensive watershed specific measures for soil and moisture conservation. A study of watershed development programme in Karnataka indicated inadequate preparatory planning for the watershed as a whole and lack of enthusiasm among the people in the efforts to improve the common property lands (Rao, Hanumappa and Erappa, 1991). The dry land agriculture in Karnataka is handicapped by a combination of three unfavourable factors: harsh physical conditions, inadequate and indifferent policies, and competition from the more productive parts of agriculture (Rao, 1991). They have an adverse influence on the thrust for growth of the new dry land technology and on the market environment for dry land crops. The strategy for development is to be based on conservation-oriented technology, use of local and, often, degraded-resources and mobilisation of people.

Agro-climatic Regional Planning

As the country has different agro-climatic regions, planning agricultural development a the macro level needs integration with micro level planning at the level of agro-climatic regions. Recognising the importance of regional planning, based on agro-climatic regions, the Planning Commission has proposed to implement its programmes through institutionalization of area-specific agro-climatic regional planning. For this exercise, the country is delineated into 15 zones, and each zone is divided into sub-regions. A sub-region consists of a few revenue districts. The ultimate micro level planning unit is the district. A study conducted for Trichur District has pointed out five main strategies to be followed for the agricultural development of the district (Hanumappa, 1993). They are:

(1) Kole (the cultivable land inundated by sea water) and land development;
(2) minor irrigation for coconut plantation;
(3) sericulture development;
(4) fruit preservation and processing; and
(5) fish culture.

As a part of the zonal planning exercises, attempts have been made to study the spatial and temporal variation in growth rates in area, production, and productivity, and forecast yield gaps for important crops during the terminal years of Ninth and Tenth Five Year plans (Bhende and Hanumappa, 1995).

Yield Gap

The yield levels of major crops in Karnataka are generally on the lower side compared with the neighbouring States of Tamilnadu, Andhra Pradesh and Maharashtra which have predominant area under dry land agriculture like Karnataka (Shenoi and Vivekananda, 1995). The yield levels and the yields of these crops are compared with yields obtained in demonstrations conducted in farmers' fields and are presented in Table 4.1.

Comparison of Karnataka's crop yield levels with the three neighbouring States show that out of the nine crops Karnataka's yield level is higher only in maize and it is lower in four crops viz., rice, bajra, tur and groundnut. The yields of jowar and bengal gram are high only compared to Andhra Pradesh and the yield of cotton is high only compared to Maharashtra. Thus, the crop yield levels in the State are, in general, lower than the yield levels of neighbouring States. The crop yield levels in the State are broadly 40 per cent of the proven yields for different crops under technology developed by the Agricultural Universities.

Table 4.2 shows the yield levels attained for Ragi in 1988 under the Kabbalanala Watershed Programme for Dry Land Agriculture. The proven yield of 2,375 kgs. per hectare of ragi is nearly 100 per cent higher than the

TABLE 4.1: **Yields of Major Crops in Karnataka and Neighbouring States in 1989-90**

(Kgs. per hectare)

	Karna-taka	Tamil-nadu	Andhra Pradesh	Maha-rashtra	Yields demon-strated in farmers' fields
Rice	2,009	3,092	2,417	—	6,240
Jowar	693	1,072	587	1,032	3,200
Ragi	1,199	1,085	1,114	1,773	1,890
Maize	2,772	1,488	1,821	1,129	2,860
Bajra	550	660	1,190	630	1,800
Tur	387	648	—	747	1,430
Bengal gram	500	—	334	533	1,010
Groundnut	793	1,153	905	1,146	2,450
Cotton	221	325	251	143	854

TABLE 4.2: **Contribution of improved Technologies to the Productivity of Ragi**

Particulars	Yield (Kgs. per hec.) Grain	Straw
1. Up and down cultivation with local variety	605	877
2. Contour cultivation with local variety	690	1,020
3. Up and down cultivation with high yielding variety	793	951
4. Contour cultivation with HYV	928	1,123
5. Contour cultivation with HYV and 50 per cent of the recommended dose of fertilizers	1,425	1,890
6. Contour cultivation with HYV and 100 per cent of the recommended dose of fertilizers	2,125	2,465
7. All improved practices with local variety	1,332	1,972
8. All improved practices with HYV	2,375	2,755

Source: *Annual Report* of the Kabbalanala Watershed Project 1989.

average yield in Karnataka. At the global level research centre for dryland agriculture, namely, ICRISAT (International Crops Research Institute for

Semi-arid Tropics), Hyderabad, the average grain yields of improved cropping systems in operative scale watersheds for the years 1976 to 84 were 4.4 tonnes per hectare for maize/chickpea sequence and 3.83 tonnes per hectare for the maize-pigeonpea inter crop, as against the traditional system yield of 720 kgs. per hectare for chickpea and 570 kgs. per hectare of sorghum with post-rainy season. These yield gaps show that the available technology at the agricultural research stations has the potential to increase the productivity of crops if the available technology is suitable for adoption in different agro-climatic regions with cost effectiveness, and if bottlenecks in delivery system of credit and other inputs are eased.

Stagnation in Agricultural Production

Karnataka experienced stagnation in production and productivity in cereals, pulses and oilseeds during the 80s (Vivekananda and Satyapriya, 1994a) The stagnation attracted the attention of the Government of Karnataka and an expert committee was appointed to identify the reason for low productivity and/or constraints and bottlenecks to accelerated growth and production. The Committee submitted its report with detailed recommendations on various aspects concerning agricultural production. The Committee felt that there were still a number of technological constraints in respect of individual crops for enhancing crop yields and recommended that the research in agricultural sciences in the State should be directed to crop and region-specific problems. The Committee also came heavily on the extension system and suggested that extension system has to undergo a change in its outlook with a view to having a target and result-oriented programmes with more emphasis on increasing the productivity of crops.

Corrective Measures by the Karnataka Government

The State Planning Board brought out a Draft Agricultural Policy Resolution (July, 1995), first of its kind in the State. It noted the recommendations given by the expert committee on stagnation of agricultural production in Karnataka and outlined an integrated approach to agricultural development, combining field crops, horticulture, sericulture, fisheries, and animal husbandry under a single entity.[2] The draft envisages opening up agriculture and its allied activities to the private sector through creation of an incentive environment and also, by permitting private sector to own and cultivate agricultural land up to 23 hectares. The draft takes note of the prevailing subsidised water rates and free supply of power to irrigation pumpsets up to 10 HP and suggests appropriate pricing of water and electricity for agricultural purposes. The draft policy takes cognisance of the decline in investment in agriculture and suggests an investment to the order of Rs.1,000 crores per annum during the next five years and that investment is to be equitably shared by the public and private sectors in order to achieve 4.5 per cent annual growth in agriculture sector. The draft agricultural policy attempts to make the small and marginal farmers partners in global agricultural prosperity through commercial farming and corporate agriculture (Thimmaiah and Hanumappa, 1995).

Prospects

Achieving the envisaged 4.5 per cent annual growth in agriculture in the short run appears to be over ambitious given the present level of farm support infrastructure. However, concerted efforts are to be initiated for the development of high yielding variety seeds suitable to the agro climatic conditions of the State through Agricultural Universities as well as private enterprises. The need for the transfer of technology arises when the technological bottlenecks are cleared. Transfer of technology from the research stations to the farmers' fields calls for a strong extension service base manned by motivated and knowledgeable extension workers. This can be achieved by strengthening and making more effective the operation of the existing extension wing through reorientation and constant up-gradation of their knowledge. This would equip the extension workers with the right kind of information to be carried to the farmers. If these are attended to, the State's hope to achieve the envisaged growth rate may be realised.

The advantages of relative prices of commodities may not really prove that advantageous in the long run. The changes in the relative prices of commodities, in the long run, with stagnating productivity of crops may bring in instability in cropping pattern which may not benefit all sections of farmers equally. As a short term policy option, one may choose consolidating the changes that have taken place in the positive direction by strengthening the efforts in providing appropriate infrastructure. For a long term policy, the State should identify the crops in which it has comparative advantage and, research and extension efforts should be specially geared to improve the productivity levels of those crops in addition to the traditional crops of the State. The change in the cropping pattern in favour of commercial crops is a clear indication that the State does not have the comparative advantage in cereal crop production. Further, when trade boundaries are shrinking under the present day liberalisation policy, there is no need for the State to strive for self sufficiency in cereals and continue with lower levels of productivity. Instead, it should go all out for the crops in which it can inject higher productivity levels through research and extension.

Even after the full exploitation of the available irrigation potential, about 60 per cent of the cropped area is likely to be under rainfed conditions in the State. The production growth in the State would depend upon higher and stable productivity levels of rainfed crops. This calls for serious efforts in the direction of retaining soil moisture with appropriate cost effective technology to harness the run off water through the watershed development programmes.

To strengthen the cooperative system, the State Government has to infuse funds of the order of Rs.500 crores into cooperative credit institutions. There is a need to rationalise the subsidised interest rates as subsidy system has led to distortions, corruption and destroyed the rural credit market.

The subsidies by the Government to farmers in various forms viz., supply of electricity, fertilizer and other input subsidies are to be phased out over the years and the amounts saved should be used for the efficient maintenance of power system and promote higher investment in agricultural assets and better extension system.

Further, to achieve a sustained higher level of production, it requires strengthening and expansion of the existing marketing institutions at various levels for assured supply of agricultural inputs and markets for the output.

Thus, the agriculture sector in the State requires big push in appropriate technology development for different agro-climatic zones of the State and its adoption and rationalization of supporting systems to bring back the agricultural sector from stagnation to the path of sustained growth.

NOTES

1. I am thankful to Dr. P.V. Shenoi for sparing his time and offering comments on the draft paper.
2. Some faculty members of ISEC were actively involved in the committee on stagnation of agricultural production as well as in the preparation of the draft agricultural policy for the State.

REFERENCES

Bhende, M.J. and H.G. Hanumappa (1995) *Agro-climatic Regional Planning for Karnataka: A Sub-Regional Analysis*, Bangalore: ISEC. Mimeo.

Giriappa, S. (1983) *Water Use Efficiency in Agriculture*. New Delhi: Oxford and IBH.

Govindaraju, K.V. (1981) *A Study of Sewage/Sullage Water Utilisation in Rural Areas in Karnataka*. Bangalore: ISEC. Mimeo.

Govindaraju, K.V. (1989) *Economic and Agronomic Factors Influencing the Use of Chemical Fertilizers—Cropwise and Regionwise in Karnataka*. Bangalore: ISEC. Mimeo.

Hanumappa H.G. (1993a) Decentralised Agro-climatic Regional Planning Proposal for Trichur District. Bangalore: ISEC. Mimeo.

Hanumappa H.G. (1993b) *Sericulture, Society and Economy*, Bombay: Himalaya Publishing House.

Hanumappa H.G. and M.J. Bhende (1994) *Planning for Full Employment: Strategies for the Small Farmers Agri-Business Consortium—Dharwad District*. Bangalore: ISEC. Mimeo.

Hanumappa, H.G. and D. Rajasekhar (1994) *Fertilizer Price—Impact on Consumption and Cropping Pattern (A study of Three Villages in Karnataka*. Bangalore: ISEC. Mimeo.

Hanumappa, H.G. and H.S. Shylendra (1990) *Whither Farm Credit? The Times of India*, December 17.

Institute for Social and Economic Change (ISEC) (1979a) *Impact of Irrigation (Canal, Well and Tank)*. Bombay: Himalaya Publishing House.

Institute for Social and Economic Change (ISEC) (1979b) *New Seeds Adoption and Yield*. New Delhi: Sterling.

Nadkarni, M.V. (1977) *Behaviour of Marketed and Marketable Surplus of Foodgrains—A Study of Farm Management Data of Ahmednagar District, Maharashtra*. Bangalore: ISEC. Mimeo.

Nadkarni, M.V. (1984) Irrigation and Rural Development—A Sceptical View. *Economic and Political Weekly*, XIX(26): A67-A73.

Nadkarni, M.V. (1987) *Farmers' Movements in India*. New Delhi: Allied Publishers Ltd.

Nadkarni, M.V. (1993) Agricultural Policy in India—Context, Issues and Instruments. *Development Research Group—Study 5*. Bombay: Department of Economic Analysis and Policy, Reserve Bank of India.

Nadkarni, M.V. and R.S. Deshpande (1980) *Rainfall and Yield Uncertainty in Karnataka Agriculture*. Bangalore: ISEC. Mimeo.

Rajapurohit, A.R. (1984) Land Reforms and Changing Agrarian Structure in India. In A.R. Rajapurohit (ed), *Land Reforms in India*. New Delhi: Ashish Publishing House.

Rao, V.M. (1979) Linking Irrigation with Development—Policy Issues: In ISEC, *Impact of Irrigation (Canal Well and Tank)*. Bombay: Himalaya Publishing House.

Rao, V.M. (1991) *Growth in the Context of Underdevelopment: The Case of Dryland Agriculture*. Bangalore: ISEC. Mimeo.

Rao, V.M., H.G. Hanumappa and S. Erappa (1991) Development Opportunities in Dryland Agriculture. *ISEC Working Paper*. Bangalore: ISEC.

Rao, V.M., H.G. Hanumappa and H.S. Shylendra (1993) *A Study of Agricultural Costs: Some Implications for Efficiency Analysis and Price Policy*. Bangalore:

ISEC. Mimeo.

Satyapriya, V.S. (1981) *Labour Utilisation in Agriculture (Tumkur District, Karnataka)* Bangalore: Shiny Publications.

Satyapriya, V.S. (1984) *Arecanut Marketing—A Case Study of Three Major Regulated Markets in Karnataka*. Bangalore: ISEC. Mimeo.

Satyapriya, V.S. (1986) *Marketing of Silkworm Cocoons in Karnataka*. Bangalore: ISEC. Mimeo.

Satyapriya, V.S. (1990) *Labour Use in Agriculture—The Case of Karnataka, Andhra Pradesh and Tamil Nadu*. Bangalore: ISEC. Mimeo.

Satyapriya, V.S. (1992) *Potentialities of Marginal and Small Farmers for Employment Generation*. Bangalore: ISEC. Mimeo.

Satyapriya, V.S. and M. Vivekananda (1996) Agricultural Development: Some Issues. In Abdul Aziz and Sudhir Krishna (eds.) *Regional Development—Problems and Policy Measures*. New Delhi: Concept Publishing Company.

Shenoi, P.V. and M. Vivekananda (1995) Agricultural Development in Karnataka: A Paper Presented at a seminar on *Karnataka Economy* held on 13-14, November 1995, at Hampi. Mimeo.

Thimmaiah, G. (1996) New Perspectives on Land Reforms: In Abdul Aziz and Sudhir Krishna (eds.) *Land Reforms in India—Karnataka*. New Delhi: Sage.

Thimmaiah, G. and H.G. Hanumappa (1995) Karnataka's New Farm Policy—Focusing on the Small Farmer. *The Hindu Business Line*, Madras, August 17.

Venkataramanan, L.S. (1985) *Agricultural Productivity Growth and Labour Absorption in Agriculture in Karnataka*. Bangalore: ISEC. Mimeo.

Venkataramanan, L.S. and M. Prahladachar (1978) Study of Cropping Pattern Changes in Andhra Pradesh During 1950-75. *Indian Economic Review*, Vol. XIII (New Series).

Vivekananda, M. (1992) *Agricultural Development and Distribution of Gains—A Regional Analysis of Karnataka*. Bangalore: ISEC. Mimeo.

Vivekananda, M. and V.S. Satyapriya (1994a) *Time Series Analysis of Agricultural Production in Karnataka*. Bangalore: ISEC. Mimeo.

Vivekananda, M. and V.S. Satyapriya (1994b) Karnataka's Changing Cropping Pattern. *Agricultural Situation in India*, September: 441-4

Vivekananda, M. and L.S.Venkataramanan (1986) *Fertilizer Use in Karnataka: A Preliminary Analysis based on Cost of Cultivation Data*. Bangalore: ISEC. Mimeo.

Vyasulu, Vinod *et al.* (1990) *Strengthening the Credit Delivery System—An Evaluation of the Pilot Project sponsored by the National Bank for Agriculture and Rural Development in Karnataka, Orissa and Madhya Pradesh*. Bangalore: ISEC. Mimeo.

5

INDUSTRIAL POLICY AND DEVELOPMENT

M. PRAHLADACHAR

The various industrial policy pronouncements of the Government of India, have, time and again, focused on: (a) commanding heights of the public sector undertakings; (b) regional dispersal of industries with a view to promoting industrialisation in backward areas; (c) employment generation; and (d) import substitution and export promotion. Many of these aspects, understandably so, do get echoed in several States' industrial policy statements also. The implications of the industrial policy—national and/or State—for industrial development, along with the strategies and programmes followed towards its realisation have been the subjects of research in the Institute for Social and Economic Change at various points of time during the last 25 years. In what follows, an attempt has been made to present, in brief, a review of studies undertaken by the researchers in the Institute, highlighting their significance and relevance to issues/dimensions relating to industrial policy and development.

These studies may be classified broadly into the following categories:

(1) Public sector undertakings;
(2) Regional dispersal of industries;
(3) Rural industries;
(4) Specific-sectors; and
(5) Other issues/aspects.

Studies Relating to Public Sector Undertakings

With many of the public sector undertakings tainted with the dubious distinction of non-performance, as reflected in their poor financial results, there has been a debate going on about their role and relevance in the country's economy. This debate assumes an added significance in the context of the new economic reforms which lay emphasis on efficiency and competition. It is to the credit of the Institute for Social and Economic Change that an attempt was made to throw light on several issues surrounding the public sector undertakings through a seminar organised in February 1987 [for details, see Aziz, 1989].

A position was taken at the above seminar that those of the public sector undertakings which were running under heavy losses, notwithstanding the active support and encouragement from the government, had no right to exist. Contrary to this was the view expressed that there was no justification for trying to evaluate the performance of the public undertakings merely in terms of their ability to generate profits as they were primarily promotional in nature. If so, the question arose as to what criterion should be followed to evaluate them. To answer this question, attempts were made to evolve an appropriate set of criteria, apart from profitability, for evaluating the different categories of public sector undertakings (Thimmaiah, 1989; Rayappa and Thippaiah, 1989). Public Sector Undertakings required to be categorised, it was suggested, on the basis of the objectives for which they were started, and the evaluation of their performance should be done in terms of whether or not the concerned undertaking fulfilled these objectives. Ample evidence of the dismal performance of the public undertakings was provided (Thimmaiah, 1989; Hemlata Rao, 1989; Nadkarni and Rao, 1989) but a need was felt for identifying constraints in the path of these undertakings turning around.

A constraint which was peculiar, and acted as an important bottleneck to better performance by the public undertakings arose out of their organisational structure (Ray, 1989). Restrictive managerial control, bureaucratic management system and lack of delegation of power and authority were identified as the basic drawbacks of the management's style, giving rise to the plea for an appropriate change in the management style and inputs.

Yet another constraint arose from the nature of personnel management and industrial relations. The State sector assuming the responsibility of being a model employer, led to over-staffing, management being soft to the workers and their unions, which, in turn gave rise to multiplicity of unions at the plant level. Also, an extraordinary situation was created by some undertakings by recognising more than one unit for collective bargaining—a situation that was not conceivable in theory and practice of collective bargaining (Aziz *et al.*, 1989).

Apart from the organisational and personnel management aspects, the other aspects which deserved attention were pricing, project planning, working capital and inventory management, sales promotion, marketing management, quality control and so on.

Studies Relating to Regional Dispersal of Industries

Proper spatial spread of industries has been accepted as one of the important means of promoting balanced regional development. This presupposes the identification of industrially backward areas in a given region/State. Although there have been efforts from time to time by State(s) to identify the industrially backward areas, it is felt that these are not based on comprehensive and scientific criterion. To remedy this situation a composite index method by taking selected indicators was offered (Rao, 1985).

Various efforts have been made towards promoting and dispersing industry widely during the last three decades. Notwithstanding these, there has been no marked regional dispersal in industry as evidenced in the specific context of Karnataka. The study by Prahladachar (1994) emphasised, among others, the crucial role of a catalytic nature that infrastructure played in the industrial development and performance of a region. It noted that within the State considerable inter-district disparities existed with regard to various infrastructure indicators and these disparities continued to persist despite the professed objective of the government to develop infrastructure facilities in the backward areas and to promote industrial development therein.

In order to reach the expected or desired level of regional dispersal of industries, starting of rural industries, among others, is proposed as a good strategy to achieve the objective of balanced regional development through industrialization.

It is not difficult to appreciate that the regional dispersal of industries including the rural areas, despite the incentives and concessions offered by the government, would remain a pious hope unless industrial entrepreneurship emerged. Such entrepreneurship would not emerge in a vacuum unless conscious efforts and initiative by the government are forthcoming to build up, nurse and tap the potential entrepreneurship, more so of a local origin. Entrepreneurs, prior to their venturing into industrial manufacturing activities, would assess the 'industrial investment climate' prevalent in a region. Accordingly, a study was undertaken with particular reference to Karnataka to profile how the prospective entrepreneurs viewed the whole question of the general industrial investment climate to assess the accessibility by the entrepreneurs to the infrastructure facilities and to examine the relative efficiency of the incentives offered by the government (Aziz, Rao and Babu, 1988).

This study was carried out with the help of both secondary and primary data. Primary data were collected through canvassing a small interview schedule among (a) intending entrepreneurs; (b) entrepreneurs who had already started industries; (c) government and financial institutions; (d) industrial organisations; and (e) knowledgeable persons.

An interesting finding that emerged from this study was that the entrepreneurial base had become diversified in its composition in that the members of the backward and depressed communities came forward to take up industrial activities. Also, non-traditional industrial communities joined this line. Factors which explained the diversification of the composition of the entrepreneurs were: (i) spread of engineering education; (ii) State's programme to assist and finance the unemployed graduates and diploma holders to start self-employment activities.

Studies on Rural Industries

The logic behind promoting rural industries is to provide gainful employment to the unskilled—unemployed and under-employed—rural labour force. The theoretical justification for the promotion of rural industries is that rural markets are small and dispersed and infrastructural facilities being under-developed, development of manufacturing activities on a small scale at the countryside will facilitate the utilisation of local resources, employment of local skills in order to meet the local needs (Balasubrahmanya, 1993).

As a part of the larger study on rural industrialisation, sponsored by the ILO, an attempt was made to review the literature on different aspects of rural industries both at the national and international levels (Vyasulu and Kumar, 1993). The review observed that the number of studies dealing with the aspects like "linkages" and "efficiency" were high compared to those on aspects like technology and employment. In other words, the existing literature on the level of technology adoption, workers' skill, training of the workers, capacity for surplus generation, etc., were relatively few and these issues were not given enough attention. Another aspect that was conspicuously lacking in the literature was the studies on environment *vis-a-vis* industries.

A study on rural industries with particular reference to Karnataka pointed out that though the rural industrial sector formed a minor part of the State economy, it had grown significantly over the years. With the result, it had gained dominance over its urban counterpart (Balasubrahmanya, 1993). Within the rural industrial sector, non-household sector was gaining prominence. However, its industrial as well as spatial distribution revealed that it had a narrow base since it was, to a large extent, confined to certain industries and districts. This base of rural manufacturing showed no signs of diversification over time. The above features of the rural industrial sector of Karnataka suggested the following policy implications: the growth of non-household sector would facilitate the diversification of rural economy; but, such a growth, if it was confined to certain industries and areas, would not achieve the goal of balanced regional development. Hence, the thrust on rural industries should aim at diversifying the base: industry-wise and region-wise, in addition to expediting the process of rural industrialization.

While planning for the location of rural industries, a pyramidical industrial structure was advocated (Aziz, 1985). Industries that would be established in rural areas could be distinguished under two types: (a) region specific industries which are specific either in respect of raw material or market; and (b) region non-specific industries being fairly universal in nature. It is the latter type of industries which held in store bright prospects for regional dispersal of industries with a slant in favour of backward areas.

In the present scenario of deregulation, it is plausible that the rural industries as well as other small scale industries have to withstand the competition from their large scale counterparts and exist without government support. In other words, a necessary condition for the existence and growth of these industrial units, under the regime of deregulation, is the "efficiency" factor. This is all the more imperative when a strategic role to the rural industries in the development process is assigned. It is in this background that a study on relative efficiency of small scale industries was envisaged (Vani, 1993).

Though it is necessary to study the problem of relative economic efficiency in total, that is, both the allocative and technical efficiency, due to limitations of data, the study concerned itself to the problem of technical efficiency. This was carried out using efficiency measures based on partial and total productivities. Data were obtained from the following sources: (a) ASI; and (b) Census of Small Scale industries.

The results of this study indicated that, in general, at the all-India level, the small scale industries used less capital per worker than large-scale industries i.e., in general, SSIs were more labour intensive than the large-scale ones. However, these observed relations required to be viewed with reservation, as the study noted, mainly due to the measurement problems of the variables under consideration. As long as the extent of the measurement error was the same for small and large scale industries (since the data were collected from the same source) the capital intensity comparisons were still valid to some extent. The analysis at the State level revealed that except in the case of two or three industry groups in each State, in all other cases the relative capital intensity turned out to be less than one. The food product industry group in a majority of the States showed capital intensity greater than one: that is, in general, manufacturing food product industry group required more capital per worker in small scale industries than in large scale industries.

The results further revealed that the relative labour productivity was less than one in almost all the industry groups at the all-India level implying that the output per worker was less in small-scale industries than in large-scale industries. The relative capital productivity was greater than one in more than 70 per cent of the industry group i.e., the capital productivity of small-scale industries was greater than that of their large-scale counterparts.

In regard to the total factor productivity measure, it was found that at the all-India level, for all the industry groups, the total relative efficiency index was less than one. Even though two or three industry groups in each State showed relative efficiency index greater than one, in a majority of the cases the index was less than one. Thus, in general, one could say that small-scale industries were less efficient than large-scale industries.

An analysis, based on Central Statistical Organisation and Annual Survey of Industries data for the year 1987-88 relating to 8 States at two digit level of industrial classification, revealed that small-scale industries had lower capital/labour ratios than the large-scale industries in almost all the cases except in one or two industry groups in each State.

To sum up, this study indicated that in a majority of the industry groups both at the all-India and at the State levels, small-scale industries were inefficient compared to large-scale industries. A significant association between relative efficiency index and relative capital intensity (both at the all-India and in a majority of the States) implied that the small-scale industries cannot be relied upon to generate more employment efficiently.

Specific Sector Studies

(a) *Food Processing Industries*

A study was undertaken to examine the growth, structure and organisation of Food Processing Industries in Punjab. The study looked at the process of industrialisation with special reference to food processing (Singh, 1992). This study observed a clear shift in the relative importance of various industries within the food processing sector. The secondary data analysis brought to the fore that the small scale sector of food processing was relatively less efficient compared to the factory sector. It not only had lower labour and capital productivity but also a higher capital intensity than that of the factory sector.

Although these industries were the major sources of employment for the unskilled and semi-skilled migrant workers, they did not generate the type of employment that suited the local needs. In fact, job opportunities in this sector contributed to a labour shortage in rural areas during peak months.

The high degree of relationship between agricultural growth and the growth of the food processing sector at the district level brought out the importance of agricultural growth in the process of agro-industrialisation/ industrialisation.

These industries seemed to have helped the rural sector by way of providing a market for their produce and certain other linkages like employment and investment opportunities in transport, trade and other sectors. However, the growth of food processing industries did not reflect adequate involvement of the rural community in it. Further, the integration of agricultural trade with processing led to no improvement in the share of the producer in the consumer's rupee which perhaps could be attributed to the form of organisation of food processing units. Therefore, if the food processing industry were to play the role of a catalyst for rural development, it had to be organised in such a manner that rural community could participate in investment, if not in jobs. In this context, cooperatives were expected to play a useful role because they could possibly efficiently link the farm sector with manufacturing.

In the case of new industries, the market may be deemed to be a crucial determinant of their viability. The question of market pertains to whether they should cater to local, national or international markets. Once the market issues come in, the question of technology becomes very crucial since at every level of market the products have different levels of technology. Should the technology be indigenous or imported? Should it be labour saving or labour augmenting? At what scale—small, medium or large—these should be organised? These questions need serious research at firm level and these results will have to be fitted into a macro strategy (Singh, 1992).

The question that requires further research is why there is lack of sub-contracting in this industry which is so prevalent in other activities, and what is the potential for such ancillarisation of production, especially in the secondary processing sector, because marketing and advertisement which are so crucial in food industry are prohibitive to the small units in terms of their cost. Thus, there is a need to look into the potential areas for tie up with the large units.

(b) *Electronics Industry*

The status and prospects of the electronics industry in Karnataka was studied in the background of the broad experiences of the countries like Korea, Taiwan and Japan, which have carved niches for themselves in the world in respect of this industry (Prahladachar and Gayathri, 1995). The special feature of this study lies in the fact that it does not view this industry as a single homogeneous entity but as comprising of five sub-sectors with distinct traits in terms of capital and labour intensity, nature and level of technology, training and skills required and so on. This study tried to understand the constraints and problems faced by this industry in the country, in general, and in Karnataka, in particular.

Unlike many of the success cases wherein predominant emphasis was laid on the development of component sector first that triggered off growth in the other sectors, India has been struggling to develop all the sub-sectors simultaneously. Although, all these sub-sectors are inter-related and the growth in one leads to the growth in another, it is no gainsaying that among all these sub-sectors the components sub-sector constitutes the vital link and therefore, the nature of development in this sub-sector determines the development of other sub-sectors. Indigenous manufacture of components, which are presently being imported, helps bring down the cost of manufacturing and also the price of the final product, thus rendering our industry competitive in the world market. Access to components is determining the location, pace and direction of manufacturing in the other sub-sectors. The study emphasised the special advantages that Karnataka (Bangalore, in particular) enjoyed in the Electronics Industry, but, at the same time, pointed out the hindrances (like quantity and quality of power supply, tax rates, etc.) that stood in the way of realising the full potential of this industry in Karnataka.

Studies Covering other Issues/Aspects

(a) *Environment vis-a-vis Industries*

A study based on 15 case studies in Karnataka which have had installed effluent treatment plants was taken up for assessing the costs of pollution abatement in relation to the economy of individual firms and also, in relation to the level of pollution abated (Ravichandran, 1989). The reference period for the study was from 1982-83 to 1984-85. The cost analysis, attempted in this study, revealed that the burden of extra cost imposed by pollution control was marginal for most of the observations. This finding exposed the hollowness of entrepreneurs' claim that the pollution control was so burdensome in terms of costs that it would affect profit levels, output and employment. This study concluded that pollution abatement would not impose an unduly large burden on industry but a burden which they could easily absorb without adversely affecting their growth. This finding is heartening, because, at least in the Indian conditions it shows that there need be no contradictions between development and environmental concerns.

(b) Employment Aspects of Manufacturing

As mentioned earlier, among various objectives spelt out in India's industrial policy and planning, employment generation has been one all along, with the New Industrial Policy (NIP) being no exception to this. The policy emphasis accorded to the generation of productive employment opportunities in manufacturing sector is understandable and possibly justified, given the concern that our very large manpower resources are utilised effectively. But, it is important to appreciate that the translation of this objective into a working reality in the given resource endowment context (with regard to labour and capital) in which we find ourselves, implies the adoption of labour intensive and capital saving technologies in whichever areas it is feasible to do so. This, in turn, "demands" an appropriate set of pricing and related policies to make sure that industrial units develop in such a manner as to combine the least investment and the maximum employment to the extent that this is technologically feasible and economically possible" (Paranjape, 1991).

In the background of this perspective, an attempt was made to analyse the growth characteristics of employment in the manufacturing sector in Karnataka, as far as possible, across industries and across districts. The data available from:

(a) Annual Survey of Industries for the period 1960-61 to 1988-89;
(b) Reserve Bank of India for the period 1970 to 1986-87; and
(c) the Directorate of Industries and Commerce, Government of Karnataka, for 1991-92, were made use of for the purpose of analysis.

The study noted that the relative share of Karnataka in the country's total manufacturing employment was not only low but also the distribution of employment in the manufacturing sector within the State across districts was quite skewed.

An examination of the industry-wise details, based on RBI data for the period 1975-76 to 1988-89, revealed that employment opportunities grew at a dismal rate of 1.9 per cent as against output and fixed capital, which grew at 6.87 per cent and 8.12 per cent respectively. However, it is crucial to recognise that the objective of employment generation *per se* will not be realised, more so on a sustainable basis unless it is backed up by right policies and facilities in several areas: factor prices, market, finance, etc., which make the industrial units economically and technologically viable. Also, there is a greater need to appreciate that employment generation prospects will receive a serious setback if questions relating to labour productivity, work culture, technology and foreign collaboration are not given adequate attention (Gayathri and Prahladachar, 1995).

(c) Industrial Potential in Karnataka

It is necessary to study the industrial growth and structure at as disaggregated level as possible in order to evaluate industrial policies and potential for growth. Such a study was attempted in the case of Karnataka (Prahladachar *et al.*, 1993) which was sponsored by the KSIIDC. An attempt was made in this study to understand and analyse the State's industrial growth pattern across industries and regions and examine the various parameters: finance, resources, infrastructure, and policy that contributed towards the process.

The growth pattern of industry in the specific context of Karnataka, notwithstanding the government's efforts towards regional dispersal (these efforts manifesting themselves in the form of varied concessions and incentives for the industrially backward areas), was characterised by the persistence of the heavy concentration of industry, prominently around Bangalore, followed by Belgaum, Dharwad, Mysore and Dakshina Kannada. The analysis identified several factors that hindered industrial growth and its regional diversification. The major bottlenecks appeared to be in the area of infrastructure, especially with respect to power and transport. The taxation policy of the State government also acted as a constrictive factor in the path of industrial development in the State. An effective portrayal of the ramifications of these several inhibiting factors for industrial development activity was made with respect to Hyderabad-Karnataka region, in general (Prahladachar, 1996b), and Bellary district, in particular (Prahladachar, 1996a).

Various concessions and incentives offered to industrialists with a view to coaxing them to move to under-developed/undeveloped districts turned out to be mere palliatives in the absence of substantive pre-conditions being fulfilled. While, on the one hand, the State seems to be serious in attracting entrepreneurs to relatively backward areas, on the other, it inadvertently discouraged them by showing laxity and tardiness in implementing many of the concessions and incentives earmarked for the backward regions. Moreover, the purpose and effect of some of these well-meaning concessions and incentives were defeated by counter-measures and steps of the government.

The study proposed that it was a good strategy to identify a few clusters within the State with industrial potential and give top priority in providing and ensuring pre-requisites necessary for industrial development.

The study discerned that the role of concessions and incentives in attracting investors was overstressed. It pointed out that the provision of concessions and incentives encouraged the tendency towards sub-optimal usage of resources.

The study came out with several recommendations to help improve the industrial status of Karnataka in the near future. These recommendations emerged out of the logic, rationale and discussions spelt out at length at various points in the study.

Conclusion

To sum up, the studies in the area of industrial policy so far mostly relate to the scenario prior to the new economic reforms including the New Industrial Policy. But the industrial scenario has changed since the mid-80s with the first round of liberalization. The new economic policy, introduced in 1991, is expected to provide a boost to the industrial sector. As part of the structural adjustment programme many State governments have come out with industrial policies for promoting industries, especially through foreign direct investments from NRIs (Upendranath, *et al.*; 1994). In short, with the launching of new economic reforms, the focus, thrust, approach and policy prescriptions have assumed a new dimension, meaning and significance. It is time the Institute undertook studies examining the impact of new economic reforms on industrial development to ensure the goals of growth, efficiency and equity.

A good beginning seems to have been made in this direction by a recent study completed in the Institute, in collaboration with IDE, Tokyo (Rao and Inoue, 1995). This study made an effort to evaluate the impact of new industrial policy measures on performance indicators like turnover, investment, employment, exports and imports of various types of industries with different types of ownership such as private or government through a field-survey of 50 industrial units covering three zones (Zone I: Highly developed; Zone II: Backward; Zone III: Growth centres). The survey found that the new industrial policy measures, along with a trade policy, foreign direct investment policy, tax and tariff policy, were widely welcomed by the industrialists and varied industrial organisations. However, the State (Karnataka) tax policies were not fully acceptable to the entrepreneurs and in their view, there, were a number of shortcomings affecting adversely the performance of the industrial sector.

REFERENCES

Aziz, Abdul (1985) Regional Dispersal of Industries through Rural Industrialization. In B.S. Sreekantaradhya (ed.), *Regional Dispersal of Industries and Industrial Development*. New Delhi: Deep and Deep Publications.

Aziz, Abdul (ed.) (1989) *Management Problems of State Public Undertakings*. Jaipur: Printwell.

Aziz, Abdul, Devendra Babu and V.K. Shetty (1989) Industrial Relations in Karnataka State Public Undertakings: Some Issues. In Abdul Aziz (ed.), *Management Problems of State Public Undertakings*. Jaipur: Printwell.

Aziz, Abdul, Hemlata Rao and Devendra Babu (1988) *Industrial Investment Climate in Karnataka: The Position Paper*. Bangalore: ISEC. Mimeo.

Balasubrahmanya, M.H. (1993) *Economics of Rural Industries in Karnataka*. A Ph.D. thesis (ISEC). Bangalore: Bangalore University.

Gayithri, K. and M. Prahladachar (1995) Employment in the Manufacturing Sector in Karnataka: Reflections on the New Industrial Policy. *Conference Volume of the 78th Annual Conference of the Economic Association.*

Nadkarni M.V., and G.V.K. Rao (1989) Public Sector for Basic Needs: The Case of Fuel Wood. In Abdul Aziz (ed.), *Management Problems of State Public Undertakings*. Jaipur: Printwell.

Paranjape, H.K. (1991) New Industrial Policy: A Capitalist Manifesto. *Economic and Political Weekly*, XXXV (43): 2472-481.

Prahladachar, M. *et al.* (1993) *Industrial Potential in Karnataka*. Bangalore: ISEC. Mimeo.

Prahladachar, M. (1994) Regional Disparities in Industry in Karnataka: Current Status and Future Outlook. A Paper presented at the Seminar on *Regional Disparities in Agricultural and Industrial Development in Karnataka*. Organised by the IIPA, Karnataka Branch, and ISEC, Bangalore, August 5.

Prahladachar, M. (1996a) Industrial Development Pattern and Location. A Paper presented at the *Seminar on Industrialisation, Socio-economic Externalities and State Policy: A Case Study of Bellary District*, held in Bellary, Aug.16-18.

Prahladachar, M. (1996b) Industrial Development: Status and Prospects. In Abdul Aziz and Sudhir Krishna (eds.). *Regional Development: Problems and Prospects*. New Delhi: Concept Publishing Co.

Prahladachar, M. and K. Gayithri (1995) *Industrial Potential in Karnataka—Phase II: Electronics Industry: Status and Prospects*. Bangalore: ISEC. Mimeo.

Ravichandran, M. (1989) *Economics of Pollution Prevention and Control: A Study of Industrial Pollution in Karnataka*. A Ph.D thesis (ISEC). Mysore: University of Mysore.

Ray, Amal (1989) Public Enterprises in India: Their Managerial Aspects. In Abdul Aziz (ed.), *Management Problems of State Public Undertakings*. Jaipur: Printwell.

Rayappa, P.H., and P. Thippaiah (1989) Criteria to Evaluate the Performance of Public Sector Undertakings in Karnataka. In Abdul Aziz (ed.), *Management Problems of State Public Undertakings*. Jaipur: Printwell.

Rao, Hemlata (1985) Intra-Region Disparities in Industrial Development. In B.S. Sreekantaradhya (ed.), *Regional Dispersal of Industries and Industrial Development*. New Delhi: Deep and Deep Publications.

Rao, Hemlata, (1989) Financial Performance of Karnataka Electricity Board. In Abdul Aziz (ed.), *Management Problems of State Public Undertakings*. Jaipur: Printwell.

Rao, Hemlata, and Kyoko Inoue (1995) *Industrial Development of Karnataka and the New Industrial Policy*. Tokyo, Japan: Institute of Developing Economics.

Singh, Sukhpal (1992) *Agro-Industrialization in Punjab: The Case of Food Processing Industries*. A Ph.D. thesis (ISEC). Bangalore: Bangalore University.

Thimmaiah, G. (1989) State Government Public Enterprises in Karnataka: A Macro Perspective. In Abdul Aziz (ed.) *Management Problems of State Public Undertakings*. Jaipur: Printwell.

Upendranath. C, M. Vijaya Bhaskar and Vinod Vyasulu (1994) Industrial Growth and Structure: Analysis of Manufacturing Sector in Karnataka, *Economic and Political Weekly*. VIIL (26): M156-M164.

Vani, B.P. (1993) *Rural Industrialization in India: Relative Production Efficiency of Small Scale Industries in India*. Bangalore: ISEC. Mimeo.

Vyasulu, Vinod and A.V. Arun Kumar (1993) *Rural Industrialization in India: A Review of Policies*. Bangalore: ISEC. Mimeo.

6

EDUCATIONAL POLICY AND DEVELOPMENTAL RESEARCH

A.S. SEETHARAMU

ISEC is the only Social Science Research Institute which has a distinctive Education Unit. This chapter is a faithful record of the research efforts in Education at ISEC in the backdrop of issues of policy, planning, strategies and problems of educational as well as overall socio-economic development in India, with special reference to Karnataka State.

Educational Policy: Issues and Problems

Karnataka State has no specific or special educational policy. It falls in line with the rest of India in adopting the National Policy on Education. At the national level, an explicit statement of a National Policy on Education was made only in 1986. The 1986 policy was, in several respects, a continuation of the policy perspectives since independence. However, national aspirations got a definite focus, direction and momentum after this period. One of the highly significant policies of the State has been the provision of "Education For All", which was initially incorporated in Article 45 of the Constitution of India that provided for the Universalisation of Primary Education. The last 46 years of educational development in India has been a story of neglect and failure of the State in the realisation of this constitutional dream and national policy. Most of the issues and problems of education configurate around this challenge. Problems of enrolment, retention and attainment in primary education, problems in the provision and popularisation of pre-primary education as a head-start for primary education, provision of a certain measure and quality of non-formal education as a supplement to primary education, specifically to solve the problems of non-enrolment and drop-out phenomenon, provision of literacy programmes for those who escape the channel of primary education, provision of post-literacy and continuing education to sustain the gains from literacy projects, special attention to girls, scheduled castes, scheduled tribes, rural areas, urban slums, reducing regional disparities in educational development, are all issues and problems that have a relevance for the realization of the dream of "Education for All" in India. The ISEC has contributed research insights on all these various issues and problems concerning pre-primary education, primary education, non-formal education, adult education and other related problems cited herein. An account of research efforts at ISEC and their relevance follows.

Pre-Primary Education

Four studies have been completed in this area. A State level survey of the availability of low-cost, flexible and indigenous play materials that may be of value for effective and meaningful transactions between the teacher and learners was made. A manual for use of these materials was also prepared (Devegowda, 1978).

A survey of Pre-Primary institutions in Bangalore City (Usha, 1979) discovered that private aided institutions had better facilities and were better managed as compared to private unaided, Government-run and corporation-run institutions.

A nation-wide programme of Integrated Child Development Services was launched in 1978 including Karnataka State. Health, Nutrition and Education were integrated in a single package at the point of delivery through a chain of institutions known as *Anganwadis*. A viable village unit was chosen to locate an *Anganwadi*. *Anganwadi* is an educational centre for pre-school age children apart from services for expectant and nursing mothers. A cluster of *Anganwadis* was constituted for departmental supervision through an intermediary supervisor known as *Mukhya Sevika*. She served as a link between the huge departmental structures of the Government and the grass-roots functionaries and clientele. There was a need to get a feedback on the problems in the role-performance of the *Mukhya Sevikas*. Such a study was required in the formative stages of the ICDS programme. A study of *Mukhya Sevikas* was taken up in the unit (Nayana Tara and Ramkumar, 1980) and concrete suggestions were offered to the Government on corrective measures in removing constraints on their role performance.

The 73rd and 74th Constitutional Amendments in the country

provided for the decentralisation of development administration through mandatory creations of Panchayat Raj institutions at District and Sub-District levels. The responsibility for school education, including pre-school education, was transferred from Governmental control to local bodies. Pre-primary schools run by the Department of Public Instruction, and *Anganwadis* run by the Department of Women and Children's Welfare came under the purview of PR institutions. It was necessary to examine the issues and problems in the democratization of powers and functions in the field of non-formal education/pre-school education/*Anganwadis*. Such an exercise was made (Seetharamu 1995a) in the unit. The study identified the tension-areas in the transfer of powers and functions from State Control to Local bodies control in the field of Pre-school/Anganwadis education.

Primary Education

Primary education has remained a global as well as national priority for the last 50 years. Still, achievements in India at this level have been sub-optimal. Problems of quantity, quality and equity have besieged the field of primary education. There has been a revival of fresh enthusiasm for universalizing primary education in the international and national contexts of globalization of the economy and structural adjustments needed for the same.

While illiteracy in India, even after the relatively sincere efforts in total literacy campaigns, has remained at 40 per cent as per certain crude estimates, the Mean educational level in India has been just 1.6 years (Human Development Report 1991, UNDP). Education for all through a policy and strategy of Universal Primary Education (UPE) has remained an enigmatic challenge. A major contribution of the Education Unit and the Institute has been in the area of Primary Education.

Non-enumeration, non-enrolment, drop-out phenomenon in schools and sub-optimal attainment levels of children are the challenging and serious problems in primary education. Several studies concerning these problems have been completed in the Institute. Three studies focused on the problems of non-enrolment and drop-out phenomenon in schools (Seetharamu, 1981; Nayana Tara, 1979; Seetharamu and Ushadevi, 1985). These studies discovered a variety of factors, both school and non-school, that worked against the participation of children in schools. Poverty and inequality that punctuate the Indian life in general also got reflected as variables in the success of primary education. Time-utilization analysis of non-enrolled and drop-out children dispelled the common thinking that they are idlers. According to the study, over 94 per cent of the children were engaged in gainful work, either paid or unpaid. While 20 per cent of the rural children were engaged in paid labour, 25 per cent of the urban children from slums were so engaged in paid labour. The scheduled castes, as a category, and girls, in general, displayed non-participative behaviour. A study of the progress of education of the Scheduled Castes and the problems therein brought to the fore the inter-district and inter-regional imbalances in primary education (Bai, 1984). This study highlighted the interplay of historical factors in the relative differentials in the success of primary education. It is wondered whether the State interventions in the form of incentive schemes contribute to educational progress. A study on this theme showed that attendance scholarship scheme did prove useful as a State intervention while the mid-day meals scheme had no such effect (Chandrashekaran, 1979). Factors of educational achievement among Scheduled Caste and Scheduled Tribe students with Kannada as the medium of instruction was the focus of a study (Aruna, 1982). This study revealed that, apart from other factors, the personal adjustment of children and the education of their parents were significant variables in achievement.

Child-labour has been a bane of India's social life. It has also affected school participation. A few studies at the Institute have focused on this problem. One of these studies revealed time-use and management of children in both paid and unpaid labour. It revealed that the difficulties in school participation were genuine for children engaged in family or paid labour (Kanbargi and Kulkarni, 1987). Another study examined the dynamics of child labour in rural areas and its relationship to school participation (Dinesh, 1985).

An estimation of working children who were not able to participate in schooling was made using secondary data (Nagaraju and Thippaiah, 1995). Case study Profiles of Working Children, including their socio-economic and educational contexts were developed. The study discovered that the earning of children in labour was absolutely essential for their families. Hence, a programme of non-formal education was recommended for these children.

Regional disparities in educational development is another important issue in school education. A few studies have thrown light on this problem. One study (Rao, 1984) on regional disparities in development, including education, brought to light inter-district variations and identified backward districts which required intensive support. One of the reasons for inter-regional variations may be attributed to levels of expenditure on education. A study (Nagaraju 1983) focused on this aspect and discovered that such an opinion could not be confirmed. Rather, the disparities in educational provisions at the village level as shown by one of the studies (Nagaraju and Ramachandran 1991), could be attributed to imbalances in rural power structures. Such a finding in the context of Karnataka State was retested (Jena 1990) for Orissa State and confirmed the view that educational distribution is determined by developmental levels and power structures in rural areas. Apart from all these studies, and keeping in mind various field problems, a Master Plan for the universalisation of elementary education in Karnataka State had been drawn up (Devegowda *et al.*, 1981).

A study of the quality of primary education in diverse village contexts was made (Anitha, 1996). A typology of teacher-pupil transaction was made viz., Domesticating, Text-book transmission and Reflective Teaching. The study, which included longitudinal observations, inferred that, by and large, transactions were mostly of the domesticating type followed by text-book transmission and rarely of reflective teaching.

By 1988, as per the Fifth All India Educational Survey, complete access to primary schooling had been achieved in the country. The attention got more and more focused on the quality of schooling as reflected mainly by the attainment levels of children. For the first time, Minimum Levels of Learning at the lower primary stage of education were identified and specified in 1993. It was necessary to prepare and field test the achievement tests for Minimum Levels of Learning. Such an exercise has been completed at the Institute (Nagaraju, 1995).

A significant contribution of the Institute in the field of primary education in current times has been in the facilitation and support for the District Primary Education Project. The Indian State adopted a new economic policy in 1991, proposing structural adjustments in the economy, which included privatisation along with shrinking of the State, globalisation and liberalization. There was a widespread perception that social sectors may get neglected in the tornado of economic reforms. It was also observed that many East Asian nations, with a high profile of economic growth and development, had accorded high priority to primary education in the early years of their growth process while in India, though values of primary education had been recognised even in the Constitution of 1950, the progress continued to be poor as reflected in the infrastructure facilities, access, enrolment, retention, attainment and investment. Hence, it was decided to set up a National Renewal Fund in 1993, supported by international agencies. The Indian State drew up a Social Safety Net strategy to invigorate the social sectors, including education, out of the National Renewal Fund (NRF). The World Bank, and other international aid agencies, began to support primary education in India. It was noted that by 1988 itself access to schooling in India had been achieved with the provision of a primary school in the village itself for 94 per cent of the children, as per the 5th All India Education Survey. The need of the hour was to improve the quality of schooling as well as attract and retain girls in schools. As such, a national programme, known as the District Primary Education Project (DPEP) was initiated in several regions of the country. Four districts in Karnataka States viz., Raichur, Belgaum, Mandya and Kolar, one each in the four divisions of the State with a low record of women's literacy, were chosen for DPEP treatment. Four hundred million rupees would be provided to each district to be spent on quality improvement and gender-specific programmes in a span of 6 to 7 years so as to universalize enrolment, retention and minimum levels of attainment in primary education. Only 24 per cent was to be spent on construction works and 6 per cent on establishment. Keeping these parameters in view, there was a need to prepare perspective plans for the 4 DPEP districts. It had to be an academic/bureaucratic/people's participative exercise. The Education Unit of the ISEC prepared perspective plans for 2, out of the 4 districts in the State (Seetharamu, 1994a; Nagaraju, 1994) which are being implemented at the moment.

Following the 73rd Constitutional Amendment by the Government of India in 1993, providing for democratic decentralisation, planning and management of School Education, including primary education, was transferred to Local Self Government bodies. There was a need to examine the issues and problems in the transfer of powers and responsibilities as well as prospects therein. A study in the unit (Seetharamu, 1995c) of this policy measure identified ways in which democratic culture has to be integrated with reconciliation of historically evolved bureaucratic centralised structures. The study also identified areas of stress and strain where such reconciliation is needed.

Secondary Education

Secondary Education is a bridge between primary education and higher education, on the one hand, and the organised employment market, on the other. It is a critical stage of education for occupational, income and overall social mobility and social change. One of the studies in the unit examined the performance of secondary education in the State, using a systems approach, the input-process-output model. The study discovered 329 schools in the State which consistently, for 11 years, secured results far below the State average, 80 per cent of them being in Old Mysore region. It also highlighted the significance of process variables in the relative levels of performance of schools (Bhatta, 1990). The results of this study regarding the importance of process variables reconfirmed the findings of an earlier study (Manvikar, 1984). This study showed that expenditure on schools in per pupil terms, an input variable, had no relationship with the efficiency of the school. In fact schools with higher per pupil expenditure were displaying lower levels of efficiency.

State interventions in the form of incentives and hostel facilities formed the focus of one of the studies. It demonstrated through follow-up of beneficiaries/path analysis and other techniques, the importance of State interventions in students' performance among the backward communities (Chandrashekar, 1990). Alternatively, State interventions in the form of audio-broadcast over the All India Radio for secondary schools revealed their limited utilization (Nagaraju and Usha, 1982). There are a large number of students who appear for the SSLC examination as private candidates. A study of this scheme showed that the beneficiaries belonged to higher socio-economic strata from urban areas (Nagaraju and Ushadevi, 1984). Plus two stage represents a twilight area in the field of education. It is considered as part of the secondary stage and referred to as the higher secondary stage. A study of vocational education at the +2 stage was taken up by the Institute in its formative stages. Vocational education was introduced as a part of a national policy in 1978 under the Fifth Five Year Plan. This study had been taken up to examine the problems and prospects of vocationalisation (Thimmaiah, *et al.*, 1981). The study showed that the programme was pro-poor though in terms of input supply and human resources supply, its status was very poor.

A study of the promotion of scientific attitude in secondary schools which was completed in 1996, developed a Scientific Attitude Scale, measured the entry and exit performance of students in secondary stage as well as correlated input and process variables with scientific attitude across diverse school contexts (Alexander, 1996). The study highlighted the importance of teaching-learning and infrastructure variables in promoting 3 components of scientific attitude viz., open mindedness, curiosity, judgements based on facts. The study discovered that it was the co-curricular activities that had a strong bearing on 3 other components of scientific attitude, namely, willingness to test and verify conclusions, suspended judgement, and faith in cause and effect relationships.

The average score of total sample on scientific attitude, out of a total score of 50, was 18.22 at the beginning of the school year while it improved to 22.02 at the end of the school year.

Adult and Non-Formal Education

Illiteracy in India has been a subject of global concern. The Indian State in 1950 planned to achieve full literacy through universalisation of primary education. India did not have a policy of adult literacy till 1978. Exclusive reliance on formal primary education to achieve full literacy proved illusory. It contributed a large number of adult illiterates apart from the non-enrolled children and drop-outs from schools at any point of time. The policy discussion paper of 1985, "Challenge of Education" referred to a World Bank warning to India that unless radical measures were adopted to eliminate illiteracy in the country, India would face a dubious prospect of sporting around 500 million illiterates by 2000 AD which would be nearly half the illiterates of the world's 180 countries. This concern has been globalised through a message of "Education For All" across the world.

The concern for adult education and full literacy was expressed in the National Policy on Education, 1986. Immediately thereafter, a National Literacy Mission was set up in 1988 by the Government of India. At this time, there was an ongoing national programme of adult education known as the Project approach. A cluster of 100 to 200 literacy centres were set up in a revenue block and run for a period of 10 months by a trained instructor. A centre enrolled 30 illiterates and ran evening/night schools. A chain of adult and continuing education centres called as Jana Shikshana Nilayas were set up to support literacy projects. Added to all this, in Karnataka State, the adult education projects had been entrusted to the local-self governments during the period 1987 to 1992. There was a need to examine the feasibility of the policy of adult education and the strategy of project approach. This was necessary because the National Literacy Mission (NLM) decided to shift its approach and strategy from project mode to a mission mode for mass literacy through campaigns for literacy. This was a novel experience for India which had to be studied in detail. Further, having realised the limitations of formal primary education in universalization, as early as in the early 70s, the Government of India had initiated a strategy of non-formal education in the Fifth Five Year Plan. Non-formal education for school drop-outs and non-enrolled children began as a centrally sponsored scheme in 1978. The Education Unit has contributed its insights on all these aspects.

A concurrent evaluation of non-formal education for the age-group 9 to 14 years for non-enrolled children and school drop-outs was made in 1988 (Sakuntala, 1988). On several indicators of educational performance, the study established the pro-poor, pro-scheduled castes, pro-girl child character of non-formal education. There have been three studies on literacy programmes in the country. Following the National Policy on Adult Education, 1978, a project approach for the promotion of Literacy had been in force. A study on the project approach (Seetharamu and Ushadevi, 1991) demonstrated the significance of grass-roots level leadership of the local self-government for successful results. A study on literacy campaigns in its formative stages (Shantha, 1992) in South Kanara and Bijapur Districts of Karnataka State revealed the importance of the threshold levels of literacy in the expansion of literacy in a region. Importance of orchestration of the State administrative effort with voluntary effort also came to surface, in this study. Another comprehensive evaluation of Total Literacy Campaigns, covering the entire Karnataka State, was also completed (Seetharamu, 1995b). This study was split up into seven components and steered at the ISEC with contributions from sister universities and institutions. Environment Building Campaigns, Quality of Primers, Organisation and Management aspects, Training of functionaries, Teaching-Learning process in literacy centres, Impact of the Programme in terms of attainment levels of learners, Post-literacy and continuing education programmes are the seven components studied herein. Practical suggestions for mid-course corrections and future strategies were made by these studies and presented at a State-level seminar on the subject. Executive summaries of all the seven studies have also been published. The study highlighted the need to differentiate between "Education for a living" and "Education For Life" in Environment Building Programmes. It underscored the crucial status of the Deputy Commissioner/District Collector/District head in the success of campaigns, as well as the total integration of efforts at the sub-district level.

Teacher Education

Teacher Education is not one of the priority areas of the Education Unit. Still, the unit has displayed marginal concern in this field. The child from 3 to 5 years is not a responsibility of the State. The State bears Constitutional responsibility for education of children after the age of six years. There is an intense interest in pre-primary education from the private sector in urban areas for various reasons, some of which are related to problems of urbanization. While Pre-Primary education is beset with several problems, the problem of training of pre-primary teachers in Karnataka State (Seetharamu and Usha, 1984) showed that the institutions being self-financing, found it hard to balance their expenditures between provision of physical and infrastructure facilities and salaries of teachers.

There was a mushrooming of B.Ed. colleges in the State and Bangalore region, in particular during 1980-81. There was a widespread feeling that they had been established as money-spinning units. It is in this context that a study of the status of teachers in B.Ed. colleges, affiliated to Bangalore University, was made (Seetharamu and Manvikar, 1982). The study revealed the pitiable, low status of B.Ed. college teachers. The teachers of aided colleges were marginally better. There was a mushrooming of not only B.Ed. but also TCH colleges in the State during 1980s. This was because of an increasing demand for trained teachers from Kerala State. That was the time when Kerala State had begun a programme of retraining the teachers through a Radio broadcast programme in the context of a thorough change in the primary curriculum. An evaluation of this programme (Nagaraju, 1982) revealed that there ware several problems of coordination within the Education Department in non-utilisation of Radio broadcasts.

Of late, the syllabi of Primary Education has been changed in Karnataka State. Added to this, a nation-wide programme of quality improvement in primary education has been launched known as the District Primary Education Project. Special orientation for Primary Teachers is also being given under a national programme called SOPT which covers such areas as Minimum Levels of Learning (MLL), Multi-Grade Teaching etc. The minimum entry qualification for primary teachers has been raised from 10th to 12th standard which is the qualification fixed for TCH Courses. In view of all these changes in Primary Education, a need was felt to look at the pre-service training programme of teachers through the TCH programme. A study of the TCH Course (Usha Devi, 1996) discovered that TCH Course did not accord special attention to the teaching-learning process at the initial stages of primary education where learning and retention problems were acute. While practical workload had increased, guidance for such increase had not been adequately planned.

Higher Education

The Bangalore University allowed the colleges to start evening colleges for the benefit of those persons who could not attend colleges during day time. A study of this programme (Ushadevi, 1981) showed that the beneficiaries were mostly from higher socio-economic strata of urban areas. Another study (Seetharamu, 1984) examined the inter-personal relationships, leadership patterns and socio-economic profiles of students from rural areas who came to pursue post-graduate courses at the Bangalore University. The study discovered that during 1979-81, out of the total number of students admitted to the post-graduate courses in Bangalore University, one-third were from rural areas. Eighty per cent of these students were from Bangalore Rural, Tumkur and Kolar Districts which comprised the jurisdiction of Bangalore University. However, one-third of the total students admitted could not enrol themselves. Lack of information about hostel facilities, inadequate hostel facilities, parental poverty, no blood relations (kinship) living in the city as they were the first generation learners and migrants were some of the reascns for non-enrolment. Those who were pursuing post-graduate studies had several interpersonal problems in the Departments and with the urban students, most of them having problems of articulation and communication through English language. It was also discovered that one out of every four students had no aspirations for employment in the organised sector. Many of them liked to get back to their villages and take up farming. They had come to pursue post-graduate education to expand their horizon of general knowledge. They were too young to look after their farms and they had an elder brother or father or uncle who was doing that job. Hence, this study called for restructuring of the university courses and provide flexibility to satisfy the aspirations of rural students. Counselling services to rural students by the university before admission and later, also was recommended.

A study of access and equality of educational opportunity to professional education in the background of social class and educational achievement of students was completed (Gowrishankar, 1995). Social class was perceived in terms of 1986 G.O. of the Government of Karnataka. A secondary analysis of time-series data of students who had entered professional education, either on 'merit' or on 'merit-cum-reservation' basis, was made. The study discovered that the average performance of students admitted to professional courses through merit-cum-reservation basis was marginally better than the average performance of unsuccessful students under the merit category. The study did not approve of the general feeling that merit has suffered because of reservation policy. Here, 'merit' is conceived in an absolute and not a relative sense.

Education and Development

The studies, reported so far, have tried to improve the system of education from within. They are spread across various levels and forms of education. Education is also considered as an instrument for social and economic change, a catalyst in development efforts and a facilitator of a better quality of life. Education is considered as a human capital in this perspective. Education is an indicator as well as a tool of development. Several studies at the Institute have examined the place and importance of education from this perspective. One of the earliest studies in the unit (Seetharamu, 1980) examined the place of formal education as a stimuli in rural response to various development programmes of the State. People who were illiterates and those with various levels of educational attainment constituted the educational stimuli. Responsiveness was defined in terms of awareness, interest and involvement. A ten-point responsiveness scale had also been used to measure rural response to several development programmes of the State, such as those of Free Distribution of Sites, Janatha Housing, Schemes of the Department of Agriculture, Horticulture, Animal Husbandry and Veterinary Services, Irrigation, Health and Family Welfare, Social Welfare, Rural Industries, etc. The study showed that lower primary education appeared as a critical and threshold level for development response. The study advocated reorientation of formal and non-formal education and training programmes to suit the developmental needs. The findings of this study formed a basis for an international study in a comparative perspective regarding the nature and dynamics of integration of education within Integrated Rural Development Projects (Seetharamu, 1985). Two development projects, one in agriculture, known as the Training and Visit System of Agricultural Extension, and another, non-agricultural programme, known as the Training of Rural Youth for Self-Employment (TRYSEM) were examined for the integration of education and training components therein. The study revealed that wherever the principles of Training and Visit System of Agricultural Extension Education had been flouted, there, education was well integrated with Agriculture, and, where it had been honoured, there it was poorly integrated. The study also discovered that formal education, up to seventh standard level, was essential for getting TRYSEM benefits. However, the poorest of the poor, and the poor rural households did not have persons with seventh standard education. The findings of this study on T and V system of agricultural extension were strengthened by a study of T and V in Sericulture (Nagaraju, 1986). This study discovered laxity in the integration of education with the developmental efforts for sericulture.

A collaborative study of the relationship between education and development was made (Ramachandran and Raza, 1988) wherein such variables as adopting scientific methods of agriculture, utilisation of health and sanitation facilities, markets, rural roads etc., were related with levels of education. The study used secondary data, generated by the IRDP study in Tumkur District of the Institute. This study demonstrated the strong relationship between education and rural development.

One of the unique studies in the Institute using longitudinal method was on "Access to Basic Needs including Education". A household survey in sample villages of Tumkur District had been completed in 1977 for a study on Integrated Rural Development directed by Professor V.K.R.V. Rao. A resurvey of the same households had been completed in another study in 1988 (Nagaraju and Ramachandran, 1991). A change in quality of life in the households of sample villages was analysed (Nagaraju and Mathiyazhagan, 1995). The study discovered that though there was growth in access to education in households under study, still this growth had been uniform across gender, caste and occupation categories indicating the continuance of initial levels of inequality. Villages with dominant castes had registered higher growth in education relatively.

Gender studies have gained their rightful prominence in recent years. A few studies have been completed in the area of women's education. One of them studied life-time returns (private returns) of income of women with different levels of education and no education (Shantha, 1983). This study identified that secondary education yielded the highest private returns to women. Length of study of general higher education, private costs and opportunity costs gave an advantage to secondary education over general higher education. The study also included non-economic returns in terms of behaviours and attitudes. Another study (Jehan, 1991) examined the relationship between social mobility, social change and education among women with different levels of education. This was a study of three generations of women: the respondent, her mother and mother's mother. The findings from this study also demonstrated that secondary education for women is a critical minimum stage for occupational and higher social mobility and desired social changes.

A study of women's empowerment through a non-formal education and mobilisation programme was completed (Shantha Mohan and Usha, 1994). This study highlighted the importance of non-formal education in awareness building, mobilisation and self-help among women.

A study of the relationship between Education and Modernity

(Sabu, 1994) was set in Kerala State, and individual modernity was defined in terms of Secular Orientation, Democratic Orientation, Scientific Orientation, Achievement Orientation and Readiness for Change. Modernity scores were obtained for a sample of 700 respondents, 100 each belonging to various levels of education. Secondary education appeared to demarcate the less modern from the more modern in significant ways, though illiterates, lower and higher primary educated were also modern to a degree. That is, the difference between the modernity scores of the secondary educated and other lower levels of educated was statistically significant.

General

A few studies have been completed which cannot be strictly classified in the foregoing framework. They cover either various levels or cut across all these levels. A Survey of Education and Vocational needs of the Physically Handicapped Children (Rohidekar and Usha, 1981) identified such needs, made an inventory of the same and suggested the setting up of special infrastructure facilities to satisfy the needs. A Consultancy Report (Seetharamu, 1988) prepared for the Government of Karnataka on Education in the State by 2000 AD, called for special efforts for the promotion of literacy. A meta-analysis was made of educational researches in the country to examine their relevance for the needs of the country. The study observed that the relevance was far below expectations (Nagaraju, 1989). A Study of Communication and decision making process of educational administration in Karnataka State (Ushadevi, 1992) discovered several dysfunctionalities therein.

It is also noted that quite a large number of studies in the Institute have used "Literacy" as one of the intervening variables in development. They are too innumerable to be listed here. The studies, spread across all the disciplines/units of the Institute. A few studies have also included educational level of the head of the household and its relationship with developmental variables. The studies converge in their findings on the relationship between literacy and developmental variables of their foci.

Overview

It is observed that, by and large, studies in the field of education are policy-oriented. They have either a direct or lateral bearing on both educational and developmental policies. While some evaluation studies have been there, a large number of them are research studies. Studies of Government policies and programmes are evaluative in nature while research studies are issue and problem focused whose inferences have a relevance for policy. Both types of studies have been completed. Perspective plans have been prepared for the State and for Districts. Only one study has been made which is purely theoretical (Seetharamu, 1993). This is a theoretical and historical analysis of the development of a field of education which is now popularly called as Economics of Education. This study identified three stages of development of education in State and nation-building efforts viz., Welfare, Human Capital and Social Choice. The study inferred that Indian Education has been a disorchestrated integration of the three models wherein welfare orientation has gained supremacy. With the analysis of limited but significant data base, the study brought out the distorted priorities in planning and development efforts in Indian education wherein higher education has been heavily subsidised at the cost of Primary, Secondary, adult, non-formal and Vocational Education.

It is also to be noted that, by and large, all the studies in Education have served as bases for planning exercises as well as inputs in training programmes. These studies at the Institute have highlighted the place and importance of education in national development efforts as well as in improving the quality of life. It has also brought to light that education easily integrates with other symbols of power in an inegalitarian society, thereby impressing upon the need for its spread in the interests of equality and social justice.

REFERENCES

Alexander, Benny (1996) *A Study of Development of Scientific Attitude through the Teaching of Science in Secondary Schools*. A Ph.D. Thesis (ISEC). Bangalore: Bangalore University.

Anitha, B.K. (1996) *Intervention of Village Characteristics and School in Terms of Quality and Utilisation: A Study of Villages in Tumkur District*. A Ph.D. Thesis (ISEC). Bangalore: Bangalore University.

Aruna, N.S. (1982) *A Study of the Factors Influencing the Achievement of Seventh Standard Students belonging to SC/ST Whose Medium of Instruction is Kannada*. A Ph.D. Thesis (ISEC). Mysore: University of Mysore.

Bai, D. Premala (1984) *A Study of the Extent and Problems of Utilisation of the Educational Facilities Offered by the Government of Karnataka to the Scheduled Castes at the Primary School with Special Reference to Bangalore District*. A Ph.D. Thesis (ISEC). Mysore: University of Mysore.

Bhatta, H.S. Ganesha (1990) *Secondary Education*. New Delhi: Ashish Publishing House.

Chandrasekaran, Rajeswari (1979) *A Critical Study in Depth of the Various Measures taken by the Government of Karnataka (Mysore) in the Field of Primary Education During the Period 1947-72*. A Ph.D. Thesis (ISEC). Mysore: University of Mysore.

Chandrashekar, U.P. (1990) *A Study of Utilisation of Various Measures Provided by the State to Promote Equality of Educational Opportunity in the Case of Other Backward Classes in a District of Karnataka*. A Ph.D. Thesis (ISEC). Mysore: University of Mysore.

Devegowda, A.C. (1978) *Educational Playmaterials of Karnataka*. New Delhi: NCERT.

Devegowda, A.C. (1981) *Universalisation of Elementary Education: Master Plan for VI and VII Plan Periods (1978-79 to 1987-88)*. Bangalore: ISEC.

Dinesh, B.M. (1985) *Economic Activities of Children: Dimensions, Causes and Consequences*. A Ph.D. Thesis (ISEC). Mysore: University of Mysore.

Gowrishankar, A.D. (1995) *A Study of Relationship Between Social Class, Educational Achievement and Access to Educational Opportunities with Reference to Medical and Engineering Education in Karnataka State*. A Ph.D. Thesis (ISEC). Bangalore: Bangalore University.

Jehan, Fatima Nusrat (1991) *Education, Social Mobility and Social Change Among Women in Bangalore City*. A Ph.D. Thesis (ISEC). Mysore: University of Mysore.

Jena, S. (1990) *Village Characteristics and Schooling: Case Studies of Some Typical Villages in the Balesore District of Orissa*. A Ph.D. Thesis (ISEC). Mysore: University of Mysore.

Kanbargi, Ramesh and P.M. Kulkarni (1987) *Child Labour, Schooling and Fertility in Rural Karnataka, South India*. Bangalore: ISEC. Mimeo.

Manvikar, Sharda (1984) *A Critical Study of Relationship Between Expenditure Pattern and Efficiency Levels of the Secondary Schools of Bangalore District*. A Ph.D. Thesis (ISEC). Mysore: University of Mysore.

Mohan, Shanta (1989) *Returns from Education: The Employed Women in India*. New Delhi: Uppal Publishing House.

Mohan, Shanta (Assisted by M.N. Usha) (1992) *Mass Literacy Campaign in Bijapur and Dakshina Kannada Districts in Karnataka—An Evaluation*. Bangalore: ISEC. Mimeo.

Nagaraju, C.S. (1982) *Evaluation of Radio-cum-Contact in In-service Teachers Training Programme in Kerala*. New Delhi: M.H.R.D.

Nagaraju, C.S. (1983) *Growth or Stagnation: Study of School Education in Karnataka from 1961 Onwards*. Bangalore: ISEC. Mimeo.

Nagaraju, C.S. (1986) *Evaluation of Sericulture Extension and Training in Karnataka Sericulture Project*. Bangalore: ISEC. Mimeo.

Nagaraju, C.S. (1989) National Concerns and Indian Educational Research, *Perspectives in Education*, 4(4).

Nagaraju, C.S. (1994) *Perspective Plan for Universalisation of Primary Education in Belgaum District*. Bangalore: Government of Karnataka.

Nagaraju, C.S. (1995) *Minimum Levels of Learning: Preparation of Teacher Support Materials, Phase III*. Bangalore: ISEC. Mimeo.

Nagaraju, C.S. and K. Mathyazhagan (1995) *Access to Satisfy Basic Needs: Analysis of Change over Time*. Bangalore: ISEC. Mimeo.

Nagaraju, C.S. and H. Ramachandran (1991) *Schooling of Rural Population—A Study of Structural and Organisational Determinants*. Bangalore: ISEC. Mimeo.

Nagaraju, C.S. and P. Thippaiah (1995) *Profile of Working Children in Belgaum Division of Karnataka State*. Bangalore: ISEC. Mimeo.

Nagaraju, C.S. and M.N. Usha (1983) School Broadcasting: Utilisation by High Schools in Bangalore District. *Journal of Indian Education*. IX(1): 20-4.

Nagaraju, C.S. and M.D. Ushadevi (1984) Multiple-point Entry Scheme—A Study of Private Candidates Appearing for S.S.L.C. Examination of Karnataka. *Journal of Indian Education*. IX(6): 44-7.

Nayanatara, S. (1984) *Education in a Rural Environment*. New Delhi: Ashish.

Nayanatara, S. and Usha Ramkumar (1980) *Integrated Child Development Services: An Evaluation*. New Delhi: Ashish.

Ramachandran, H. and Moonis Raza (1988) *Schooling and Rural Transformation*. New Delhi: Vikas.

Rao, Hemlata (1984) *Regional Disparities and Development in India*. New Delhi: Ashish Publishing House.

Rohidekar, S.R. and M.N. Usha (1988) *Educational and Vocational Needs of Physically Handicapped Children: A Study in Karnataka*. Bangalore: ISEC.

Sabu, K.C. (1994) *Relationship Between Education and Modernity: A Study in Kerala State*. A Ph.D. Thesis (ISEC). Bangalore: Bangalore University.

Sakuntala, S.N. (1988) *A Critical Study of Non-Formal Education for Dropouts and Non-enrolled Children in the Age Groups 9-14 Years in Karnataka State*. A Ph.D. Thesis (ISEC). Mysore: University of Mysore.

Seetharamu, A.S. (1980) *Education and Rural Development*. New Delhi: Ashish.

Seetharamu, A.S. (1981) *Education in Slums*. New Delhi: Ashish.

Seetharamu, A.S. (1984) *Rural In-migrants to Higher Education: A Case Study of Bangalore University*. Madras: CLS.

Seetharamu, A.S. (1985) Planning and Management of Education within Integrated Rural Development Projects. In D. Berstecher *et al.* (eds). *Education and Rural Development: Issues for Planning and Research*. Paris: IIEP.

Seetharamu, A.S. (1988) Education in 2001 A.D. in Karnataka. *Journal of Educational Planning and Administration*, 2, NIEPA.

Seetharamu, A.S. (1993) *Economics of Indian Education*. Bangalore: ISEC. Mimeo.

Seetharamu, A.S. (1994) *Perspective Plan for Universalisation of Primary Education in Raichur District*. Bangalore: Government of Karnataka.

Seetharamu, A.S. (1995a) *Structure and Management of Non-Formal Education in Karnataka State*. ISS, New Delhi.

Seetharamu, A.S. (1995b) *Comprehensive Evaluation of Total Literacy Campaigns in Karnataka State*. Bangalore: Government of Karnataka.

Seetharamu, A.S. (1995c) *Structure and Management of Education in Karnataka State*. Bangalore: ISEC. Mimeo.

Seetharamu, A.S. and Sharada Manvikar (1982) *A Study of the Status of Teacher Educators in the B.Ed. Colleges of Bangalore City*. Bangalore: ISEC. Mimeo.

Seetharamu, A.S. and M.N. Usha (1984) *Pre-Primary Teacher Training Centres in Karnataka—A Status Study*. Bangalore: ISEC. Mimeo.

Seetharamu, A.S. and M.D. Ushadevi (1985) *Education in Rural Areas: Constraints and Prospects*. New Delhi: Ashish.

Thimmaiah, G., A.S. Seetharamu, Abdul Aziz and P.H. Rayappa (1981) *Vocationalisation of Education in Karnataka: Problems and Prospects*. Bombay: Himalaya.

Usha, M.N. (1979) *A Survey of Pre-Primary Institutions in Bangalore City*. Bangalore: ISEC. Mimeo.

Ushadevi, M.D. (1981) *A Study of the Motivational Pattern of Evening College Students Studying in Bangalore University and its Constituent Colleges*. Bangalore: ISEC. Mimeo.

Ushadevi, M.D. (1992) *A Study of Communication Process in Relation to Decision Making in the Offices of the Education Department*. A Ph.D. Thesis (ISEC) Mysore: University of Mysore.

Ushadevi, M.D. (1996) *A Study of the Teacher Training Programme for Primary Education*. Bangalore: ISEC. Mimeo.

7

HEALTH AND DEVELOPMENT IN INDIA: TRENDS AND PROSPECTS

RAMESH KANBARGI

Health status of a population is determined by several factors including health care services. It is closely associated with genetic, social, economic, environmental, cultural and political factors which also jointly shape the quality of life of the people. Although interaction among these factors is multi-directional and too complex, it is increasingly being realised that an integrated approach to development would minimise the conflicts and undesirable side-effects of sectoral approach. But, what should be the critical mix of these interventions to obtain the expected results is not clear and planning in most of the countries is dominated by sectoral approach. The distressing disparities observed in the key health indicator—expectation of life at birth or in simple terminology, 'human longevity', brings this out clearly. While the more developed nations today are approaching to a life expectancy of 80 years, many of the less developed nations are still struggling to reach a longevity of 60 years. The global differentials in longevity indicate the efforts put in and the extent of success achieved by countries in health and development. In order to address these issues, representatives of 134 countries assembled at Alma-Ata in the then USSR at the initiation of the World Health Organisation and UNICEF in 1978. The world assembly articulated the historic consensus on the goal of "Health For All by A.D. 2000". The conference declared that health is a fundamental human right and defined it again as a 'state of complete physical, mental and social well-being' and not just a state of absence of disease as is generally believed. The meeting at Alma-Ata is a milestone in the international efforts to reduce the global disparities and improve the health status of all.

One of the basic objectives of the national and international initiatives in health sector is the conviction based on the experience of several decades that good health of a population promotes economic and social development. Better health of labour force would reduce significantly the production losses attributable to labour sickness. It provides resources for investment in other development programmes which, otherwise, would have been spent on treating the sicknesses. Better health improves school enrolments and performance of children in schooling that accelerates the process of human resource development. Healthy labour force improves labour outputs and efficiency leading to rising earnings which tends to reduce mortality. Declining mortality leads to acceleration of the process of demographic transition by reducing fertility and population growth rates. In brief, mortality decline sets in motion a series of changes and therefore, health status is considered as an important input by itself in development.

Health in India

India has made remarkable progress in the field of health since independence. The Crude Death Rate (CDR) today is less than half of what it was in 1947. As a result, expectation of life at birth which was estimated to be just about 27 years in 1947 has risen to about 60 years in the early nineties.

The declining mortality, as noted earlier, brings in several far reaching changes both at macro and micro levels. While the rapid population growth in India mainly attributed to the declining mortality attracted considerable attention of researchers, surprisingly, very little attention has been paid to study what happens at the family level particularly to children. A research study, undertaken at the Population Research Centre of the Institute for Social and Economic Change (ISEC), tried to explore this and came out with several surprising findings. It found that the survival chances of children had improved significantly from 56.6 per cent during 1901-11 to 82.9 per cent during 1961-71 period. Similarly, orphanhood incidence showed a considerable decline—children by age 5 not having mother alive came down from 32.8 per cent during 1901-11 to just 16.0 per cent during 1961-71. Percentage of children not having father alive was reduced from 13.3 to just 2.9 per cent during the same period. As a result, the study pointed out, the process of socialization of children improved because of greater interaction between parents and children on the one hand and also, among siblings, on the other. However, the most alarming finding was that consumption level among children of poor households was on the decline because of the upward trend observed in producer/consumer ratio (Bhat, 1979). Later, several studies that examined the nutritional status of children in India found that a large proportion of children suffered from varying degree of malnutrition in the country.

Data on vital events such as birth, deaths are very poor in most of the less developed countries, including India. They are collected by untrained officials at village levels and suffer from many deficiencies. Such deficient data cannot provide robust estimates so essential for development planning and initiating necessary effective health programmes. Under the circumstances, the Demographers have to depend on census data and indirect statistical techniques to derive robust vital estimates. One such technique, widely known and used, is Coales method. A flaw was noted in this technique and an improved method of estimating life expectancy and age distribution was proposed in a research paper which appeared in the well known Population Index as a special article (Bhat, 1977).

Another methodological contribution from the Population Research Centre was of estimating the incidence of widow and widower remarriages in India from census data. It was strongly believed that during the course of the evolution of Hinduism, a total prohibition on widow remarriages was enforced among the priestly and noble castes in India and no such restrictions were imposed on lower and depressed castes. In the absence of any strong evidence, many western scholars and some intellectuals and elite circles at home had false impression that the proportion of widows remarrying is insignificant. An effort was made to develop a methodology based on life tables to derive estimates of widow and widower remarriages from census data. The analysis showed that about one-third of the widowed women and close to two-thirds of ever widowed men were in remarried status in 1971 (Bhat and Kanbargi, 1984).

The impressive decline in mortality and rise in longevity noted earlier, pale into insignificance against the great strides made by developed and even a few other not so developed countries. It is argued by several experts that the observed decline came in India mainly because of the disease specific public health interventions such as eradication of malaria, small pox, plague etc., that used to take a heavy toll of human lives. It is also argued that the increased longevity in India hides more than what it reveals because the relation between longevity and general health status is not that simple. A person may survive despite being sick. So, the prevalence and incidence of diseases in the population, case fatality rates and the type of health care facilities available to the public all do play a significant role in shaping the health status of the surviving population. The observed wide differentials in mortality among different States, by rural-urban residence, by age, sex, do support this observation. For example, while Kerala State reports that lowest death rate of 6 per 1,000 population, most of the Hindi speaking north Indian States report over 10 deaths per 1,000 population. Deaths among women and children under five years age are significantly large. Women suffer increasingly from health problems associated with pregnancy and child birth. Therefore, Maternal and Child Health (MCH) has been given top priority in the present health programmes. Recently, the government expanded the scope of the programme renaming it as "Reproductive Child Health (RCH)" services which include promotion of family planning, child survival and safe motherhood, prevention of reproductive tract infections/sexually transmitted diseases and AIDS, with a stress on "client approach" rather than the "target approach", followed earlier.

One of the important issues in reproductive health is the problem of abortions—terminating of unwanted pregnancies. Prior to 1972, abortions in India were illegal except when it was done to save the life of a pregnant woman. Despite the law, clandestine or illegal abortions did take place and their number was estimated to be around four million per annum. The associated health hazards, loss of lives and wastage of medical infrastructure forced the government to re-examine the law. In 1964, the Central Government constituted a committee under the chairmanship of Shantilal Shah to study the question of liberalising abortion laws. Based on the report, the Termination of Pregnancy Act (MTP) was passed by the Parliament in 1971. In the wake of the enactment, MTP services were made available to the needy women in approved medical institutions. The Population Research Centre of the Institute for Social and Economic Change conducted a study of various aspects of 996 MTPs performed in 3 hospitals in Bangalore City during 1972-1974 (Kanbargi, 1975). The number of MTPs in Karnataka was rising fast and it was felt necessary to examine systematically the impact of liberalisation on the illegal abortions, on the one hand, and the magnitude of maternal deaths caused by illegal abortions, on the other. But, the data available were very limited. Therefore, a study was conducted on a large scale, whose objectives were to assess the trends in legal abortions in the State, to understand the composition of women who had abortions, to know the trends and differentials in gestation and to study the question of post-abortion acceptance of contraception (Rao and Kanbargi, 1980).

The analysis of 8,073 abortions in Karnataka that took place between April 1972 and March 1975 indicated that the number had increased rapidly since the liberalisation of the law. During this period, age of women obtaining abortions, their family size, duration of pregnancy had declined while the proportion of less educated women had increased. The study observed that if there were more rural approved hospitals and greater diffusion of information, there would have been more demand for abortions in the State (Rao and Kanbargi, 1977).

The liberalization of MTP Act has brought in many issues that require debate and discussion. Whether the women in need of abortion know about the liberalization? If they know about the liberalization, do they know where to seek the abortion services? If they know the place where the services are available, are they able to avail themselves of the services? These questions were tackled in an innovative study conducted in one of the approved government hospitals in Bangalore city. The study pointed out the role of personal communication in disseminating basic information about MTP facilities among the acceptors of MTP in the hospital studied and highlighted the need of using mass media imaginatively not to encourage abortions but to bring out an awareness among all women about the existence of facilities where safe abortion services are provided so that they need not endanger their lives by visiting back-street abortionists or delay their visit to an approved place due to their ignorance (Kanbargi and Kanbargi, 1977).

In the study, it was also found that a large proportion of poor and illiterate women's request for MTPs were rejected on one or other ground while most of the educated women from higher income groups obtained MTP suggesting that the criteria for denying legal abortions were not medical or failure of contraception as the act stipulates but were more of social in nature (Rao, Kanbargi and Kanbargi, 1977).

The primacy given to maternal and child health in the health programme needed continuous feedback to the health bureaucracy on the way they were functioning so that effective measures were taken to maintain some quality. The Population Research Centre was entrusted with the task of evaluating health and family planning including MCH services in Karnataka. Each year a district was selected for an in-depth study, and a confidential report was submitted to the Ministry of Health highlighting the drawbacks in the delivery of the services and suggesting remedial measures (See Appendix A, for details of these studies). In addition to these routine investigations, special studies were initiated on specific research issues. One such study was the Situational Analysis of

Child in Karnataka that examined the various aspects of children—nutrition and health, education, labour disabilities and destitution (Rao and Rayappa, 1989).

The family planning programme in India faced several criticisms for not achieving the desired goals. A new dimension was added to the drawbacks of the programme that the Crude Birth Rate (number of births per 1,000 population) in India remained almost stagnant hovering around 33 while the per cent couples protected observed to be increasing continuously though at a moderate rate. Among the several explanation offered by researchers to this phenomenon, one important issue was the reliability of the service statistics itself compiled by the Ministry of Health. In order to explore the reliability of service statistics, a field investigation was carried out in Bangalore Rural District. The investigation revealed that about 15 per cent of the sterilised cases and 32 per cent of the IUD acceptors could not be traced (Kanbargi, 1991). The study also highlighted the lacklustre delivery of health care services and several other problems in the effective functioning of PHCs (Kanbargi, 1990).

The health policy in India is guided by several reports submitted by the Expert Committees constituted by the Government from time to time. The most influential and widely known among them is the Bhore Committee Report which contains a comprehensive set of recommendations dealing with preventive, curative and promotional aspects of nation's health services. It highlighted the need to develop health infrastructure in the vast rural areas and also suggested ways to form norms for health facilities (GOI, 1946). Later, in 1959, 1962 and 1973, other committees were constituted which suggested ways and means to organise and improve the health care services. Some of the recommendations of these committees were innovative and are being implemented.

The modern health care system in India is based on the western technological institutional model which the rich developed nations have adopted. It needs heavy investment in infrastructure building and training of medical and para-medical personnel which many less developed nations find difficult to manage with. Though, in principle, public health care is accessible to all, in practice, it is used by a majority of those who cannot afford or have access to other better services. The amount of government expenditure on these services is meagre. India occupies middle level position both in public and private care expenditure among countries. The budgetary allocation for health care in India is not only meagre hovering around 2 to 3 per cent of the total outlays from First to Fifth Five Year Plan periods, but has declined to less than 2 per cent thereafter. The World

Bank has been pleading for larger allocation for health care services and a realignment of public-private responsibilities to reduce supply constraints in the delivery of these services, save government's money and improve outcomes to patients (World Bank, 1987).

At the State level also health care services are not given the priority they deserve in resource allocation. A large proportion of the resource allocation goes for disbursing salaries to the staff while the quality of care has been deteriorating. Lack of drugs, non-working equipment and inefficient services have become the hallmark of government health services. Research studies have pointed out that people, particularly in remote rural areas, who depend only on government services are losing faith in them (Kanbargi, 1991).

Several suggestions have been made to improve the accessibility of health care services. K. Mathiyazhagan (1993) through an intensive study has examined the issue of health insurance for rural population in Karnataka. T. Krishna Kumar and Ramesh Kanbargi (1993) have examined in detail the issues involved in pricing and financing of health care services in India through systems approach. They have assessed the present situation of health sector with its demand sub-system, production sub-system, input sub-system including health, manpower and its training. The pharmaceutical industry, the public sub-system that incorporates State regulation of the private services, the interaction of all these subsystems with each other and the linkages of this entire health sector with other sectors of the socio-economic environment have also been studied. This study has tried to answer several relevant questions after assessing the present situation of health sector such as what policy instruments — pricing, regulation and financing—does the State have, in order to bring about a change in the status of health sector from a less desirable position to a more desirable one? What is the optimum choice among alternate policy instruments? etc. The study has also presented an agenda for research so that the gaps in knowledge can be filled up. The items in the agenda have been classified into three groups—to understand clearly the conceptual issues in health economics; setting the basic right; to compile reliable and comparable data across time and regions to get clear and comprehensive picture of the entire health sector; and getting the right tools of analysis; to understand the facts well and to get to the right picture of the underlying structures in order to design the health policies (Krishna Kumar and Kanbargi, 1993).

It was noted earlier that increased longevity in India was achieved mainly through disease specific public health intervention. Any further improvement in health and mortality situation would be a slow process. For example, further decline in mortality and morbidity among women and children is closely associated with their nutritional level. The available information shows that the proportion of low birth weight babies in India (33%) is one of the highest, next only to Bangladesh (where 50 per cent of the babies are of low birth weight). Several other studies also have highlighted severe under-nutrition among Indian children (Gopalan, 1985) and the role of maternal factor in this as an important issue. Babies born to poorly nourished mothers have to suffer increasing susceptibility to diseases and perpetuate poor nutritional status because of their Vitamin 'A' deficient breast milk. This leads them to greater exposure to the risk of several infections. Experts in nutrition argue that human body adopts to continued low nutrient intake by reducing its rate of growth and thereby maintain an equilibrium of physiological functioning. This leads to shortened stature and low body mass index, as observed in India.

Though India not only claims self sufficiency in foodgrain production but also has the potential to export food and this is indeed a creditable achievement. But, it has not helped reduce nutritional deficiencies in the population in a significant way. Several explanations are offered for this and the most important among them is the lower purchasing power of a large section of population. Though food consumption rose in the eighties, Indian diet seems to have deteriorated in terms of protein intake (Evenson, 1986). Nutrition experts have pointed out that though cereal consumption has increased among low income households, health promoting food items like pulses, milk/milk products, oils/fats, meat, poultry or vegetables have remained more elusive in their diet (Rao and Shastri, 1985). To combat nutritional deficiencies and their serious consequences, the government has initiated several intervention programmes such as distributing iron and folic acid tablets to pregnant women and nursing mothers, high potency Vitamin 'A' tablets to prevent blindness among children, providing mid-day meals to school going children etc. However, several evaluation studies, carried out by the Population Research Centre in the Institute, have reported that these programmes are poorly run and often fail to reach the target population to have any visible impact. There are other programmes like Public Distribution System (PDS) of foodgrains at subsidised rates through fair price shops mainly intended to help the poor to improve their food consumption. The PDS suffers from poor targeting, encourages large leakages to the open market, thereby subsidising consumers who are capable of buying in the open market (Bhalla, 1994) and is beset with organisational and management problems

(Sivanna, 1994).

Significant improvements in nutrition and health can be expected when adequate food at affordable price is made available to the low income households. It has to be noted here that during the last four decades per capita net availability of pulses itself has declined, leading to steep rise in its price and the poor just cannot afford pulses in their diet. Many researchers have examined in detail the state of pulse production in India. V.S. Satyapriya's (1989) analysis has shown that pulse production has remained stagnant for over 35 years and the rapid population growth during the period has reduced their per capita availability. This has affected more adversely the consumption among the low income households and the rise in the cereal consumption observed is achieved at the expense of pulses. Similarly, an examination of oil seeds production in India presents a gloomy picture. An exhaustive study of oil seeds concludes "low rates of growth in production, high instability in production and prices, virtual stagnation in yield levels, considerable speculative trading in oil seeds and its products are some of the conspicuous features of Indian oil seed economy" (Ninan, 1989). Several measures taken to improve the situation have not been very fruitful. Like pulses, prices of oil/fats have reached an all-time high and are beyond the reach of low income households. It is worth recalling VKRV Rao (1982), who cautioned in early 1980s for reorienting agricultural production and planning in the light of nutritional requirements for a balanced diet instead of being directed by mere market demand. His analysis considered long term food policy in relation to immediate food problems that confronted India in the early eighties.

Under the present circumstances, further improvements in health status and mortality decline are intricately interlinked with not only the extent of success in direct nutritional interventions but also the overall improvement in the economic condition, particularly that of low income households.

Another major hurdle in further improvement in health and mortality is the problem of drinking water. The relation between drinking water and certain diseases are well documented and widely known since long. Cholera, typhoid and diarrhoea that affect large number of people every year can be significantly reduced if the water supply is improved in quality and quantity. Finding more water from rivers and lakes has become almost impossible because of large-scale pollution from sewage, industrial affluents, pesticides and chemical fertilizers run off, and the water resources are choked with weeds and silt. While the Eighth Five Year Plan reports that there are still 1.5 lakh villages/ habitations having either low per capita water availability (less than 40 litres per capita) or part of the population uncovered (Eighth Five Year Plan, 1992-1997), a study in selected districts of Karnataka found that only 15.4 to 37.5 per cent of habitations were provided with potable water supply (Rao, 1991; 1995).

The situation regarding sanitation is still worse. The Eighth Five Year Plan document indicates that only 2.7 per cent of the rural households have latrine facility but generally the sanitary situation has remained neglected in urban areas also. Rapid urbanisation is responsible for this, to a large extent, as it has put enormous pressure on infrastructure and administration. Large proportion of urban poor live in squatter settlements established on low lying areas, in houses constructed by scrap material or rags and straw, and suffer from several infections and diseases. While disease specific interventions initiated in India were able to eliminate major killer diseases like small-pox, influenza, malaria, plague etc., new more deadly diseases have appeared. AIDS is one such disease that still does not have a cure. It spreads mainly through sexual intercourse and the available evidence shows that the risk of AIDS is high among persons afflicted with sexually transmitted diseases (STDs). A research study conducted in Bangalore reported large proportion of pre-marital and extra-marital sex mainly with commercial sex workers to be an important route of infection. The proportion of students among the patients is large and alarming. However, the number of women among STD cases is found to be too small (Kanbargi and Kanbargi, 1996). The study highlights the urgent need of sex education to adolescents which is the only way to reduce the incidence of STDs in the light of western cultural invasion through electronic media in the country.

A major challenge to the health sector in the coming decades will be of managing the health problems of the growing number of elderly persons. Geriatric health services are yet to grow in India. Though most of the health problems today fall under the domain of public health, epidemiology transition is slowly setting in. Chronic diseases like cancer, tuberculosis, and heart diseases are affecting more and more persons who need expensive curative services, including hospitalization for longer duration. Reproductive health would put enormous pressure on the existing system of care. Scarcity of resources would be a major hurdle in bringing any significant improvement in the accessibility of quality care to all. Alternatives to the present system need to be found and further research can go a long way in this direction.

APPENDIX-I

REPORTS OF RESEARCH STUDIES COMPLETED AT ISEC, BANGALORE—UNPUBLISHED

Jorapur P.B. (1978) *Health, Nutrition and Family Planning Programme: A Study of ICDS.*

Kulkarni, P.M. and Deepak Grover (1982) *Evaluation of Family Welfare Programme in Karnataka.*

Mutharayappa, R., A. Prakash Rao and M. Lingaraju (1992) *An Evaluation Study of Health and Family Welfare Programme among Selected Scheduled Tribes in Dakshina Kannada, District of Karnataka.*

Narayana, M.R. (1994) *An Evaluation of the Family Welfare Programme in Chitradurga District of Karnataka State*, Part 1.

Raju, K.N.M., T.N. Bhat and K.S. Umamani (1993) *Evaluation of Family Planning and MCH Services in Mandya District, Karnataka.*

Ram, Foujdar, Jyothi Girimaji and K.S. Umamani (1983) *Infant and Childhood Mortality: Levels, Trends and its Determinants in Karnataka.*

Rao, N. Baskara (1980) *Use Effectiveness of IUD: A Follow-up Study of IUD Users in Bangalore City.*

Rao, N. Baskara, T.N. Bhat, K.S. Umamani and Jyoti Girimaji (1984) *Evaluation of MCH and Family Planning among Scheduled Castes and Others.*

Rao, N. Baskara (1988) *Evaluation of Health and Family Welfare Programme in Mysore District.*

Rayappa, P.H. (1984) *Village Health Guide Scheme in Karnataka: A Study of Two Primary Health Centres in Kolar District.*

Rayappa, P.H. and M. Johnson Samuel (1990) *Universal Immunization Programme in Karnataka: An Evaluation Study in Hassan District.*

Shariff, Abusaleh (1986) *Child Survival: Some Cultural Factors associated with Morbidity and Mortality in South India—A Village Level Investigation.*

Shariff, Abusaleh (1987) *Evaluation of MCH and Family Planning in Coorg District.*

Veeramatha, C.S. and Shanta Kanbargi (1991) *Evaluation of Family Planning and MCH Services in Bangalore City.*

REFERENCES

Bhalla G.S. (1994) "Globalisation and Agricultural Policy in India". A Presidential Address delivered at the *54th Annual Conference of the Indian Society of Agricultural Economics*. Bombay.

Bhat, P.N. Mari (1977) Estimation of Vital Rates and Age Distribution under Quasi-Stability: A Case of India - 1961 Re-Examined". *Population Index*, 43(2).

Bhat, P.N. Mari (1979) On the Impact of Declining Mortality on Children in India. (In K. Srinivasan, P.C. Saxena, Tara Kanitkar (eds.), *The Child in India*. Bombay: Himalaya Publishing House.

Bhat, P.N. Mari and Ramesh Kanbargi (1984) Estimating the Incidence of Widow and Widower Remarriages in India from Census Data. *Population Studies*, 38(1).

Evenson, Robert E. (1986) *Food Consumption, Nutrient Intake and Agricultural Production in India*, Occasional Paper No. 3. New Delhi: USAID India.

Gopalan, C. (1985) The Mothers and Child in India. *Economic and Political Weekly*, XX(4).

Government of India (GOI) (1946) *Report of the Health Survey and Development Committee* (Bhore Committee Report). 4 Volumes, Delhi: Manager of Publications.

Government of India (GOI) (1992) *Eighth Five Year Plan, 1992-1997*, Vols. I and II. New Delhi: Planning Commission.

Kanbargi, Ramesh (1975) *Induced Abortions in Bangalore City: 1972-1974*. New Delhi: Allied Publishers.

Kanbargi, Ramesh (1990) Lunges at Birth Boom without Conviction. *Deccan Herald*, Bangalore, July 21.

Kanbargi, Ramesh (1991). *Health and Family Planning Programme in Two Primary Health Centre Areas in Karnataka: An Evaluation*. Bangalore: ISEC. Mimeo.

Kanbargi, Ramesh and Shanta Kanbargi (1977) Some Aspects of Communication in Legal Abortions: A Case Study. *Journal of Family Welfare*, 34(2).

Kanbargi, Ramesh and Shanta Kanbargi (1996) Sexually Transmitted Diseases in Bangalore City: Some Findings from an Exploratory Study. *Journal of Family Welfare*, 42(1).

Krishna Kumar, T. and Ramesh Kanbargi (1993) *Pricing and Financing of Health Care Services in India: Problems, Priorities and Policies*. Bangalore: ISEC. Mimeo.

Mathiyazhagan, K. (1993) *Financing Health For All: The Validity of a National Rural Health Insurance Policy in India—A Report*, London: London School of Hygiene and Tropical Medicine.

Ninan, K.N. (1989) *Edible Oil Seeds*. New Delhi: Oxford and IBH Publishing House.

Rao, M. Negeshwara (1991) *Evaluation of Handpump Programme in Karnataka*. Bangalore: ISEC. Mimeo.

Rao, M. Nageshwara (1995) *Validation Study on Not Covered Rural Habitation (in Five Districts of Karnataka)*. Bangalore: ISEC. Mimeo.

Rao, N. Baskara and Gowrinath Shastry (1985) *Nutritional Profile in India Over a*

Decade. Hyderabad: National Institute of Nutrition.

Rao, N. Baskara and Ramesh Kanbargi (1977) Legal Abortions in an Indian State. *Studies in Family Planning*, 8(2).

Rao, N. Baskara and Ramesh Kanbargi (1980) *Medical Termination of Pregnancies: An Analysis of Trends and Differentials in Legal Abortions in Karnataka*. Bombay: Himalaya Publishing House.

Rao, N. Baskara, Ramesh Kanbargi and Shanta Kanbargi (1977) Criteria for denying Legal Abortions. *Economic and Political Weekly*, XII(48).

Rao, N. Baskara and P.H. Rayappa (1989) *Child in Karnataka: A Situational Analysis*. Bangalore: ISEC. Mimeo.

Rao, V.K.R.V. (1982) *Food, Nutrition and Poverty in India*. New Delhi: Vikas Publishing House.

Satyapriya, V.S. (1989) *Pulses in India*. New Delhi: Oxford and IBH Publishing Company.

Sivanna, N. (1994) *The Public Distribution System in Karnataka: A Study of its Organisation and Management Aspects*. Bangalore: ISEC. Mimeo.

World Bank (1987) *Financing of Health Services in Developing Countries*. Washington: The World Bank.

8

IRRIGATION AND DEVELOPMENT

M. VENKATA REDDY

Introduction

The role of irrigation in the development of a country is primarily that of increasing agricultural production by way of higher intensity of cropping as also higher productivity of crops. Keeping these objectives in view, efforts were made to develop irrigation projects on a large scale with increasing levels of public investment, particularly after independence. The era of big storage dams started to supplement the traditionally important systems like tanks, wells and diversion weirs, which were not adequate enough for increasing agricultural production to keep pace with the fast growing population. A major proportion (about 65 per cent) of the public investment in irrigation during the post-independence period was on major and medium storage reservoirs. Such expansion of investment in major irrigation underscores its pivotal and potential role in accelerating agricultural development.

While higher levels of investment in irrigation and the consequent increase in the number of large storage dams is justified, as they are deemed to be temples of modern India, its impact on socio-economic and environmental conditions has become a matter for debate. For, the ramifications of irrigation impact have given rise to a number of theoretical and empirical questions. It is now generally acknowledged that the 15 billion dollars that used to be poured into the irrigation subsector in less-developed countries annually have not produced more than 50 per cent of the anticipated output (Nijman, 1993). The problems of environmental deterioration such as waterlogging, salinity and other adverse effects on socio-economic conditions are said to be due to the disjunction between increasingly large scale complex and modern irrigation network and still largely traditional peasant farm users of that system (Shepperdson, 1981).

The benefits from irrigation are alleged to be cost-ineffective and inegalitarian in their distribution across space and among the target groups. This process, if not corrected, tends to create negative externalities like income inequalities and other socio-cultural problems, camouflaging the positive role of irrigation as an agent of economic development. Furthermore, the major irrigation projects in India are beset with a variety of problems which have led to the questionable validity of the very importance and thrust given to its development in the successive plan periods.

One of the main problems with major irrigation projects is their unduly longer gestation periods; projects go on lingering for years without completion. It is then natural that it leads to cost overruns and the consequent uneconomic returns. It is no doubt acknowledged that political compulsions and other social factors sometimes arising out of inter-State water sharing, necessitates undertaking a number of projects simultaneously, spreading thinly the available funds. This tends to increase the cost per hectare of irrigation potential created, which is generally played against major irrigation projects, undermining its potential as growth-promoting factor.

In spite of long gestation periods, the irrigation potential created under the major and medium projects is said to be under utilised. The gap between irrigation potential created and its utilisation has increased in the successive plan periods. The gap is expressed as the difference between the targeted area for irrigation for a particular crop pattern and the actual area irrigated. Despite the theoretical nuances about the definition of irrigation potential, as it is defined variously, it is important to identify the factors, if any, contributing for such a gap. The limitations of some of the design parameters like water duty, cropping pattern envisaged and crop-water requirements need a fresh look based on field realities in various projects.

Even the potential utilised is believed to have created distribution problems. There has been inequitable distribution of water among farmers. The farmers at the head-reaches and other influential ones generally get more water than they are entitled to, depriving the tail-end farmers of their legitimate share. Such inequitable distribution of water seems to have created social tensions in the countryside apart from widening the income inequalities between the rich and poor. Hitherto, irrigation planners perhaps thought that it is enough to build a dam to store water and construct canals to release water to the fields. The relevance of building an equally, if not more, important DAM (Distribution, Allocation and Management) was paid much less attention. The result is the poor performance of irrigation projects. The primary concern of the planners now is how to ensure equitable distribution of water in major irrigation projects.

On-farm development (OFD) is another neglected aspect in canal command areas which seems to be one of the contributing factors for the gap between irrigation potential created and utilised. Farmers are generally expected to develop their lands before water is actually released for irrigation. Ensuring scientific OFD is even one of the main objectives/ mandate of Command Area Development Authorities (CADAs). It is also one of the imperatives for promoting scientific water management. But the experience so far is that even after several years of irrigation, a substantial part of the localised area remained undeveloped in many projects, which is said to be a contributing factor to the adverse effects on soil.

Scientific water management is conspicuous by its absence in many command areas. As pointed earlier, farmers may not be knowledgeable about irrigated farming as they have had no exposure to it. With the result, they tend to overuse water which affects the productivity of crops adversely, apart from creating environmental problems. It is, therefore, necessary to identify the constraints, if any, to ensure scientific water management practices which help increasing productivity of crops and minimise adverse effects.

Agricultural development options are expected to closely follow the introduction of irrigation through a well-knit network of extension activities. Farmers should be equipped properly to take on to irrigated farming with the help of agricultural extension agents. Therefore, the question of committed and farmer-friendly agricultural extension arises. But, the experiences in many command areas seem to be much less encouraging, in spite of the training and visit (T & V) system being introduced.

Low rate of irrigation water charges followed by its poor collection is yet another problem associated with major irrigation projects. It is expected to meet the entire operational cost of a project, besides a small percentage of interest on fixed capital through irrigation charges. But, in reality, not even 50 per cent of the operational costs are met out of the irrigation charges, let alone interest on fixed capital. It is, therefore, necessary to have a fresh look at the irrigation fee structure to formulate strategies to increase the returns on investment in irrigation without jeopardising farmer's income.

Negative externalities of large storage dams in the catchment as well as command areas are many and varied. Millions of people are being displaced, thousands of hectares of forests are being submerged, some of the rare species of flora and fauna are getting wiped out, millions of hectares of land all are going out of cultivation due to waterlogging and salinity, water-borne diseases are increasing, to mention a few. Unable to understand the complex nature of causal relationship between irrigation and some of these externalities, anti-major irrigation protests have started emerging in the recent past. Keeping in view the critical need to harness available water resources in the country to augment agricultural production, how to build and ensure environment-friendly irrigation systems has become the major concern of the irrigation planners.

In view of the several problems allegedly affecting the efficiency of major irrigation, a change in the policy thrust from major to minor irrigation is contemplated in the recent past. This is a larger question which should be based on a rational approach taking all the possible techno-economic and social considerations into account and not based on any naive emotional overtones. The latest thinking on Participatory Irrigation Management (PIM) in the agency-managed large systems is, however, a silver lining. There are adequate evidences to show that the participatory management has ensured irrigation efficiency in many developing countries. Farmer-managed irrigation systems are well known for their efficiency and sustainability in this country. But how to ensure beneficiary participation in the Government managed large systems is an important question. It is relevant to ponder over the kind of structural changes and adjustments required in the design, operation and maintenance of the systems to introduce participatory irrigation management.

A brief account of some of the issues and problems presented so far brings out the limitations of irrigation as an important input to gear economic development as perceived, planned and expected by the planners. In the forefront of a move to make irrigation, particularly major irrigation projects, more efficient and productive to accelerate the development lies an enormous task of identifying the constraints, if any, and incorporating corrective measures. This calls for a comprehensive problem-specific research at the micro-level, encompassing a variety of technical, socio-economic, political and environmental considerations. Adequate efforts are already being made by national and donor agencies to study the problems of water utilisation.

Keeping some of the above mentioned contemporary problems associated with irrigation and its role in economic development as a backdrop, an attempt has been made in the following pages to highlight the policy research so far undertaken in the ISEC during the last two decades.

II. EMPIRICAL RESEARCH ON IRRIGATION: AN OVERVIEW

The research at ISEC on irrigation could, broadly, be grouped into five phases:

(a) Socio-economic Benchmark Studies in the command areas of Karnataka;
(b) Concurrent Evaluation of Programmes undertaken by the Command Area Development Authority (CADA);
(c) Action research on Water Management and Distribution;
(d) Irrigation Impact Assessment; and
(e) Issue-based Specific Studies.

The policy research on irrigation at ISEC covers a wide range of issues and problems associated with the distribution and utilisation of irrigation water in the canal command areas, besides the programmes and processes related to water use efficiency. The major findings of various studies and their relevance in the contemporary scenario of irrigation are discussed below.

Socio-Economic Benchmark Studies

The impact of developmental programmes is generally measured by using cross-section (with and without) or longitudinal (before and after) approach. While the limitations of the cross-section approach are well articulated in irrigation literature, the longitudinal approach is hardly adopted, for want of pre-irrigation socio-economic benchmark studies. Realising the contemporary relevance and importance of such studies in almost all the major irrigation projects of Cauvery and Krishna Basins, benchmark studies were undertaken during the post-independence period, an advantage for longitudinal studies, which are conspicuous by their absence in many other States.

The Benchmark studies addressed four distinct, but interrelated, aspects, namely:

(a) Farm Economy;
(b) Income, Savings and Investment;

(c) Social Framework; and
(d) Demography.

This was done with a view to enabling comprehensive measurement of irrigation impact on the socio-economic conditions of the beneficiaries.

The Methodology adopted for benchmark studies had its own significance. It provided for measuring the impact not only between irrigated and unirrigated villages but also between the villages with relatively longer period of irrigation (stabilized) and the villages where irrigation is of shorter duration (newly irrigated):

(1) The villages which were irrigated just on the eve of initiating a Benchmark survey, were categorised as 'A'-villages (irrigated);
(2) The villages which were not irrigated at the time of Benchmark survey, but scheduled to receive irrigation in due course, were categorised as 'B'-villages (To be irrigated); and
(3) The villages which were not irrigated at the time of survey and remained so in future, were categorised as 'C'-villages (unirrigated).

When an ex-post evaluation of irrigation impact is carried out, 'A' villages reflect a stabilised irrigated farming scenario, followed by newly irrigated or unstabilised scenario in 'B' villages and unirrigated farming status in 'C' villages. Such comparative analysis might help drawing lessons from stabilized irrigation systems, and incorporating efficiency-promoting corrective measures in newly irrigated tracts to accelerate the benefits of irrigation. This type of stratification is very uncommon and hardly found elsewhere in irrigation research.

The benchmark studies, by very definition, were meant for studying the socio-economic status of the beneficiaries in particular, and the village as a whole, in general, before the introduction of irrigation, to provide watermarks for measuring the impact at a future date. The studies on Farm economy, Demographic Features and Social Framework (Narayan, *et al.*, 1978) presented a broad spectrum of agricultural development in terms of cropping pattern, yield rates, input application, employment of labour (owned as well as hired) followed by demographic indicators like population growth, literacy, infant mortality, female and child work participation and sociological problems related to living conditions, marriages and other cultural traits. For instance, in Ghataprabha and Malaprabha command areas, crops like jowar and bajra were traditionally the important ones grown in all the three categories of villages (A, B and C). Hardly any high-yielding varieties (HYVs) were grown. In villages where irrigation was introduced just one or two years before the Benchmark Survey (BMS), HYVs were grown on a limited scale. But, the yield differentials between HYVs and local varieties were found to be very insignificant. In some cases, local varieties fared better than HYVs. This was essentially due to lack of experience to the farmers in irrigated farming. While the application of chemical fertilizers was much lower than the recommended levels, the combination of farmyard manure and chemical fertilizers had significantly improved the productivity of crops. This explains the need for educating farmers in newly irrigated areas on improved technology before actually water gets released for irrigation. It is only an illustrative example as to how the benchmark studies could be useful to formulate policy interventions, apart from providing watermarks for measuring the impact.

It was interesting to note that the per capita debt was more in "A" villages. Interesting because, in spite of irrigation being introduced, farmers were more indebted. This could be due to more initial investment requirements for irrigated agriculture. But none of the farmers availed long term loans. It was not clear whether it was due to lack of need or farmers' reluctance to avail loans as it generally called for innumerable procedures and formalities. The per capita and also per household expenditure of small and marginal farmers were much less encouraging.

The non-cultivators, small and marginal farmers from "A" and "B" categories of sample villages, had invested more in the purchase of agricultural lands, while it was conspicuous by its absence among big landholders. Anticipating assured and sustainable income under irrigated conditions, the landless and also small holders were found to be channelling all their resources towards purchase of land, if and when available. Barring big landowners, all other cultivators and non-cultivators were below poverty line. Though the poverty line was chosen arbitrarily, it was closer to the officially accepted figure of Rs. 70 per capita per month for 1978-79. The intensity and spread of poverty observed in the command area may hopefully be reduced by the introduction of irrigation.

Irrigation is known for triggering off multi-dimensional spread effects through forward and backward linkages in various sectors in a command area. It becomes, therefore, necessary to channel the growth processes to optimise their multiplier effects with minimum transaction costs. The study on Integrated Development of Malaprabha and Ghataprabha Command Areas (Narayan, *et al.*, 1977) analysed various aspects of command area development covering land development, irrigation, agricultural support programme, markets and warehouses, provision for inputs and socio-economic infrastructure. The approach broadly covered an estimate of requirements and location of necessary functions/services. The study pointed out that it was not desirable to spread the economic activity too thinly over a large space; it was necessary to limit the dispersal of economic activity to a few selected centres built on the basic principles of decentralization and selectivity.

The central place theory was adopted to identify the growth centres. The method for delineating hierarchy of settlements was based on statistical, empirical, cartographical and irrigation potential analysis. The study first identified central places in the command areas in the order of their hierarchy, earmarked their hinterland/service area and estimates the potential of the hinter-land and requirements of service areas. The central places and their service areas were identified, based on a detailed field data on linkages, critical functional distance, commodity flows, functional hierarchy, geographical centrality, availability and utilization of services, and estimated agro-industrial potential of the region. The plan prepared for area planning was considered by the Planning Commission, Government of India, as one of the best.

> "The commission finds that some of these plans, particularly the one prepared by the Institute for Social and Economic Change, Bangalore, for the integrated development on Malaprabha and Ghataprabha project areas to be of exceptionally good quality" (*The Hindu*, August 25, 1977).

Concurrent Evaluation Studies

Concurrent evaluation is the analysis of continuing relevance of an activity, its efficiency and effectiveness, present and future potential benefits. This helps provide information to the decision makers for the adjustment of objectives, strategies and other related factors, besides providing information for future planning. It also helps them to examine the appropriateness and relevance of the assumptions and hypotheses based on which the project was formulated and actual technology, skills and resources available locally.

As pointed out earlier, the major irrigation projects are subjected to criticism on account of the gap between irrigation potential created and its utilization, which has increased in the successive plan periods. On the recommendations of the Irrigation Commission 1972, Command Area Development Authorities (CADAs) were started in the country in 1974 to initiate and co-ordinate various programmes in major irrigation projects to improve water-use efficiency by reducing the gap between irrigation potential created and utilized. Among various activities of CADA, On-Farm Development (OFD), which included systematic levelling and bunding of land, providing field irrigation channels, drainage etc, and scientific water management were given priority. Even so, the results were said to be much less encouraging.

The study on concurrent evaluation of Land Development and Water Management (Narayan and Reddy, 1979b) addressed the techno-economic and other issues related to timely and efficient implementation of these two important programmes. Farmers were expected to complete OFD before the water was released into the canals for irrigation. But it was found that no single farmer had taken up land development work before the release of water.

Several factors seemed to have contributed for the slow progress of OFD. Farmers had no confidence about the timely and adequate supply of water. Since OFD is a cost-intensive activity, farmers did not venture to take up land development work. This is particularly so with the tail-end farmers. Furthermore, non-availability of mechanical equipments like bulldozers and tractors, followed by inadequate and untimely supply of institutional credit, have restricted the progress of OFD. Owing to non-upgradation of land records, many farmers became ineligible for availing institutional credit for want of proper ownership titles and also due to some loans already outstanding against the mortgage of lands. The question of ineligible farmers was, therefore, found to be an important one calling for immediate attention of the planners. Non-availability of adequate labour and bullock power also contributed for the dismal progress of land development in the command areas. The study highlighted some policy interventions to augment the supply of mechanical implements, credit and most of all, assuring timely supply of water to expedite OFD works.

As expected in a newly irrigated tract, many farmers were not aware of scientific water management practices. Overuse of water in the head-reaches was rampant, resulting in lower yields than expected. None of the farmers had proper knowledge about crop-water requirements. The methods and materials used by the farmers for water distribution and control on the field were crude and did not help in any way to ensure water use efficiency (Reddy, 1982b).

It is natural that inexperienced and illiterate farmers when exposed suddenly to new technology find it difficult to understand, assimilate and adopt it successfully at the farm level. The question of committed and farmer-friendly agricultural extension, therefore, becomes important and relevant. The study on Agricultural Extension (Narayan and Reddy, 1979b) analysed the limitations of the existing extension programmes in the command areas to meet a wide range of farmer's needs and suggested some ways and means of improving the services.

The study pointed out that the extension agent had become more and more an adviser to the farmer. The age-old system of guidance and advice should have given place to learning and teaching process. It was not enough if a number of programmes were administered; success, in fact, depended a great deal on the persuasive role of extension agent through teaching and training. Furthermore, the importance of endogenous development efforts in the form of an extension leader, in addition to extension agent, from within the village or group of villages was emphasised with an indication that the present "contact farmer" concept should lead gradually to extension leader approach. Lack of perceptible impact of agricultural extension on agricultural production was attributed to the multifarious activities of the extension agent, lack of single line of control and direct line of technical support. Added to this, unduly larger jurisdiction covering roughly about 6,000 farm households, spread over extensive areas, was also one of the contributing factors for poor performance of agricultural extension. It suggested that farm management, storage, processing, transportation and marketing of agricultural produce should be made an integral part of agricultural extension in the canal command areas.

The basic philosophy in building a competent extension agency in the command areas should take into account the limitations in a rural setting, difficulties of covering too many farmers as also too many crops and finally, the farmer's resistance and limited knowledge. It was suggested that the minimum qualification for an extension agent should be a degree. For, it is believed that higher qualification enables better comprehension and grasp of problems, despite commanding more respect from the farmers. Further, both in learning from and teaching to the farmer, a graduate is better equipped and is likely to leave definite and sustainable impact.

The extension, to be successful, should be based on the advice, experience and proven success. It is desirable to teach farmers the new technology based on extensive field trials to create confidence in them. The programmes in the command areas tend to be successful only when one idea is driven home through many methods rather than many ideas through one method. The acceptance rate among the farmers was fairly good, as recommended cropping pattern was readily accepted by a majority of the farmers irrespective of their landholding. However, inadequate and untimely package of practices and inputs resulted in lower yields as reported by the farmers. It is, therefore, emphasised to take sufficient care before introducing new technology, as farmers tend to accept recommendations since they will be new to irrigated farming. Any failure or adverse effects in the initial period makes the task difficult to change farmers' attitude towards new technology.

Farmers wanted the extension agents to teach them water management practices, techniques for conserving soil fertility, and other related irrigation technology which, according to them, was not forthcoming from the extension services. Small and marginal farmers were, in particular, not happy with the extension services as they could hardly get any help or guidance. Finally, the study revealed that the impact of extension on agricultural production in the command areas varied from indifference, low and in some sections, fairly good across the beneficiary farmers, which calls for more vibrant, committed and unbiased extension system to ensure optimum and productive use of water for irrigation.

Action Research on Water Management and Distribution

The concept of irrigation development as a process did not seem to have given adequate importance to the Distribution, Allocation and Management (DAM) issues while designing an irrigation project. It was, perhaps, thought enough to build the dam, construct the canals and release water to the fields, leaving the distribution aspects to farmers whose rational behaviour was taken for granted. But, in reality, this did not happen. The non-recognition of management and distribution problems seemed to have led to a variety of avoidable social, economic and environmental problems. Keeping this contemporary situation/problems in view, an action research study on water management was conducted (Narayan and Reddy, 1981).

Warabandi (rotational supply of water) system of irrigation to ensure equitable, timely and dependable supply of water is widely practised in Punjab, Haryana, U.P. and other parts of northern India. An attempt was made to introduce this system for the first time in Karnataka on an experimental basis in one of the major irrigation projects, namely, Hemavathy Command Area in the Cauvery Basin. The detailed objectives and operational plan which included technical details, rotation schedules, rules, regulations and strategies to organise farmers were prepared and implemented (Reddy, 1982a).

The advantages of Warabandi System were many. Tail-end farmers, who never got adequate water, could get water for irrigation on par with head- and middle-reach farmers. The area irrigated per unit of water had increased. Farmers could save substantial time in watering the fields, as predetermined irrigation schedules and timings were known to them in advance, and used the same for other activities enhancing the opportunity cost of their labour. Water-related litigations and squabbles had come down drastically. Over and above all, the productivity of crops had increased substantially after the introduction of Warabandi System. The demonstration effect of such benefits made farmers from rest of the command area to voluntarily adopt Warabandi System which was extended subsequently to many distributaries in the command area and also, to other command areas in Karnataka.

The success story of Warabandi was, however, short-lived. The retrograde process seemed to have taken place after the ISEC withdrew from action research. The limitations of research organisations for continuous associations need to be appreciated. It was expected that the system would be able to sustain as it was kept on a sound footing for two years, with all the technical and institutional backup. Unfortunately, that did not happen and on the contrary, reverted back to the same old method followed by indiscipline and inefficient use of water. Many factors contributed for the failure of the system (Reddy, 1988a or ab or c). Among other reasons, the transfer of executives, who were trained and motivated to operate the system scientifically, was considered, even according to the irrigation officials themselves, responsible for operational lapses in an otherwise successful system. Such lapses were successfully exploited by the influential head-reach farmers to break the system which was not to their advantage. This showed that the ISEC had not only ventured into policy research but also followed it up, may be in a limited way, to analyse the constraints and drawbacks, which enabled the formulation of corrective measures.

There are not many studies which have addressed water distribution problems in major irrigation projects, especially at the micro-level. The assumption of water duty and cropping pattern, based on which Culturable Command Area (CCA) of a given project will be delineated, is expected to be as closer to the field realities as possible. But, in reality, one does not know to what extent they would be realistic and conform to the field conditions. Because, it depends upon farmers adhering to the cropping pattern assumed in the project design and other related factors. The Study on Water Distribution and Management in Ghataprabha Command Area

(Reddy, 1987) brought out in detail the problems and constraints in ensuring efficient utilisation of water.

The study was a comprehensive one where discharge of water in three distributaries (one each from head, middle and tail-reaches of Ghataprabha left bank canal) was measured daily during the rabi season of 1985-86 agricultural year. Similarly, crops irrigated by the given discharge in a day was also recorded. Demand for water was worked out by taking crop-water requirements into account. The difference between demand for and supply (actual discharge) of water was worked out. The study came out with specific solutions to improve water use efficiency in the command areas.

The study indicated that the water duty (100 acres per cusec of water) assumed for the project did not hold valid under the existing field conditions. Violation of cropping pattern was quite perceptible in the command area which explained, to a larger extent, the non-conformity of duty with field situation. Furthermore, the demarcation of command area into kharif and rabi zones, an apparently realistic strategy to enforce 40:20:40, was not practicable. Because, in several cases kharif and rabi blocks overlapped in the same distributary which had led to indiscipline in water use, apart from damaging irrigation structures by the farmers. Rotational Water Supply (RWS) system prevalent in some parts of the command area had several advantages over Continuous Water Supply (CWS) system. Wastage of water under the former system was almost nil, when compared with latter one. The dependability was assured under RWS system and night irrigation was compulsorily followed by all the farmers, which was conspicuous by its absence in the CWS system. Water use efficiency, measured in terms of output per acre-inch of water, was found to be highest under RWS system.

Conjunctive use of canal groundwater is one of the best strategies for improving water use efficiency. However farmers faced several constraints the practising Conjunctive Use of Water (Reddy, 1987). Inadequate and untimely institutional finance was reported by a majority farmers as one of the main constraints for constructing wells in the command area. For small and marginal farmers and for those whose plots were fragmented, well irrigation was not economically viable. Lack of proper technical advice on groundwater quality and its availability discouraged farmers to go for well irrigation. The productivity of farmers practising conjunctive use of water was invariably high and almost equal to theoretically expected levels under irrigated conditions. It also enabled them to grow high value commercial crops. Adverse effects like waterlogging and salinity were at the minimum.

The study suggested several policy measures. The present system of notifying the area for irrigation survey number-wise, should be replaced with sharing of time on *pro rata* basis of landownership. Instead of notifying that a farmer gets water for 'X' acres, it could be notified as 'X' hours. Given the "water-hour" entitlement and known quantity of water flow in the canal, farmers would be able to decide the type of crops and the extent of area that could be irrigated. Accordingly, they can plan their cropping pattern. Another alternative that could be considered is a shift from the present supply-based system to demand-based system, with the necessary modifications in the canal network. The need for enforcing accountability of water released and actually utilised was suggested, based on the experimental results in the command area on water distribution. It was recommended to introduce RWS in the entire command area, followed by construction of appropriate structures to regulate water. Construction of "Farm-ponds" was suggested to utilise water flowing during nights (For a detailed list of recommendations and policy measures, see, Reddy, 1991).

Irrigation Impact Studies

It would be logical to initiate ex-post evaluation after a reasonable period of at least a decade to measure the impact of irrigation in the command areas where benchmark surveys were already completed. This would provide for a longitudinal study enabling more realistic assessment of the impact of irrigation. The study on "Impact of Irrigation on Economic, Social and Environmental conditions in Ghataprabha Command Area" (Reddy, 1990a), was the first to be carried out in a command area, eleven years after completing the socio-economic benchmark survey. The same set of villages and households that were covered for BMS were revisited to assess the impact.

There had been, as revealed by the study, a perceptible change in the agricultural scenario in the command area. An obvious, but disturbing, change was observed in the cropping pattern. Obvious because, whenever irrigation is introduced there would be a shift from traditional low value crops to modern high value hybrid varieties of crops, which is a welcome change to optimise agricultural production. Disturbing because, in the command area under reference, a crop, namely, sugarcane which was not provided for in the project design had gained overriding place in the post-irrigation cropping pattern. Since the project is designed for protective irrigation where lightly irrigated crops are expected to be grown, it is natural that water-intensive crops like sugarcane and paddy are prohibited. But, it was found that sugarcane accounted for almost 40 per cent of the area irrigated. This had led to not only scarcity of water for tail-enders but also to adverse effects like waterlogging and salinity. Sugarcane cultivation was more in "A" villages (stabilised irrigation) when compared to "B" villages (newly irrigated villages). Another paradox was a mushroom growth of sugar factories in the command area. As many as six sugar factories were started. The very fact that government gave licenses for sugar factories, in a command area which is designed only for protective irrigation, indirectly encouraged farmers to violate the cropping pattern. At the same time farmers are blamed for all possible ills in irrigation management. The twists and turns in government policies also contribute to the emergence of less efficient irrigation systems.

The productivity of crops was 3 to 4 times more than under rainfed conditions. But, the cropping pattern and productivity were positively related to the location of the plot in the canal. The productivity of crops in the head-reach plots was much higher, almost equal to, or, in some cases, more than theoretically expected levels, than in the tail-end plots. While high value hybrid varieties were grown in the head-reaches, low value traditional varieties continued in the tail-end areas. Such imbalance in the cropping pattern and productivity has led to income inequalities among the beneficiaries. While economic status in terms of assets, income, savings and investment had improved among all sections, including landless people, the improvement was more perceptible among large farmers, in spite of small farm efficiency being high with relatively higher productivity. The debt burden was more in "B" villages (newly irrigated) when compared with BMS status. This was, as brought out by the study, due to more investment in land development, purchase of farm equipment and other related activities in irrigated farming. The institutional loans in 'A' villages were mainly availed as crop loans. But the investment priorities were distinctly different; mostly for consumer durables and other luxury items.

There had been a perceptible change in the levels and styles of living, including consumption habits. A clear shift from inferior cereals to superior serials like wheat and rice was found in both "A" and "B" villages, while the near *status quo* continued in "C" villages. The expenditure on non-food items was higher in "A" villages than in "B" villages. Health consciousness among the beneficiaries had increased when compared with BMS. This was demonstrated by relatively higher nutritious food, including fruits and vegetables, consumed by the people, apart from consulting expert doctors in specialised hospitals outside the village, which was totally absent at the time of BMS. It is pretty clear that irrigation contributed for a better quality of life in the command area.

Irrigation did affect the environment adversely. Waterlogged area had increased, particularly in 'A' villages. This was more so in the head-reaches of canals where water was used liberally for crops. Social environment and outlook also changed perceptibly. Alcoholism among farmers had increased which was considered as a social taboo at the time of BMS. It was observed that people preferred matrimonial alliances from the educated and rich families settled in the towns or even villages, transgressing the traditional boundaries of native or neighbouring village and kinship preferences. Furthermore, it is interesting to note that the traditionally established dominant caste-based or lineage-based village leadership is being questioned and not given much importance which they used to enjoy earlier. All this was possible because of the economic stability and affluence brought about by irrigation.

Another study in a large, but stabilised, irrigation system, namely, Krishna Raja Sagar (KRS) was significant enough (Deshpande and Iyyam Pillai, 1986). This is one of the oldest reservoir projects in the State completed in 1930s, and there was no benchmark data available. Therefore, a cross-section approach (with and without irrigation) was adopted to measure the impact. The project under reference, unlike others in the State, was not designed for protective irrigation, violation of cropping pattern was, therefore, not a major issue. The study, however, addressed some of the issues related to farm-business income and increase in the wastage of water over a period of time and the consequent environmental problems.

In the wake of emerging controversy in the recent past about the relative efficiency of minor and major irrigation projects, if one looks back in retrospect shows the kind of vision late Professor Rao had in initiating impact studies under canal, tank and well irrigation systems way back in 1970s (Nadkarni, *et al.,* 1979). These studies were conducted in Bellary, Tumkur and Kolar districts respectively. The study on canal irrigation in Bellary district stated that the existence of protective type of irrigation was the result of geographical constraints on the process of supplying water to irrigate all lands equally in the district. As a consequence, three main patterns of cropping were followed by farmers in the district. The extent of irrigated area in the villages varied from one to another. Within the villages—Dry-cum-wet (DCW), or Wet, or perennial—the extent of irrigated area also varied from one farm-size to another. The inter-farm extent of irrigated area at the inter-village level showed that the smaller the size of an operational holding, the greater the proportion of cultivable or gross cropped area irrigated, and *vice versa*. This was, as brought out by the study, due to the existence of a large part of the total area as unirrigated for large farm households. At the inter-village level, the inter-farm extent of irrigated area showed that all categories of farm households in perennial villages had a higher proportion of irrigated area than was found in all categories of farm households in Wet and DCW villages. Such variations were attributed to the prevalence of three different characteristics of canal irrigation.

The study on tank irrigation revealed that the availability of irrigation had affected adversely the traditional crop, namely, Ragi in the district both in terms of area and productivity. Further, it stated that there was no change in the consumption pattern of the beneficiaries, except they became more self sufficient in food production, which otherwise used to depend on market to supplement the inadequate production. There had been a substantial increase in the value of land after irrigation. Many farmers became better off than they were without irrigation. Another interesting finding of this study was, unlike in large canal irrigated areas, the tank irrigation helped the small farmers proportionately more, and helped to narrow down income inequalities among the farmers to some extent. There had been two to four-fold increase in crop production, and related positively with landholding size. Employment opportunities had increased, followed by substantial increase in farm business income for all categories of farmers. Marketable surplus also has increased substantially. In view of more positive gains from tank irrigation the study offered several policy measures to improve the existing tank commands and also to plan for new tanks in the district.

Well is one of the traditionally important sources of irrigation. The study on well irrigation highlighted a number of advantages. While the shift in cropping from traditional to modern varieties is a natural and obvious process, irrespective of the source of irrigation, what interests more is multiple cropping pattern that was adopted under well irrigation, which was conspicuous by its absence under other sources of irrigation. Even the operational holdings had increased by bringing under cultivation the hitherto uncultivated marginal and submarginal lands through appropriate reclamation measures. Well irrigation seemed to have made farmers neglect the dry land farming, as they concentrated more on irrigated farming. This was observed even by some other studies

(Nadkarni, 1984; Reddy, 1991a) in canal command areas. The crop intensity was more with small holdings when compared to large holdings. Large farmers seemed to have kept more area as fallow. The productivity of crops was, however, more in large holdings, contrary to many findings in canal command areas where small farm efficiency was generally high (Reddy, 1990b). Irrigation, not only promoted an increase in cereal output, but also gave an opportunity to the farmers to raise cash crops. It is interesting to note that marginal and small farmers were the ones who benefited most from well irrigation.

The rise in farm incomes was accompanied by a perceptible improvement in the economic conditions of the farmers, which was reflected in the assets acquired, change in the consumption pattern and lifestyles. The differential rise in incomes in respect of the size class of farmers was, however, discouraging as it tended to increase income inequalities. The need for increased use of purchased inputs for irrigated crops and the marketable surplus generated by higher output of agricultural produce had resulted in the rural-urban nexus, which had influenced the lifestyles of the rural farmers. Such a situation was observed even in canal command areas (Reddy, 1990b). It is significant to note that none of the farmers using well irrigation remained below the poverty line, which was not the case with other sources of irrigation. What is disturbing is the increase in the number of smokers and consumers of liquor because of higher incomes under irrigated farming. This was observed even in some of the canal command areas also (Reddy, 1990b). Well irrigation appears to be more efficient and productive when compared to other sources. But, the possibilities of its expansion are limited owing to less groundwater availability.

The study on the impact of irrigation on rural development (Nadkarni, 1984) adopted a different approach. The impact was measured through a comparison across villages, not by the usual method of comparing output and income from irrigated and dry holdings within a village or irrigated and dry plots within a holding. This was done with a view to assessing the impact on the development of the village as a whole, including its weaker sections. The study covered 15 villages in Karnataka, Andhra Pradesh and Tamil Nadu and presented a comprehensive picture of irrigation impact. The impact, as brought out by the study, was not significant enough as claimed usually by the irrigation enthusiasts. It was observed that the impact, even in terms of stabilisation of yields and increased cropping intensity, was found to be less than expected, and it also had an opportunity cost in terms of parts of holding left idle, suggesting that reliance only on a 'technocratic strategy' was not enough.

Furthermore, the impact in terms of improving the incomes and quality of life, particularly of the poor, was not significant and sometimes even dampening. While the positive impact of irrigation was certainly conceded in a few aspects, its spread was limited and also had opportunity costs. Apart from the need to make irrigation management itself more efficient and meaningful by making it a part of an overall strategy for co-ordinated management of land and water, involving popular group action were necessary, irrigation has also to be viewed only as a part of an overall strategy for rural development and cannot be wholly identified with it.

Command Area Development Authorities (CADAs) were started to improve water use efficiency in major irrigation projects by implementing several on-farm development programmes. But the experience seems to be not very encouraging. The study on "*Command Area Development: Problems and Prospects of Irrigation*" (Reddy, 1991a) brought out the limitations of CADA to ensure irrigation efficiency and the consequent impact on the economic conditions of farmers. This was a longitudinal study where the impact of some of the critical programmes of CADA like land development, water management and agricultural extension was evaluated at two points of time (first, in 1975-76 and second, in 1984-85) covering the same set of villages and households in Malaprabha command area in Karnataka.

On-farm development (OFD), water management and agricultural extension were found to be far from satisfactory. More land remained undeveloped even after a decade of irrigation. Majority of the farmers still continued with unscientific water management practices. Agricultural extension services were not effective enough to help small and marginal farmers in particular. Irrigation has, no doubt helped farmers to ameliorate their economic conditions through higher incomes brought about by higher yields. But the benefits, as revealed by the study, are not distributed equitably. With the result, income inequalities have increased. The CADA is yet to appreciate the complex nature of inter-relationship between the irrigation-related technologies like OFD, water management and agricultural extension. This is revealed by the kind of mismatches between theoretically envisaged project objectives and field realities. The failure of CADA to strike a balance in accomplishing irrigation programmes has contributed a great deal to widen income inequalities.

Issue-Based Problem-Specific Studies

The hallmark of policy research at ISEC is not only the comprehensive studies with longer duration and wider coverage but also problem-specific short-term studies. Such studies include farmer-managed irrigation systems surface as well as groundwater, environmental issues, irrigation administration, women and child labour, irrigation water rates etc.

While irrigation has a positive impact, may be less than the expected levels, on the economic development of an individual and also the community at macro-level, its impact on women and child labour do not seem to have adequately been highlighted. According to the study on "*Female and Child Work Participation in the Integrated Development of a Command Area*" (Srikantan, *et al.*, 1978), the female work participation rate was only about half the male rate in corresponding age groups. There was substantial child work participation. Two major findings emerged from this empirical study of a command area. Female work participation was linked to a larger degree with the extent of irrigation and the norms regulating the functional and sex division of labour and only to a much lesser degree to occupational distribution and caste composition. Schooling and work participation made competing demands on children so that child earners were less literate and had less education than children who were dependents. The study offers some policy measures to augment employment opportunities for female, particularly during the off-season periods and enable the literacy rate to improve by adjusting the school year and school hours according to the needs of rural agriculture for supplementing labour in farm and household enterprise, especially in the peak season.

The study on '*Minor Irrigation Development Administration*' (Bhargava, 1980) addressed the key organisational deficiencies, administrative problems and issues involved. In minor irrigation administration, most of the organisational and administrative problems, as brought out by the study, arose due to the fact that the traditional department-type of organization handled minor irrigation programmes, which were essentially development programmes. In order to improve unified control, the study suggested: (a) to have an independent separate organisation exclusively for investigation, construction and maintenance of minor irrigation works at all levels up to the level of the Chief Engineer; (b) to have a separate organisation of minor irrigation up to the level of Chief Engineer, delinking from Communication and Building (C & B) division as there is no commonality between the two. At each level, starting from circle down to the sub-division, there should be a separate minor irrigation wing headed by the officers of the same cadres but specialized in minor irrigation.

Among the environmental problems in the catchment areas of major reservoir projects, soil erosion and the consequent sedimentation in the reservoirs is considered as one, albeit important one, of the problems. The study on *Catchment Area Treatment in Canal Command Areas: Problems and Issues* (Reddy, 1993) analysed the technical, economic and administrative problems and constraints. It was an exploratory study to find out the status of catchment area treatment programmes in Karnataka. According to the available data the rate of sedimentation in almost all the reservoirs in the State was found to be much higher than what was estimated in the project design, the intensity being very high in Tungabhadra reservoir. No specific plans or strategies were incorporated in the project design for catchment area treatment. As a result there was no co-ordination between various departments involved in the catchment area development. The cost of development was found to be very high. Then the question of sharing costs, particularly when a project covered more than one State even when the benefits were enjoyed by another, has been a debatable issue. Mining and other development projects, which were not envisaged at the time of project design, coming up in the catchment areas and their failure to build silt dams to arrest silt flow into the reservoirs, have aggravated the problem. It was, therefore, suggested to prepare a comprehensive catchment area development programme and integrate it with the project design to reduce the intensity of sedimentation in the reservoirs.

Irrigation water charges in major irrigation projects are said to be very low and not recovered fully. With the result, many State governments are believed to have suffered huge financial losses on account of gigantic storage reservoirs. An empirical study on '*Irrigation Water Rates*' (Reddy, 1988a) brought out the possibilities of increasing irrigation water charges without jeopardising farmer's income. As revealed by the study, the existing water rates in Karnataka, as a proportion to the gross income per acre for different crops, varied from 1.5 to 2.6 per cent, which was much lesser than the rate proposed by the Irrigation Commission. There was ample scope to double the existing water charges, the study stated. Farmers reaction for increasing the water rates was found to be favourable. A majority of the farmers showed their willingness to pay higher charges for irrigation water provided the service was improved in terms of adequacy and reliability. The study emphasised the need for some structural changes in irrigation water release and distribution and motivate farmers to form water users societies and purchase water on volumetric basis.

The study on Environment-friendly Irrigation Systems (Reddy,

1991b), stated that the problems like waterlogging, salinity and alkalinity were essentially due to the mismatches between theoretically well-perceived plans and programmes and field realities, which included farmer's perception and understanding. Non-recognition of the importance of on-farm drainage was found to be one of the main reasons for adverse effects on soil, besides farmer's ignorance about scientific water management practices. The percentage of waterlogged area to the irrigated area was more in head-reach farms, which perhaps explained over use of water. The need for rational distribution of water and educating the farmers on water management practices was emphasised, apart from maintaining natural drains in the command areas and other technical interventions to ensure environmentally sound irrigation systems.

Conjunctive use of canal and groundwater in major irrigation projects has gained much importance as a strategy to reduce adverse effects of irrigation on soil, and also to ensure reliable supply of water by supplementing canal flows. The study on "*Development of Well Irrigation in Canal Commands: The Prospects and Some Emerging Issues*" (Reddy, 1988a), addressed some of the important socio-economic and technical constraints associated with well irrigation in canal command areas. Inadequate institutional finance to dig wells and erratic power supply to lift water, followed by lack of technical advice on groundwater aquifers, hard-rock bottom are some of the constraints, as reported by the farmers, to practice conjunctive use of water. Farmers who were able to go for well irrigation were better off as reflected by their cropping pattern, productivity of crops and the consequent income. More importantly, the proportion of waterlogged area was much less in the fields where conjunctive use of canal and groundwater was practised. The extent of benefits, however, depended, to a great deal, on scientific planning and proper adaptation of canal operation procedures to suit soil conditions in the command area. The study also emphasised the need for community tubewells to solve a number of problems such as the non-viability of separate wells for small holdings, financial constraints to digging wells, and the overflow of wells during canal operation periods.

In view of the increasing concern to involve farmers in irrigation management, a comparative study of farmer-managed irrigation systems in India and Philippines was done (Reddy, 1988a). Another study on farmer-managed irrigation systems (Reddy, 1989b) brought out how, traditionally, farmers were able to design, construct, operate and maintain irrigation systems more efficiently on a sustainable basis. The kind of social sanctions that farmers built into operational procedures helped drawing lessons for incorporating corrective measures in agency-managed large systems. The study on river pump systems in India and Philippines brought out how farmers organised themselves to use available surface water by using the local skills and locally available resources. These studies helped drawing lessons for organising water users' associations in major irrigation projects which have high significance and value in the context of contemporary situation of irrigation water management.

Groundwater irrigation is one of the chief sources of irrigation in drought-prone areas. On account of the excessive use of groundwater in the recent years, the groundwater sources seem to have depleted beyond critical levels. The study on *Socio-economic Dimensions of Groundwater Management in Drought-prone Areas* (Reddy, 1992) highlighted the strategies adopted by the farmers to optimise groundwater use on a more sustainable basis. As revealed by the study, the farmers used groundwater more carefully to ensure that the levels did not go down beyond the limits perceived by them as unsafe from the viewpoint of sustainability. They were able to manage such balance through changes in the cropping pattern appropriate to suit the water levels in the wells. The technological advancement in groundwater exploitation through deep tube wells had its negative impact on the traditional shallow dugwells mostly owned by small farmers. Lack of proper technical guidance on the availability of adequate groundwater affected several farmers adversely. For, they had invested in digging wells where no water was available; consequently, many became indebted and caught up in a vicious circle of perpetuating poverty. It was suggested that farmers should be properly guided in exploiting groundwater without subjecting them to use scarce resources in an unproductive way.

III. A RESUME

An overview of the research studies on irrigation as presented in the foregoing pages, clearly indicates the conscious efforts made by ISEC to address most of the contemporary problems faced by irrigation sector. The empirical research studies not only analysed the micro level issues and problems but also spelt out a wide range of policy options taking into account the socio-economic ground realities, as identified by various studies. While pre-irrigation benchmark studies were useful in conducting ex-post impact evaluation of irrigation more realistically, concurrent evaluation of CADA programmes helped identifying social, economic and technical constraints to ensure optimum and sustainable benefits from irrigation. Those studies are particularly relevant in the context of growing pessimism about the role of major irrigation projects in the economic development. For, they present a systematic analysis of the field level problems and issues limiting the efficient and productive use of water available for the formulation of appropriate corrective measures to accelerate the benefits from irrigation.

The mismatches between theoretically well-conceived and designed irrigation water distribution strategies and actual field realities were identified by the action research studies and a number of practical solutions were suggested to formulate location-specific corrective measures. The limiting factors to ensure much talked about farmers' participation in irrigation management have been documented well which would hopefully serve as guidelines for future planning of water user's associations. The difficulties and limitations of enforcing cropping pattern in the canal command areas are highlighted. An alternative strategy to distribute water on the basis of time sharing is suggested to solve the problems allegedly caused by the violation of cropping pattern by farmers.

Augmentation of agriculture production has been the ultimate objective of irrigation development all through the ages: be it an individual, community or nation . In order to achieve this objective, different kinds of irrigation systems were evolved depending upon the local needs and resources. The irrigation impact studies have brought out the differential impact of irrigation not only between types of irrigation sources but also between various socio-economic and locational factors within a system. This has brought out the complex nature of irrigation systems and the need for treating an irrigation project as a social system dealing with people, their aspirations and attitudes and not necessarily a technocratic system. A blend of social systems and technical options would accelerate and sustain the role of irrigation in economic development.

The possible reasons for environmental problems in major irrigational projects have also been well documented. They include farmer's ignorance about water management practices, lack of scientific OFD, drainage including non-maintenance of drains etc. Some of these findings are useful as policy guidelines to design environment—friendly irrigation system in future, apart from rehabilitating the existing systems with appropriate corrective measures. The strategies adopted by the farmers in the drought-prone areas, as brought out by empirical studies may help drawing lessons for managing groundwater. Quite a few lessons could be drawn from the studies on farmers managed irrigation systems to improve water distribution and management in the agency-managed large irrigation systems. The empirical research on irrigation discussed so far is essentially based on contemporary problems faced by the irrigation sector and has tried to identify policy options to increase its positive impact on economic development.

REFERENCES

Bhargava, B.S. (1980) *Minor Irrigation Development Administration—A Study in an Indian State*. New Delhi: Ashish Publishing House.

Deshpande, R.S. and Iyyampillai (1986), *Impact Study of KRS—A Report on Cropping Pattern*. Bangalore: ISEC. Mimeo.

Nadkarni, M.V. *et al.* (1979) *Impact of Irrigation: Studies of Canal, Well and Tank Irrigation in Karnataka*, Bombay: Himalaya Publishing House.

Nadkarni, M.V. (1984) Irrigation and Rural Development: A Sceptical View. *Economic and Political Weekly*, Review of Agriculture.

Narayan, B.K. and M. Venkata Reddy (1978a) *Concurrent Study I: Land Development and Water Management*. Bangalore: ISEC. Mimeo.

Narayan, B.K., D. Vasudeva Rao and N.R. Jagannath (1978b) *Benchmark Survey I: Demographic Features*. Bangalore: ISEC. Mimeo.

Narayan, B.K., D. Vasudeva Rao and N.R. Jagannath (1978c) *Benchmark Survey III: Farm Economy*. Bangalore: ISEC. Mimeo.

Narayan, B.K. and M. Venkata Reddy (1979a) *Benchmark Survey IV—Income, Saving and Investment in Ghataprabha and Malaprabha Command Areas*. Bangalore: ISEC. Mimeo.

Narayan, B.K. and M. Venkata Reddy (1979b) *Concurrent Study II: Agricultural Extension*. Bangalore: ISEC. Mimeo.

Narayan, B.K. and M. Venkata Reddy (1981) *Warabandi Systems of Water Distribution*. Bangalore: ISEC. Mimeo.

Narayan, B.K., D. Vasudeva Rao and D.K. Narayan Rao (1977) *Integrated Development of Malaprabha and Ghataprabha Command Areas*. Bangalore: ISEC. Mimeo.

Narayan, B.K. and Pushpamala Prasad (1978) *Benchmark Survey II: Social Framework*. Bangalore: ISEC. Mimeo.

Nijman, Ch. (1993) *A Management Perspective on the Performance of the Irrigation Sub-sector*. A Ph.D. thesis. The Netherlands: Wageningen Agricultural University. (Quoted in Geert Diemu and Frans P. Huibens (eds.), (1996), *Crops, People and Irrigation*. Plan? Internurote Technology Publication.

Reddy, M. Venkata (1982a) Equitable Distribution of Irrigation Water. *Kurukshetra*. XXX (9).

Reddy, M. Venkata (1982b) Water Use and Management: An Illustration from a Command Area. *Productivity* XXIII(1).

Reddy, M. Venkata (1987) Conjunctive Use of Water in a Traditional Irrigation System: Some Perspectives. In *Conjunctive Use of Surface and Groundwater for Agriculture*. Vol.I. Lahore: Pakistan, Centre of Excellence in Water Resources Engineering.

Reddy, M. Venkata (1988a) Irrigation Water Rates need increase. *The Economic Times*. Bangalore: July 7.

Reddy, M. Venkata (1988b) Development of Well Irrigation in Canal Commands: The Prospects and Some emerging Issues. *Irrigation Management Network*

Paper 88/2b - IIMI/ODI, London.

Reddy, M. Venkata (1988c) *Comparative Perspectives of Farmer-Managed Irrigation System in India and the Philippines*. Sri Lanka: IIMI. Mimeo.

Reddy, M. Venkata (1989a) Theoretically Well-conceived and Operationally Ill Operated Water Management Systems. In J.R. Rydzewski and C.R. Ward (eds.), *Irrigation: Theory and Practice*. London: Pentech Press.

Reddy, M. Venkata (1989b) River Pump Irrigation Systems in the Philippines—An Indian Perspective. *FMIS News Letter*, No. 6, Sri Lanka.

Reddy, M. Venkata (1990a) *Dynamics of Irrigation Water Management*. New Delhi: Ashish Publishing House.

Reddy, M. Venkata (1990b) *Impact of Irrigation and Multi-Purpose Projects on Economic, Social and Environmental Conditions—A Study of Ghataprabha Command Area*. Bangalore: ISEC. Mimeo.

Reddy, M. Venkata (1990c) Farmer Managed Irrigation Systems: A Case Study from India. In Robert Yoder and Juanita Thurston (eds.) *Design Issues in Farmer Managed Irrigation Systems*. Sri Lanka: IIMI.

Reddy, M. Venkata (1991a) *Command Area Development: Problems and Prospects of Irrigation in Malaprabha Ayacut*. A Ph.D. Thesis. ISEC. Mysore: University of Mysore.

Reddy, M. Venkata (1991b) Environmentally Sound Irrigation System Development: Problem and Prospects—A Case Study. In Richard Wooldridge (ed.), *Techniques for Environmentally Sound Water Resources Development*. London: Pentech Press.

Reddy, M. Venkata (1992) Sustainability of Farmer Managed Groundwater Irrigation in Drought-Prone Areas: Role of Socio-Economic Conditions. In *Groundwater Farmer Managed Irrigation Systems and Sustainable Groundwater Management*. Vol. I. Sri Lanka. IIMI.

Reddy, M. Venkata (1993) *Catchment Area Treatment in Canal Command Areas—Problems and Issues*. Bangalore: ISEC. Mimeo.

Reddy, M. Venkata. *Irrigation Water Distribution Systems in Ghataprabha Command Area: A Diagnostic Study*. Bangalore: ISEC. Mimeo.

Shepperdson, M.J. (1981) The Development of Irrigation in the Indus River Basin, Pakistan. In Suranjit K. Sha and Christopher J. Barrow (eds.), *River Basin Planning: Theory and Practice*. John Wiley and Sons.

Srikantan, K.S., B.K. Narayan and D. Vasudeva Rao (1978) *Female and Child Work Participation in the Integrated Development of a Command Area*. Bangalore: ISEC. Mimeo.

The Hindu (1977) More Funds for Area Level Planning. Bangalore: August, 25.

PART THREE

GENERAL ISSUES

9

ISSUES IN RURAL DEVELOPMENT*

H.G. HANUMAPPA

The scope of the rural development theme is too vast as it is interdisciplinary in nature. All the activities carried out in the rural areas generate interest in varied forms for researchers to understand the processes of rural development. From this point of view, the researchers in ISEC are no exception. They have tried to study different dimensions of rural development efforts both by the governmental and non-governmental agencies. An attempt is made in this Chapter to identify some of the issues arising out of a few publications brought out by the ISEC faculty. Since the number of studies/papers are many, the present paper discusses, on a selective basis, some of the significant contributions. The work of researchers can be broadly grouped under the following themes:

1. basic needs of the rural people;
2. provision of social and economic infrastructure;
3. institutional intervention (ACRP work);
4. evaluation/impact studies;
   (a) poverty issues;
   (b) other issues; and
5. other studies.

Even though broad themes are identified, the presentation followed here does not stick to any definite frame. This is because the issues pertaining to rural development are so vast, divergent and inter-disciplinary in nature, that it is difficult to go according to the scope of a given theme. There is always a possibility of overlapping of discussion on certain

*The author wishes to thank P. Thippaiah for providing research assistance.

issues across themes.

The studies on basic needs dealt broadly with issues relating to housing conditions and social and economic infrastructure like health, education, social amenities etc. A study on rural housing situation based on data collected from 30,000 households in Tumkur district highlighted the inter-village differences among different socio-economic groups by using house types as control variable (Hanumappa and Ninan, 1984). This study indicated a clear relationship between type of housing on the one hand, and caste-occupation nexus on the other. A typical rural poor household normally belonged to a depressed/backward community, depended more on wage labour, and lived in a *kutcha* house without basic amenities. Here, the *kutcha* house is defined (as per the census of India classification) as one with mud walls and thatched roof. As one moved upwards on the ladder of caste, the type of house also changed from semi-*kutcha* to *pucca*. The study made a number of suggestions to give priority to the housing conditions of the rural poor. While housing and amenities have to be treated as one package, what one finds in the rural scenario is the dominance of better types of houses which need not necessarily imply the presence of better amenities.

Another study on housing, entitled '*The Rural Roofless: A Profile*', explored the status of houseless people (Johnson Samuel, 1993). Based on the 1981 census data available for Raichur, the study came to the conclusion that the incidence of "rooflessness" was quite high in rural areas and this could not be attributed to physical shortage in housing in the study area. The houseless as a category were too poor to pay the price for housing as determined by market forces.

A study on the distribution of social amenities outlined the relationship between levels of agricultural activities (development) and that of the availability of amenities of different order (Hanumappa, 1991a). This study was undertaken in two taluks of Kolar district. These taluks were selected on the basis of ranking by a development index. Detailed data on social amenities of two blocks representing the highest and lowest rank in the district from the point of view of the development index were collected and analysed to find out the relationship between the availability of amenities of different order with that of the level of agricultural development. The study very clearly brought out the fact that wherever irrigation played a dominant role, it brought in better facilities in terms of higher order social amenities. The study concluded that even within a backward district differences in the provision of amenities depended on the level of development across taluks or blocks. A couple of other studies on this theme highlighted the importance of clustering villages for providing social amenities in a more meaningful manner (Vivekananda, 1980; and Ramachandran, 1980).

A study which is of importance, attempted to understand the status of rural water supply in Karnataka (Nageshwara Rao, 1989). Among the major findings of this study, the one which startles any reader is the absence of even a single source of water in a majority of sample villages. Further, it points out that in each village SC/ST groups are segregated and have been provided with separate borewells, but their maintenance is poor. The SC/STs are not allowed to use the borewells meant for other castes. One of the important suggestions made by this study is to improve the present system of maintenance and repairs, and transfer this responsibility to the village community itself. The study also finds that the domestic use of water for alternate purposes, other than for drinking purpose, needs to be taken into account while planning for any rural water supply scheme.

For the first time, various research institutions and agricultural universities in the country are involved in preparing documents to facilitate adoption of agro-climatic regional planning framework for designing agricultural projects in the country. A research team at ISEC has been assigned the work of not only preparing an inventory for one of the Zones (Zone XII) based on agro-climatic regional planning principle, but also to prepare area-based plans highlighting the importance of soil, water and climate for agricultural development (Hanumappa, 1995). An innovative institutional intervention has been envisaged by the Planning Commission, Government of India, for bringing about changes in the planning mechanism for the promotion of agricultural activities. Accordingly, a number of studies have been undertaken under the ACRP to highlight the importance of resource based planning for rural areas. The work began looking at broad zones of the country (15) delineated by the Planning Commission and these 15 zones are further divided into 73 sub-zones and finally, the sub-zones which are identified with each of the State have been taken as ACRP units. However, due to administrative and also constitutional requirements, the ACRP work has bogged down to district level agricultural planning exercise. In fact, in the 73rd amendment to the Constitution, District Planning Committees (DPC) have been given the constitutional status. In recognition of this, on a selective basis, the ACRP research teams have been asked to prepare district agricultural plans by involving the district level functionaries (including NGOs) on the identified priorities of the districts concerned. As the work is still ongoing on an experimental basis, it may take some time to come to any definite conclusions on the outcome of this exercise.

Some important research work, carried out at ISEC, deal with a number of issues relating to the implementation of anti-poverty programmes (Rao and Erappa, 1987). Most significant of these studies is the evaluation of the impact of IRDP programmes by V.M. Rao in which the development programmes for the poor have been grouped as follows:

(1) relief and support measures;
(2) programmes for the creation of new economic opportunities;
(3) programmes for investments in human resources; and
(4) programme for reforming the structure and relationships.

Among these four categories, according to Rao, the last category is possibly the weakest in its implementation and impact.

Given the weaknesses of the third and fourth category of programmes, the movement of rural societies towards the broad based development would inevitably be very slow. What one can foresee in the immediate future is substantial participation of the poor and middle class strata; and some readiness on the part of the elite to accommodate these strata. Understanding of this scenario would help the policy makers, political parties and voluntary agencies to strengthen the rural development process. One would tend to agree with the observation that, if the growth in the macro economy is substantial, the elite find it easier to work for the rural poor and to mobilise their energies for positive and constructive purposes. If, on the other hand, the macro economy remains stagnant, the rural change may only lead to sharper conflicts in rural communities among the contending groups and factions.

A number of papers of V.M. Rao looks at the nature of transformation and the constraints in the village structure. In his paper on "Changing Village Structure: Impact of Rural Development Programmes", (Rao, 1987), he has tried to understand the rural change that has been brought about by rural development programmes and also, to bring the empirical studies closer to the emerging theoretical issues in development economics. The basis for the study is mainly the studies conducted in Karnataka by the ISEC. It points out that rural economic research, where generalisations are difficult and projections hazardous, gives only a modest picture.

The ISEC conducted a large-scale survey of a backward district (Tumkur) covering over 30,000 households in 245 villages. This survey was undertaken in order to capture the various socio-economic dimensions of rural change in a backward district. The data, both primary and secondary were enormous. But, the various scholars associated with this research project prepared a series of studies under the general guidance of Professor V.K.R.V. Rao. The range of themes varied from preparing a socio-economic inventory of a single block (Hanumappa, 1981) to themes which studied village contrasts. Social amenities, tribal issues, agricultural labour problems and the like, were researched into under this project. Even though the findings of these studies varied, one could see a common thread in these findings, viz., backward rural areas could not record faster development due to structural disabilities suffered by the existing institutions. Four per cent of these households belonged to service artisans category by their main occupation. Only a third of the young adult males (ages 16 to 35) in these households had taken up the artisan activity as their main occupation. The survey data also provide extensive evidence of the sharp rural disparities among different strata of people and villages. This is mainly due to varying capabilities. Locational disadvantages have also contributed to the disparities. This kind of situation needs State intervention to realise the positive impact of change.

Studies on the impact of programmes concerning employment generation (RLEGP) (Vivekananda, 1986) and skill formation (TRYSEM) (Sangeetha, 1990) indicate certain positive results. The Government attempted to implement employment generation programmes as relief measures. The findings of some of these studies indicated that the official machinery has shown commendable capacity to organise the employment programmes (RLEGP and TRYSEM). The RLEGP study highlights the significance of employment generation programmes in creating rural community assets like, roads, school buildings and housing.

Diversification in Rural Economy is another researched area where V.M. Rao found, by citing an ISEC study, that the proportion of beneficiaries belonging to richer sections was meagre (6%) (Rao, 1985). Seventy per cent of the beneficiaries benefited from agricultural and animal husbandry schemes. It is interesting to note that the petty trade benefited under the industry-service-business (ISB) schemes. In spite of this, programmes under ISB revealed the in-built constraints on rural diversification. Thus, poverty alleviation among the ISB beneficiaries seems to have remained a myth. Secondly, the study observed that the rural elites were losing hold on the poor. Thirdly, the agricultural labourers felt more secured and they moved to the areas where wages were more attractive. However, the study points out the weaknesses of these schemes. The State intervention through IRDP is short lived, partial and reversible by other forces impinging on the rural economy. The intention of the exercise was to show how the State intervention could help rural communities who enter the mainstream of growth and development.

Writing on "Barriers in Rural Development", V.M. Rao felt that rural development activities ought to have received higher resources than what has been given until now, and secondly, that a decentralized pattern of organisation for formulating and implementing rural development programmes needs to be evaluated (Rao, 1983a).

V.M. Rao focuses on the factors which are likely to hinder the spread of development process across a typical planning area like a district or a block. The data for the study have been drawn from Tumkur district in Karnataka. The study is purely descriptive rather than theoretical and statistical, because of the absence of models in economic theories focusing on the factors noticed in the field studies. The study points out that where the large economy began to grow, lack of linkages posed a barrier to the villages in two ways: (1) the state of subsistence in relative isolation could tempt to continue with that state in preference to the hazards of seeking links with the larger economy about which they know little; (2) the linkages that emerge (in an improved form) in the course of the growth of the larger economy are likely to disturb the settled modes of living rather than helping the villages in getting integrated with the growth process. This study presents the overall findings of the Tumkur study: (1) isolation of villages is a barrier to development; (2) a bigger village has all facilities and development and the benefits percolated to the villages located near the towns; (3) those who lack assets with poor economic base are living below poverty line. This shows that they have been excluded from the State sponsored programmes; (4) lack of their diversification due to depressed market penetration. The study concludes that the growth and development and modernisation in the economy do not automatically reach and percolate evenly within the local rural economy. Secondly, the present modes of intervention seem to be quite weak in their thrust. Thirdly, the State has only succeeded in bringing into being a group superior in status and having limited penetration beyond the large villages. Fourthly, several schemes implemented do not have much relevance to the agricultural labourers in the study area. Lastly, the study suggests additional strategies needed to be formulated to involve the local people and NGOs for the development of villages.

Some of the research efforts raised issues relating to the organisational and implementation problems of IRD Programmes (Rao, 1986, 1987, 1988b; and Hanumappa, 1986). The paper entitled "IRD Programme on Rural

Poverty: Brasstacks" reviews the findings of several evaluation studies and has come to the conclusion that IRD Programmes have not been able to accomplish the much cherished goal of reducing rural poverty. The findings of this study are quite interesting and it is observed that: (1) IRD Schemes have, by and large, benefited more non-poor than poor; and (2) traditional bureaucracy has not been able to help in reducing the poverty. In view of these findings, the paper suggests the need to integrate the positive qualities of bureaucracy and Non-Governmental Organizations to bring about the much desired reduction in poverty. Thus, at one stroke, the regulatory system of administration and the decentralised system of NGOs should come together and evolve appropriate strategies for reducing poverty.

Another study entitled *Rural Inequality and Poverty in India: A Survey of Selected Contributions of ISEC* (Venkataramanan and Satyapriya, 1983) covers work on this theme up to 1980s. The study observes that the inequalities in consumption among the rural households arise largely because of the inequality in the landholding pattern. However, it also concludes that there is a reduction in the inequality especially among cultivator households. The validity of such findings require further probing.

Another important paper, entitled "The Broad basing of Karnataka Society: A Note on Forces at Work" (Nadkarni, 1989b) highlights the trends in social and religious movements and governmental efforts for changing the socio-economic scenario of the Karnataka people. These movements and the anti-poverty programmes of the government have made some effect in countering the marginalisation process, but it is still a long-way to go to improve the working conditions of the weaker sections.

A number of studies have been conducted on the condition of rural labour. One of the important papers on this theme is on "Organisation of Rural Labour—Role of Government, Unions and Voluntary Agencies" (Nadkarni, 1990a). This study analyses carefully, the problems of organising the rural labour and the role played by NGOs, government and trade unions. The main recommendation of the study pertains to the observation that amelioration of rural poverty is not one of extending aid to the poor, but essentially its aim is to empower the rural weak.

There is another interesting report entitled "The Study Group Report on Land Reforms and Common Property Resources" (Rao, 1990). This study identifies the policies and programmes which need to be implemented with high priority to achieve the goal of improving the access of rural labourers to marginal, agricultural lands and common lands. The study examines the impact of land reforms on rural labour and the poor in a comparative regional framework. The study observes that the process and constraints hampering structural reform measures vary from region to region. The study concludes that the failure of policies in the area of common property resources has been more glaring with more tragic consequences for the poor.

There are also certain exercises conducted at ISEC on issues relating to rural energy. These exercises, by and large, highlights the significance of conserving non-renewable resources and the dangers of denudation of forests. Some of the exercises in this regard indicate alternative sources of rural energy which could be utilised optimally.

In conclusion, it may be said that the ISEC researchers, coming from different disciplines, focused on studies concerning different dimensions of rural problems. These include problems of housing, amenities, poverty, labour, land reforms, rural energy and the like. During its 25 years of existence, the ISEC has been able to contribute significantly to the development of literature on rural areas quite substantially.

REFERENCES

Aziz, Abdul, P. Thippaiah and M. Devendra Babu (1986) Beyond IRDP: Making Entrepreneurs out of the Rural Poor. *SEDME*, September, XIII.

Babu, Devendra M. and P. Thippaiah (1986) Tackling Rural Poverty. *Yojana*, 30: (22).

Bharghava, B.S. and Vijaya Kumar N. Torgal (1983) Need for an Effective Evaluation in Rural Development. *Panchayat Sandesh*, XXIII (9): 12-3.

Hanumappa, H.G. (1981) *Socio-economic Inventory for Block Planning*. Bangalore: Shiny Publications.

Hanumappa, H.G. (1986) IRD Programme and Rural Poverty: Brasstacks. *Indian Journal of Agricultural Economics*, XIV (4): 651-54.

Hanumappa, H.G. (1990) Rural Development and Co-operation: A Note. *Rural Development and the Role of Co-operatives*, Karnataka State Co-operative Agricultural and Rural Development Bank, Bangalore.

Hanumappa, H.G. (1991a) Social Amenities Spread in Rural Karnataka: A Study of Two Taluks. *IASSI Quarterly*, 9 (3): 110-30.

Hanumappa, H.G. (1991b) Issues in Rural Development for the 1990s. *Productivity* 32 (1): 8-12.

Hanumappa, H.G. (1995) Agro-climatic Regional Planning and Watershed Development. *Yojana*. Republic Day Special Issue, 39 (1-2).

Hanumappa, H.G. and John Q. Adams (1983) "Two Karnataka Villages and the Outside World, Internal Characteristics, Movement Linkages and State of Development". In B. Peter Robb (ed.), *Rural South Asia*. SOAS: University of London.

Hanumappa, H.G. and T.M. Sujatha (1983) "Mahila Mandals and Rural Women"

Kurukshetra, 31 (19).

Hanumappa, H.G. and K.N. Ninan (1984) "Socio-economic Dimensions of Rural Housing in Karnataka". Bangalore: ISEC, Mimeo.

Nadkarni, M.V. (1987) "Poverty Alleviation and the Natural Resource Base in Rural Areas". *Bangalore Theological Forum (Special Issue on Development)*, 19(3).

Nadkarni, M.V. (1989a) "The Resource Context of Rural Poverty: Poverty Alleviation in India". In Abdul Aziz and V.M. Rao (eds.), *Poverty Alleviation in India (Programmes and Action)*. New Delhi: Ashish.

Nadkarni, M.V. (1989b) "Broad basing of Karnataka Society: A Note on Forces at Work". *Pondicherry Papers*. Pondicherry: French Institute.

Nadkarni, M.V. (1990a) *Organisation of Rural Labour*. Bangalore: ISEC. Mimeo.

Nadkarni, M.V. (1990b) "New Character for Poor (Review)". *Economic and Political Weekly*, XXX (18 & 19): 1033-35.

Nadkarni, M.V. and G.V.K. Rao (1981) "Rural Development, Poverty Alleviation and Natural Resources". *Economic Times*, August 1.

Nanjundappa, D.M. (1987) "Viability of Regional Rural Banks". *Proceedings of Bank Economists Meet*, Bangalore.

Nanjundappa, D.M. (1989) "Planning from Below". *Yojana* (1-2).

Prahladachar, M. (1987) Some Aspects of Asset Structure in Rural Karnataka—1971-81. *Indian Journal of Agricultural Economics*, XLII (3): 301-6.

Rajasekhar, D. and Vinod Vyasulu (1992) The Rural Credit System in 1990s. In Vinod Vyasulu and S.N. Chary (eds.), *Managing India's Planning*. Jaipur: Printwell.

Ramachandran, H. (1980) *Village Clusters and Rural Development*. New Delhi: Concept.

Rao, M. Nageshwara (1989) Rural Community Water Supply System: Some Observations. *Kurukshetra* XXXVII.

Rao, V.M. (1983a) Barriers in Rural Development. *Economic and Political Weekly*, XVIII (27): 1177-90.

Rao, V.M. (1983b) Rural Diversification and the Strategy for the Rural Development. In Austin Robinson, P.R. Bramhananda and L.K. Deshapande (eds.), *Employment Policy in a Developing Country: A Case Study of India*. London: Macmillan.

Rao, V.M. (1985) Diversification of Rural Economy. *Indian Journal of Agricultural Economics*.

Rao, V.M. (1986) Percolation of Development in Rural Environment: A Discussion Note. In N.K. Thingalaya (ed.), *Rural India Real India*. Bombay: Himalaya Publishing House.

Rao, V.M. (1987) Changing Village Structure: Impact of Rural Development Programmes. *Economic and Political Weekly*, XXII (13): A2-A5.

Rao, V.M. (1988a) Decentralised Planning: Critical Economic Issues. *The Indian Economic Journal*, Conference Volume.

Rao, V.M. (1988b) Interventions for the Poor: Critical Dimensions, Potentialities and Limitations. *Economic and Political Weekly*, XXIII (45-7): 2409-20.

Rao, V.M. (1990) Study Group Report on Land Reforms and Common Property Resources. New Delhi: National Commission on Rural Labour.

Rao, V.M. (1991) Village Studies from the Economic Perspectives: Some Priority Issues and Themes. *The Administrator*, XXXVI (3): 1-6.

Rao, V.M. and S. Erappa (1987) IRDP and Rural Diversification: A Study in Karnataka. *Economic and Political Weekly*, 22 (52): A151-A110.

Samuel, M. Johnson, (1993) *The Rural Roofless*. Bangalore: ISEC. Mimeo.

Sangita, S.N., K. Vijayalakshmi and N. Vishwanath (1990) Training of Rural Youth for Self-Employment in Karnataka: Some Policy Considerations. *Man and Development*, XII (1): 10-25.

Thimmaiah, G. and R.M. Hadimani (1990) New Technology and Rural Development: The Social Impact—Indian Experience. In M.J. Campbell (ed.), *New Technology and Rural Development: The Social Impact*. London: Routledge.

Thippaiah, P. and T. Govindaiah (1988) Impact of Irrigation on Household Income. *Times of India*, Bangalore, December 18.

Thippaiah, P. and M. Devendra Babu (1990) Impact of IRDP on Agricultural Labourers: A Case Study. *Kurukshetra*, XXXVIII (9).

Venkataramanan, L.S. and V.S. Satyapriya (1983) *Rural Inequality and Poverty in India: A Survey of Selected Contributions*. Bangalore: ISEC. Mimeo.

Vivekananda, M. (1980) *Planning Unit Areas for Integrated Rural Development: An Exercise*. New Delhi: Ashish.

Vivekananda, M. (1986) *Rural Landless Employment Guarantee Programme in Karnataka: An Evaluation*. Bangalore: ISEC. Mimeo.

10

URBANIZATION AND URBAN DEVELOPMENT

M. JOHNSON SAMUEL

Introduction

The process of modernisation and economic development involves the shift of workers from agriculture to non-agricultural sectors and transfer of people from rural to urban areas. This leads to increasing share of urbanites in a country's total population. The pace and pattern of urbanization in a country reflect on how the society is transforming itself. In India, the role of urbanization in the transformation process is very much in evidence.

The contribution of urban sector to Gross Domestic Product (GDP) is on the increase from 29 per cent in 1950-51 to 47 per cent in 1980-81. It is estimated that it would further rise to about 60 per cent by the turn of the century. India's urban population was 62 million in 1951 accounting for 17 per cent of the total population. It has risen to 217 million in 1991 increasing its share in the total population to 26 per cent. The urban population, by the turn of the century, is likely to be around 300 million. The number of million plus cities is also likely to more than double from 23 at present to 49 by the year 2001. Although the percentage of India's population living in urban areas is small compared to developed countries, the number of urban dwellers is large. Urban India alone is bigger than the total population of all but the three largest countries of the world. It is difficult to grapple with the problem of this massive urban humanity.

Defining Urbanization

A great deal of analysis of urbanization process crucially hinges on how an urban area is defined. Almost all studies on urbanization rely on census data on urban places. According to census definition, all settlements which have corporation, municipality, cantonment board or notified area committee are eligible to be classified as urban. Settlements which satisfy three demographic criteria: (1) a minimum population of 5,000, (2) a density of at least 400 persons per sq. km., and (3) at least 75 per cent of male workers in non-agricultural activities can also be treated as urban. Besides, the Director of Census Operations in every State is given discretionary powers to declare a place as urban if the place has distinct urban characteristics even though it may neither possess a municipal administration nor satisfy the demographic criteria.

With illustrative examples from the State of Karnataka, Baskara Rao (1991) has demonstrated that arbitrary creation of municipalities by State government and subjective declaration of certain places as urban by census authorities have introduced certain amount of spuriousness to urban statistics. This has made the analysis of urbanization process across States and over time a difficult exercise. He has felt that certain places have been declared as urban under pressure from various lobbies. N. Baskara Rao has also suggested that when a census Director used his discretionary power to confer urban status to settlements, which did not pass the demographic test, he must clearly spell out for each such town, the reason as to why it was graduated to urban class. Similarly, the State governments should strictly adhere to the provisions of the municipal Act while constituting municipalities.

Regional Dimensions in Urbanization

V.L.S. Prakasa Rao and V.K. Tewari (1978) found regional differences in the degree of urbanization in India. There are highly urbanized tracts such as Kerala coast, Krishna-Godavari tract and Coimbatore-Mettur tract. There are also poorly urbanised tracts such as the delta cores, the forested hills and the hard core famine areas. Urbanization patterns differ in other respects as well. At one end of the spectrum, there are metropolitan cities which are a part of the national metropolitan city system. Metropolitan cities are linked through inter-city flows of money, commodities and metropolitan services and these links require further strengthening. At the other end of the spectrum are small agricultural and market towns, their main function being collection of agricultural surplus and distribution of agricultural inputs. They are randomly distributed and stagnant or slow growing. These towns need to be rooted to the local resource base. In between, lie the medium towns which are more diversified functionally with commerce as an important function.

Unlike in industrially developed countries, the cities, medium towns and small towns in India are integrated neither functionally nor spatially. In Rao and Tewari's (1978) views, the strategies of planned urban development should be used to minimise the inter-regional and urban scale differences. The sharply varying regional patterns of urbanization call for the adoption of region specific urbanization policies. Separate urban development strategies must be adopted for the metropolitan regions, the linear urbanized belts along the main transport routes, the agriculturally dynamic regions with a strong rural-urban nexus and the mountainous forest and drought-prone areas with a few and widely spaced towns.

Trends in Urbanization: Karnataka

Karnataka is one of the highly urbanised States in India. The level of urbanization at 31 per cent in 1991 is higher than the national average of 26 per cent but lower than those for the advanced States such as Maharashtra (39%), Tamil Nadu (34%) and Gujarat (34%). The rate of growth of urban population at 51 per cent during 1971-81 was among the highest in the country, the national average being 46 per cent. The decade 81-91, however, has witnessed a drastic decline in the growth rate of urban population in the State to 29 per cent. With 14 million population living in urban areas, Karnataka accounts for 6.4 per cent of the urban population in the country. Several factors have contributed to the sluggish pace of urbanization in Karnataka during the eighties. Commuting from a rural residence to urban workplace has gained popularity as a result of the high cost and limited stock of urban housing, and the availability of relatively inexpensive mass transportation. Rural areas gained more population through natural increase than did urban areas. Also, fewer villages were graduated to town status during the eighties than during the previous decades.

The distribution of population by size classes of town is important from the point of view of industrial location. According to 1991 census, 65 per cent of the Karnataka's population live in its twenty-one cities, each having at least one lakh population. Thus, almost seven out of every ten urban dwellers in Karnataka are residents of a city. Class II (17) and Class III (82) towns together account for 25 per cent of the total urban population. In other words, medium towns account for about one-fourth of the urban population. Class IV (70), Class V (40) and Class VI (24) towns share the remaining 10 per cent of the urban population. This implies that only one out of every ten urban dwellers is a resident of a small town in Karnataka.

One of the disconcerting features of urbanization process in Karnataka and elsewhere in the country is, that population and industrial activities continue to concentrate in big cities. Medium and small towns languish for want of industrial investment in them. As a result, small towns have recorded decreasing share in the total urban population. The small towns' (Class IV, V and VI) share in the total urban population came down from 17 per cent in 1981 to 10 per cent in 1991. The share of medium towns (Class II and III) has not changed much with 24 per cent in 1981 and 25 per cent in 1991 of the total urban population. But the share of the cities in urban population has increased from 59 per cent in 1981 to 65 per cent in 1991. This tendency has been a continuation of the trend set in during the last fifty years.

The above estimation of the growth by size class was done by considering the proportion of the total urban population that lived in different size classes at different census dates without paying attention to which particular towns or cities constituted particular size class at any particular census. In this method, the proportions are affected by the movement of towns into and out of the size classes and also by declassification and emergence of new towns during the decade. N. Baskara Rao (1987) employed a more refined method to study growth differentials by size class of towns. He took the towns and cities so designated at a certain previous census and traced them through all the subsequent censuses and examined how their population grew irrespective of the size class to which they may successively belong. This refined method also showed that cities and larger towns have grown faster than the smaller ones, though the growth differentials have somewhat narrowed down.

Besides, there are glaring growth differentials among individual cities and towns, within each size class. In terms of their population size, some towns have lost their ranks while many others have improved their ranks. In Baskara Rao's (1987) view, a town whose economy is diversified, will have consistent and steady growth. On the other hand, if a town is mono-functional, its growth will fluctuate widely, depending upon changes in the fortunes of its main function. He called for closer scrutiny of extreme variations in growth rates experienced by individual towns.

Urban growth rates vary among different districts and regions in Karnataka. Bangalore Metropolitan region, Bangalore-Belgaum transport corridor, Tungabhadra Valley have experienced high growth rates. In contrast, the rate of urbanization in the whole of Malnad region is tardy.

Raichur district in Tungabhadra basin has witnessed fast growth of its urban population. Some of its towns have recorded 4 to 6 per cent growth per annum during 1961-81. N. Baskara Rao (1989) identified irrigation development and agricultural prosperity as the causes for accelerating town growth. Increase in marketable surplus of agricultural produce gives rise to trading activities and emergence of agro processing industries. The fast growing towns of Raichur, according to Baskara Rao, are essentially market towns with deep-roots in the countryside around them.

Primate City in Karnataka

The most striking feature in the urban scene of Karnataka is the dominance of Bangalore Urban Agglomeration. In 1991, 4 million people lived in Bangalore Urban Agglomeration that is about 30 per cent of the total urban population of Karnataka. The secondary cities of Karnataka, Mysore with 6.52 lakh population, and Hubli-Dharwad with 6.48 lakh population look like pigmies before the primate city, Bangalore. The dominance of Bangalore is not confined to demographic sphere alone. It accounts for more than 20 per cent of the industrial and service employment available in the entire State (Samuel, 1991). This reflects a polarised pattern of development and a spatial imbalance in the urbanization process in Karnataka.

The pace at which Bangalore has been growing is also alarming. Through a process of cumulative causation, growth led to further growth and still further growth. Bangalore city grew from a city of 1.6 lakhs in 1901 to 4 lakhs in 1941 and 26.5 lakhs in 1991. The population of Bangalore urban agglomeration grew from 12 lakhs in 1961 to 41 lakhs in 1991. M.J. Samuel (1991) estimated that migration alone was responsible for 61 per cent increase in the population of the urban agglomeration during the period 1941-91. Another 21 per cent increase was due to changes in the agglomeration boundaries as neighbouring villages got sucked into the urban sprawl. A mere 18 per cent of the increase was attributable to natural increase in population.

V.L.S. Prakasa Rao and V.K. Tewari (1979) have felt that Bangalore's growth must be regulated. They have suggested creation of satellite towns and ring towns outside the shadow region of Bangalore, to serve as counter magnates to the metropolitan city. They have identified Tumkur and KGF-Bangarpet towns which are within one hour travel distance from Bangalore as ideal locations for the counter magnates. To remove the imbalance in the urban structure of Karnataka, they have recommended the development of Hubli-Dharwad and Gulbarga as second tier regional cities.

Medium and Small Towns in Karnataka

A more balanced mix of cities and towns will help in reducing economic and social disparities prevailing among people and across regions. By strengthening the rural-urban linkages, small towns can help injecting growth impulses into the countryside. The towns, when developed, can act as counterpoints of attraction for villagers who are prone to leap-frog to metropolitan cities.

In this context, several studies have been conducted focusing on individual towns with a view to understanding their growth dynamics. R.N. Hadimani (1982; 1983) has done a case study of Mahantpur, a medium size town with 30 thousand population located in a relatively backward district of Bijapur. The town specialises in hand-loom weaving. The chemical composition of water and dry air prevailing most of the year in the town provide it with natural advantage for textile dyeing. Marwaris, the local money-lenders in the town, have brought in capital and entrepreneurial abilities in marketing the finished products. The industry draws its labour force of skilled workers from a traditional caste of weavers known as *Neygi.* Yet, suffering from disadvantages inherent in mono-industrialisation, the town's economy is not flourishing. The handloom goods produced in the town face stiff competition from power loom and mill-made goods. Most weavers are steeped in poverty and unable to pay even the property tax, the main source of income for the local municipality. With meagre funds at its disposal, the municipality is not in a position to develop infrastructure and civic amenities in the city.

H.G. Hanumappa's (1981) study of Hospet contains a wealth of materials on the social and economic structure of this medium size town with 65 thousand population. The retrenched migrant workers from Tungabhadra irrigation project were resettled in the vicinity of Hospet leading to doubling of the towns population within a span of twenty years between 1941 and 1961. After a lull for a decade or two, the city has again picked up tempo in growth, in the wake of setting up of a steel plant there. Unless ambitious infrastructural development programmes are taken up in the town immediately, Hospet may not be able to cope with pressures arising from rapid industrialisation of the area.

The government have taken several measures to ensure urban and industrial dispersal in the country. These include ban on location of industries in congested metropolis like Bangalore, setting up of public sector undertakings in smaller cities and towns, encouragement to small scale industries, creation of industrial estates in backward regions and direct investment to improve infrastructure in medium and small towns. Government interventions have not, so far been, very successful in altering the urban structure. For developing medium and small towns, it is necessary that an integrated development programme for each town is drawn up and implemented. The development programme should be geared to the unique characteristics and functions of the individual town and its region taking note of its stage of development in the development continuum and differences in its socio-economic set-up.

Morphology of Cities and Towns

A good knowledge of the present morphology of a city can help in unravelling its past and predict its future. The usual city surveys concentrate on physical aspects of the city in order to prepare the master plan for the city. In the late seventies, an ambitious survey of Bangalore city was carried out using a very innovative methodology. The survey sought to gain insights into the city's socio-economic and ecological structure. Besides, it aimed to provide a frame and perspective for the city planners to plan for the city in regional and national context.

The survey data revealed that Bangalore's ecological structure was not a simple rich centre and poor periphery of the classical model. It had a complex structure composed of middle class centre and with high status and low status periphery (Hanspal, 1978). The city did not exhibit concentric zonation in geometric form. Rather it was a mixture of both zonal and sectoral patterns. The city core was dominant and decay function operated with increasing distance from the city core. In the eastern and western parts of the city, zonation had occurred through the interplay of social and economic forces, religion and historical accidents. The core, the intermediary and peripheral zones were discernible in these parts of the city. Along the transport corridors, the sectoral pattern was dominant with industries dotting the landscape. V.L.S. Prakasa Rao and V.K. Tewari (1979) recommended a polycentric structure for the city. To bring relief to the overburdened city core, they suggested setting up of two or more centres in the north-eastern and north-western parts of the city. The study also showed that Bangalore's morphology today is a mosaic of the pre-British, colonial and post independence periods.

Madhushree Majumdar's (1982) study of Durgapur city in West Bengal shed a great deal of light on the evolution of an industrial town.

The spatial form of the city was controlled by the physiography of the terrain with river Damodar forming the southern boundary and transportation routes especially G.T. Road and Eastern Railway's main line controlling the location of industries. It had a rich centre of industrial townships and a poor periphery of urbanising villages. However, Durgapur could not be called a pre-industrial city since socio-economic gradient from the city centre was not very steep. Its spatial structure was a combination of axial and multiple nuclei patterns. Along major transportation routes, three distinct strips of land-use had evolved: industrial, residential and an inter-mixture of the two. Discrete and self contained urban industrial neighbourhoods were found embedded within the axial sector. There were discontinuities in land-use patterns which indicated that Durgapur was in a transitional phase of urban growth. To put it differently, Durgapur was still then a city in the making.

K. Balasubramanian (1988) found that the structure of a town is closely tied up with the nature and extent of specialisation of its functions. He studied two industrial towns in Karnataka-Davanagere, specialising in cotton textile and oil extraction industries, and Bhadravathy, specialising in iron and steel, and paper production industries. Davanagere has evolved indigenously with strong spatial linkages with the surrounding countryside. The city has a large number of wholesale merchants and commission agents dealing in agricultural produce grown in the region. Even the industrial units are small in scale and most people earn their bread through self-employment. The workforce is drawn from within the region, through kinship networks. Primordial loyalties are cherished and residential segregation is along caste and communal lines. The city populace has a sense of belonging to the place and the city has many traits reminiscent of pre-industrial towns.

In contrast, Bhadravathy's industrialisation was imposed from outside and the city has only tenuous links with its hinterland. The city is heterogeneous in its caste, religious and linguistic composition. Compared to Davanagere, Bhadravathy offers higher income to its residents and much of it is earned through wage employment. Recruitment to jobs is through formal channels (Employment Exchange) and achieved status rather than ascribed status is important for securing jobs. The catchment area for labour is much wider and the demand is for skilled workers. The two public sector industrial units (Visveswaraya Iron and Steel Plant, and Mysore Paper Mills) control the distribution of residences to their workforce. The residential segregation is along class and economic status lines. Many city residents are birds of passage and view their stay in the city as a transitory one.

In larger cities, various types of goods and services are sorted out into specialised areas. While units transacting in wholesale business have very large trade areas, units dispensing with retail business have smaller trade areas. These units are supplemented by countless hawkers and pavement vendors with no site overhead costs. G.S. Sastry's (1981) study of spatial distribution of retail trade outlets in Bangalore city, has shown that it has a hierarchical structure. Shops selling specialised goods such as jewellery are concentrated in a few high order shopping localities in the city. On the other hand, vegetable and provision stores are widely dispersed all over the city. Shops selling textile goods are neither concentrated nor ubiquitous. Besides, the location of retail outlet for any given commodity is not at random. The size and income level of the population in an area determines whether the area will have a shop dealing with that particular commodity. Low income consumers buy most of their requirements of goods from the nearest neighbourhood shops. But high income consumers tend to buy even articles of daily consumption from high order shopping centres, though they may be far away from their residences. Their shopping behaviour often aggravates traffic problem in the city. His study underscores the need for locational planning for trade sector as well.

Urban-ward Migration

The movement of people into metropolitan cities is caused by the gravitational pull of the cities and the push of poverty stricken rural areas. N.D. Kamble's (1982) analysis of migration into Madras City showed that men outnumbered women among migrants. The migrants were, by and large, youthful adults. They had higher labour force participation than the locals. The male and youth selectivity of migration streams would suggest that the region surrounding the city was stripped of its young and more energetic elements. On the other hand, the city was not able to absorb the migrants and provide them settled family life. Women who wish to migrate, encounter several problems in getting decent jobs and safe accommodation in the city (Samuel, 1995).

M.J. Samuel and M. Lingaraju (1992) found from their study of census data on migration that the migrants who had 'just arrived' in the city (during the census year) were distinct from those migrants with long residence in the city. Illiterates and barely literates formed a disproportionately larger component among "just arrived" migrants. They were concentrated in low status service occupations or some other nondescript occupations. A majority of the 'just arrived' migrants were, in fact, circulating migrants. Since their stay in the city seldom exceeded one year at a stretch, census scheme of classification of duration of residence in the city, clubs them together with "just arrived" migrants. The circulating migrant moved interminably between the city and his home village in response to the fluctuations in the demand for his labour in the two places. During peak crop season when work was available for everybody in his family, the migrant stayed in the village working in the farms. During off season, he came to the city and created work for himself as hawker, pavement side vendor or cooly. His wife and children stayed back in the village where they could live relatively cheap. The dual participation in urban and rural labour markets ensured the survival of the migrant and his family. Looked at from another angle, this type of migration enabled the urban sector to accumulate capital, by passing on, a part of the cost of reproducing labour power to the rural sector.

Inter-regional migration and migrant's dominance in the city's economy are often cited as the reason for the rise of regionalism and nativist movement in the country. M.J. Samuel (1995) looked at the phenomenon from the opposite side and tried to assess the impact of regionalism on inter-regional migration. His study of migration and language data pertaining to nine top million plus cities, each dominating a major linguistic region in India showed that inter-regional migration streams flowing into these million plus cities have been on the decline after the reorganisation of States on linguistic principle in 1961. The million plus cities, however, continued to grow faster than the natural increase in their population would allow. Their growth was fuelled by the influx of people from within the region itself. One fall-out of this is, that million plus cities have become linguistically more homogeneous than ever before.

The militant nativist movements and the language policy of State governments appear to have frightened away potential migrants from venturing out of their home States. The presence in a city of a large body of inter-regional migrants, speaking different languages and practising language based customs, would enrich cultural life and serve as a bridge between linguistic States in a federal set-up. To promote national integration, the policy makers must understand to what degree the linguistic groups living in a city are antagonistic to each other. The administration must make sincere efforts to convince the groups that none of them will be discriminated and that all will be treated equally.

Urban Poverty

The positive role of urbanization in India is overshadowed by pervasive urban poverty. As per the 1983-84 estimate of the Planning Commission, the incidence of urban poverty was 29 per cent in Karnataka which was slightly higher than the all-India figure of 28 per cent. The proportion of population living below poverty line in rural areas was much higher both at the National level (40%) and Karnataka State level (38%).

H.G. Hanumappa (1991) studied the poor as a segregated group in urban society and found that poverty was the result of deprivation arising from a combination of social, economic and demographic factors. While protecting the poor from hunger and starvation, the State must endeavour to improve the marketable skills of the poor through education and appropriate training programmes. In his view, the poor's access to housing, basic infrastructure and social services must also be increased.

Informal Sector

Many observers of India's urban scene feel that India is over-urbanised. The growth of employment in the organised industrial sector is not commensurate with the growth of population in the cities. This has led to the emergence of the informal sector of coolies, hawkers, domestic help and similar workers in every city. Entry into the informal sector is relatively easy as it requires very little capital and low skills. Consequently, labour productivity is also low.

The share of informal sector in urban workforce is relatively high in Karnataka (68%) as against the national average (53%). P. Thippaiah's (1993) estimate of informal sector in Bangalore urban agglomeration in 1991 put it at 67 per cent of the total workforce in the city. Literature on informal sector have often romanticised the informal sector as a holding or transitory sector where rural migrants find jobs immediately on their arrival in the city. After getting a foothold in the city and acquiring marketable skills and work experience, they move upwards into high income formal sector. P. Thippaiah's study (1993) of Bangalore's informal sector contradicts this view. He found it to be a terminal sector. Those who found jobs in the informal sector remained there trapped for ever. Besides, it had a large proportion of locally born workers not just recent migrants from rural areas. Bangalore's informal sector produced goods and services that were consumed mostly by middle and low income groups. There was no social security, job security, leave benefit or minimum wage rates for the wage-earners in the sector. The self-employed in the sector were no better either. They experienced difficulty in marketing their products and had little access to credit facilities even for working capital. There was no separate department or any special scheme to protect the sector. P. Thippaiah suggested that the informal sector must be given all incentives on par with small scale industries.

Most studies on informal sector assume it to be a homogeneous entity and have made sweeping generalizations about its characteristics. Abdul Aziz (1984) who made a study of waste recycling industry in Bangalore noticed the existence of dualism within the informal sector itself. Those in the industry earned their living by producing useful articles out of discarded materials. Rag-pickers in the sector, for example, were poverty stricken and constituted the unorganised segment of the sector. The manufacturers and dealers in waste recycled products were relatively better off and formed into an organised segment in the sector. Either segment of the sector had its own problems calling for different policy measures. Abdul Aziz suggested that the more enterprising among rag-pickers must be helped to move into those segments where earnings are higher. The prosperous segment must be helped to establish a more enduring linkage with formal sector, by way of technology transfer and also in marketing the output through ancillarization.

Housing and Slums

The housing situation in urban areas has worsened over the years. Housing needs must, therefore, figure prominently in urban development programmes. The total backlog of housing in urban India in 1991 has been put at 10.4 million dwelling units. Based on trends in population growth and household formation, Samuel (1987) estimated that there would be 35 lakhs households in urban Karnataka by 2001 AD. To clear the backlog of housing in Karnataka's towns and cities by that time, his calculations indicated, that every year from 1981 onwards some 38 thousand new houses should be built under public housing programme alone and added to the existing stock. His study showed that the actual allocation for housing sector in the Five Year Plans was too meagre to wipe out the housing shortage in the State in the foreseeable future.

In fact, the gap between housing needs and housing supply is widening in India as well as Karnataka and the influx of poverty stricken migrants from rural areas into urban places has worsened the situation. With their meagre earnings from informal sector, they cannot compete in the urban market for housing. Collecting flimsy scrap materials like tin, cardboard and gunny bags, they build for themselves a ramshackle shelter wherever they find a vacant site in the crowded city. These unauthorised habitats lack water and power supply and sanitation facilities. Being squalid, they become breeding grounds for diseases, crime and vice. The estimates of India's urban poors living in slums vary. According to estimates made by the Task Force on Housing and Urban Development appointed by the Planning Commission, at least 23 per cent of the country's urban population lived in slums in 1981. Karnataka is characterised by a low proportion of urban population living in slums.

H. Ramachandran's study (1985b) showed that there were 282 notified slums in Bangalore Corporation area. They provided shelter to 1.3 lakhs population constituting about 10 per cent of the city's total population. Compared to other metropolitan cities, the situation is not too bad. Since slums meet the housing needs of low income people, Ramachandran argued that the slums must be brought under the ambit of urban planning rather than be condemned outright.

M.J. Samuel's (1984) assessment of government sponsored slum clearance or slum upgradation projects, site and services programme of the 1970s and urban housing finance scheme of the 1980s showed that their impact on housing situation was only marginal. The rate of slum proliferation far exceeded the scale of urban development programmes. Many schemes, designed with the ostensible purpose of helping the poor to build their own houses, have in fact, benefited only the rich. The actual price of tenement and the housing loan was beyond the paying capacity of the slum dwellers. The price of land is the largest component in the cost of an urban house. In his view, the private ownership of urban land militates against solving the housing problem of the poors.

It is commonly believed that education services are in much more ample supply in urban than in rural areas. The urban averages often hide the fact that in cities there are sizeable pockets of poor households which are much worse off than the rural households in their access to education. To take the case of slum dwellers, they are caught in a vicious cycle of low income leading to poor education, low skill formation and low productivity culminating in low income again. Public action can help to break this vicious cycle but as often as not public interventions have been limited in effectiveness by poor design and implementation.

A S. Seetharamu (1983) made a comparative study of the behaviour of school drop-outs and regular attendants among slum children. He examined the extent and problem of utilisation of special facilities such as mid-day meals, scholarships, free text books by students attending the school regularly. With regard to school drop-outs, the focus was on their participation in labour force. A.S. Seetharamu suggested that complementarities within and between welfare services must be exploited to improve enrolment and school attendance among slum children. "Earn while you learn" scheme, "setting up of mobile offices for the issuance of caste and birth certificates" and involvement of NGOs in the programmes, in his opinion, may go a long way in bringing slum children to schools.

Open Spaces and Density of Population

Existence of open spaces and water bodies lend the city an aesthetic appeal. They play an important role in recharging the depleting groundwater resources and in pollution abatement. Ramachandran (1985a) found from his study of old documents, that open spaces were shrinking in Bangalore city, particularly in low income areas. They were encroached upon for building houses. As the study pointed out, vanishing open spaces have serious health and environmental implications for the city.

In 1981, the density of population in urban Karnataka was 2,913 persons per sq. km. which was somewhat lower than the national average of 3,000 persons per sq. km. Karnataka urban density is more than seven times the qualifying density of 400 persons per sq. km. for a settlement to be graduated to town status by Indian census. Bangalore city has recorded a density of 7,991 persons per sq. km.

Within Bangalore city, the population density varies from ward to ward. Usually, urban studies look for causes for intra-city variations in densities. But Malini (1988) sought to assess the impact of population density in a locality, on the cost of providing infrastructural services to that locality. In her search for optimum density which can minimise the cost of providing infrastructure and maximise its accessibility to the people, she found that the per capita cost of providing a basket of infrastructural services is over fifteen times, at a density of 50 persons per acre as compared to a density of 400 persons per acre. An interesting finding from her study is that the density in Bangalore city can be raised from the existing 66 persons to 140 persons per acre which would result in substantial cost reduction without aggravating congestion in any part of the city. Bangalore is characterised by low rise residential buildings. Malini's calculations showed that by increasing the average number of floors to two per residential building, Bangalore can save a substantial area of land and costs on land development.

Urban Environment

Indian cities face serious environmental problems caused by growing population and increase in motor vehicles and factories. The problem is exacerbated by the poverty of the people and an inadequate system for urban waste disposal. Polluted water, air and land threaten the health of city dwellers.

The cars, trucks and factories spew out hydro-carbons and other toxic substances affecting the quality of air in the cities. G.S. Sastry (1985) worked out composite indices of air pollution for major metropolitan cities in India taking into account four pollution parameters—suspended particulate matter, sulphur dioxide, sulphation rate and dust fall. He found that the concentration levels of pollutants are on the increase in every city. Calcutta emerged as the worst polluted city followed by Bombay, Kanpur, Hyderabad, Delhi, Ahmedabad and Madras in that order. Jaipur appeared as the least air polluted metropolitan city in India. Within each city, industrial areas were severely polluted. Commercial centres were moderately polluted. Air pollution levels were relatively low in residential localities.

Over the past two decades, India has enacted a series of laws to prevent and control pollution. However, these laws and regulations are not strictly enforced. The often touted excuse is that many Indian industries cannot meet pollution control standards because they lack necessary funds and technology. M. Ravichandran (1990) studied 15 industrial units, most of which are located in Bangalore city and some others located in industrial towns like Bhadravathy, Harihar, Nanjangud and Chennapatna. He collected from the firms, information on investment, production cost, pollution abatement cost and profit levels. With these data, he demonstrated that the burden of extra cost imposed by the pollution control was marginal for most of the firms. Pollution control measures did not affect the size of employment in the concerned industries either.

Residents' Perception of a City

An urban planner's image of a city is influenced by the layout of its streets, business centres and parks and the architecture of its buildings. The people who live and work in the city day in and day out may have an altogether different perception of the city. A study of their perceptions may help in uncovering latent problems.

In the Bangalore city survey, residents were asked to rate their residential locality in terms of its accessibility, street lighting, sanitary condition, availability of water and power and its proximity to shopping, educational, medical and entertainment facilities. On analysing the data Ramachandran (1982) found that different income classes had different perceptions on what constituted good living condition. Dissatisfaction with urban living was the least in areas where population was moderately dense, ranging between 100 and 150 persons per acre. The average of the ratings indicated that neither low density nor high density areas were the favoured location for residence in the city. Obviously, people looked for a trade off between congestion and dispersion.

Conclusion

While urbanization is helping the process of economic development and social change, it is not being managed properly.

Steady inflow of migrants from rural areas, coupled with natural increase in the urban population itself, causes unmanageable increase in the size of cities and towns. Therefore, any strategy of urban development should focus itself not merely on the migration question but also on the high rates of natural increase in population.

Rapid deterioration in urban environment and infrastructure is a matter of great concern. Recent outbreak of plague in Baroda and Bhopal gas leak tragedy are all grim warning that all is not well in our cities. Streamlining of metropolitan transport, provision of housing, increase in protected water supply, improvements in drainage sanitation and solid waste disposal system are all necessary to make our cities and towns liveable.

Ambitious urban infrastructural development programmes and expensive city beautification schemes often produce unintended effects. They widen rural urban differentials and consequently, increase the inflow of migrants into the city. They run the risk of being counter productive in the long run. Concern for civil problems of metropolitan cities like Bangalore, therefore, must be tempered with realism. In order to resolve the complex problem, it seems desirable to evolve a strategy which will stimulate the growth of satellite towns at some distance from the city to function as counter magnates and relieve the central city from congestion and excessive strain on its overstretched infrastructure.

There is need for a deliberate policy of encouraging medium and small towns and placing of some effective restrictions on the growth of big cities. Ban on the location of industries in congested cities, fiscal incentives for setting up of industries in backward areas, promotion of small and cottage industries, use of labour intensive technologies, more investment in infrastructural facilities in small towns and identifying and nurturing the growth centres and growth poles, all must form part of a package for industrial and urban dispersal. The medium and small towns must develop economic complementarities with large cities on the one hand and rural settlements on the other and act as a vital link between villages and cities. The town's economic functions must be integrated vertically and horizontally leading to optimum organisation of economic activities over space.

Above all, urban development, to be effective, must maintain a certain harmony with rural development. Making rural life better would help keep the villagers stay put in their villages. It could be a more effective way of solving the problems of insanitary conditions, over crowding and slum living—the bane of developing world's urbanization.

REFERENCES

Aziz, Abdul (1984) *Urban Poor and Urban Informal Sector*. New Delhi: Ashish.

Balasubramanian, K. (1988) *City Functions and City Structure*. A Ph.D. Thesis (ISEC). Bangalore: Bangalore University.

Hadimani, R.N. (1982) Some Perspectives on Planning for Urban Development. *Nagarlok*, XIV (3): 48-56.

Hadimani, R.N. (1983) Socio-ecological Factors in the Emergence of a Weaving Town: A Case of Mahantpur. *Indian Journal of Regional Science*, XV (1): 19-27.

Hanspal, Ranjana (1978) *Urban Structure of Bangalore City: A Spatial Analysis*. A Ph.D. Thesis (ISEC). Mysore: University of Mysore.

Hanumappa, H.G. (1981) *Urbanization Trends in India: A Case Study of a Medium Town*. New Delhi: Ashish.

Hanumappa, H.G. (1991) *Urban Poverty*. Jaipur: Print Well.

Kamble, N.D. (1982) *Migrants in Indian Metropolis: A Study of Madras Metropolis*. New Delhi: Uppal.

Majumdar, Madhushree (1982) *The Structure of an Industrial City: A Case Study of Durgapur*. A Ph.D. Thesis (ISEC). Mysore: University of Mysore.

Malini, R.S. (1988) *Residential Densities and Living Conditions in a Metropolis: A Case Study*. A Ph.D. Thesis (ISEC). Mysore: University of Mysore.

Ramachandran, H. (1982) *Living Conditions in Bangalore: An Analysis of Residents' Perception*. Bangalore: ISEC. Mimeo.

Ramachandran, H. (1985a) *Greening of a Metropolis: An Analysis of Open Space in and around Bangalore*. Bangalore: ISEC. Mimeo.

Ramachandran, H. (1985b) Slumming of a Metropolis. In V.Vyasalu and A.K.N. Reddy (eds.), *Essays on Bangalore*, Vol. 2 Bangalore: K.S.C.S.T.

Rao, N. Baskara (1987) *Growth of Towns and Cities in Karnataka, 1961-81*. Bangalore: ISEC. Mimeo.

Rao, N. Baskara (1989) *Irrigation, Agricultural Development and Urban Growth: Some Linkages*. Bangalore: ISEC. Mimeo.

Rao, N. Baskara (1991) Census Criteria for Rural-Urban Classification: A Need for Reexamination. *Nagarlok*, XXIII (3): 50-60.

Rao, V.L.S. Prakasa and V.K. Tewari (1978) *Urbanization in India: Spatial Dimensions*. Bangalore: ISEC. Mimeo.

Rao, V.L.S. Prakasa and V.K. Tewari (1979) *The Structure of an Indian Metropolis: A Study of Bangalore*. New Delhi: Allied.

Ravichandran, M. (1990) *Economics of Pollution Prevention and Control: A Study of Industrial Pollution in Karnataka*. A Ph.D Thesis. (ISEC). Mysore: University of Mysore.

Samuel, M.J. (1984) The Poor's Struggle for Shelter in Urban India. *Samata*, 2: 15-32.

Samuel, M.J. (1987) Housing Needs in Urban Karnataka 2001 A.D. *Nagarlok*, XIX (1): 96-107.

Samuel, M.J. (1991) Some Aspects of Bangalore's Growth—1941-1991. *Demography India*, 20 (1): 53-64.

Samuel, M.J. (1995) Growing Regionalism as a Barrier to Inter-regional Migration: Evidence from Metropolitan Cities in India. *Indian Journal of Regional Science*. XXVI (1 & 2): 1-10.

Samuel, M.J. (1995) *Life Cycle and Female Migration: A Study of the Pattern and Causes*. Delhi: B.R. Publishing Corporation.

Samuel, M.J. and M. Lingaraj (1992) Bangalore: A City of Migrants. *Loyala Journal of Social Sciences*, VI (2): 26-43.

Sastry, G.S. (1981) Retail Trade Structure of an Indian Metropolis: Bangalore. *Annals of National Association of Geographers, India*, 1 (2): 57-73.

Sastry, G.S. (1985) Metropolitan Cities Environment: India. *Nagarlok*, 17 (3): 1-11.

Seetharamu, A.S. (1983) *Education in Slums*. New Delhi: Ashish.

Thippaiah, P. (1993) *Informal Sector and the Urban Poor in a Metropolitan Area: A Case Study of Bangalore*. A Ph.D. Thesis (ISEC). Bangalore: Bangalore University.

11

RESEARCH ON EMPLOYMENT AND LABOUR*

P. HANUMANTHA RAYAPPA

Employment has been an important area of concern for the planners in India. Hence, several plans, programmes, and strategies have been evolved to tackle the problem of unemployment, under-employment and seasonal migration searching for employment. There are no dearth of studies on these aspects in the country. As a premier research institute in the country, several research studies on various aspects of employment have been carried out at the Institute for Social and Economic Change. The studies have, particularly, concentrated on areas of employment generation to suggest different policy measures. They are essentially field based, mainly exploring the situation in rural areas. Broadly, the studies can be classified under following groups: methodological studies, employment situation with regard to specific groups, labour scenario in different sectors, programme impact on employment, policy-oriented studies and others. Even though it is quite difficult to restrict the scope of one study to a specific issue, it has been done here for better comprehension. However, it should be mentioned at the outset that this review is neither exhaustive nor includes all the studies. The attempt here is to identify major areas of focus in our research work on employment and labour during the last two decades.

Methodological Studies

There are very few studies on methodological aspects of employment and labour. How much does a given unit of investment generate employment?

* The research assistance of Dr. T.V. Sekher is gratefully acknowledged.

Aziz and Rayappa (1980), in their paper, present an outline of the methodology for estimating the employment potential of individual plan schemes in Karnataka. The authors identify many methodological problems in the operationalisation of the concepts at the stages of data collection and data analysis, and put forth some workable solutions. The attempt has been to evolve an alternative conceptual framework where employment generation is regarded as a function of creation, maintenance and operation of production asset. Apart from direct employment that the implementation of any scheme would generate some employment is likely to be induced, which may be termed as indirect off-site employment. The study mainly concentrates on two problems that arise at the analysis stage, relating to the nature of capital-labour ratio to be worked out and the kind of composite index of employment to be evolved. The study indicates that the employment potential (both direct and indirect) of different plan schemes not only varies but is different at each phase of each category (manual, skilled, etc.) during construction, operation and maintenance phases. Estimation of such parameters is very crucial in the process of planning for employment generation.

In another study (Kamble, 1973), two models have been developed to explain spatial variations in the utilisation of manpower in Transport, Storage and Communication sector (T-Sector). The explanatory variables of Model-I are based on land-use as well as cropping pattern and those of Model-II are based on the level of economic activities. It is found that land-use and cropping pattern provide explanation, to some extent, for the spatial variations in manpower utilisation in the T-Sector in rural areas. But they fail to explain the situation in which the urban component is added. On the whole, it is observed that acceleration of employment in T-Sector largely depends on the expansion of employment opportunities under the manufacturing industry in both rural and urban regions.

Employment Situation in Different Segments of Population

Where is the concentration of workers in different age and sex groups? What are the activities they are engaged in, and how much is their contribution? The employment aspect of different segments of population has also received considerable attention. There are many studies with regard to child labour and related issues. A study on the situation of children in Karnataka (Rao and Rayappa, 1989) observes that when family support system breaks down in conditions of extreme poverty, illiteracy and social backwardness, it necessitates governmental and voluntary agencies to intervene and fulfil the basic requirements of children. With rapid urbanisation and industrialisation, child labour, with all its inhuman characteristics, has become more visible in towns and cities. Child workers miss educational opportunities, the pleasures of childhood are denied, and adult responsibilities are thrust on them so early in their lives. Child labour has also certain debilitating effects on the physical and mental developments of children, the consequences of which become visible much later in life. Children in some occupations are exposed to fatal accidents and diseases such as asthma, bronchitis and tuberculosis. A child's health, nutrition and the overall well-being depend much on the mother's health, nutritional standard and social status. According to this study, even though Karnataka has a number of programmes for the benefit of women and children, all programmes do not work effectively and coverage levels also vary. There is need for continuous monitoring and evaluation, and modification of these programmes. Regarding child labour, the study suggests that provision of the Child Labour Act with respect to hazardous occupations have to be implemented more effectively.

A study by Dinesh (1988) focuses on the dimensions, causes and consequences of economic activities of child labour in a rural set-up and their contribution towards household economy. It examines the compatability of work and schooling of children and the causes for the child work participation. The analysis is mainly based on primary data collected from three villages of Karnataka. Children in the schoolgoing age (6 to 15 years) have been grouped into four mutually exclusive categories according to school-work status. He suggests that the economic contribution of children have to be understood in terms of their current and future utility to their parents. A large number of parents expect their children to start helping their family economically by the time they are eight years old. They also consider children as the major source of financial support in their old age. Any policy measures to improve the schooling rate of children in rural areas should take into account the current economic utility of children to their parents. The measures in this direction not only bring down the incidence of child labour but also influence the fertility rate in rural areas.

Ramesh Kanbargi and P.M. Kulkarni (1984) analyse the extent and the manner in which child labour and schooling affect fertility. The data have been collected from 45 villages of Karnataka State. They find that the direct effect of child labour on fertility is insignificant. A possible reason for the observed weak relationship could be the presence of family planning programme. A couple take fertility decisions not solely based on their own perception of costs and benefits of children but are influenced by what other couples have been doing and what is being advocated by the family planning workers and others. Any intervention like banning child labour, the study notes, is not likely to bring down fertility dramatically. The study also points out that by reducing child labour, there is a possibility of improving school attendance. Another study focussing on the child labour in the silk reeling industry of Karnataka (Acharya *et al.*, 1992), based on intensive field work through participant observation, brings to light the problems and compulsions of children. It is observed that children constitute about 25 per cent of the workforce in the silk reeling industry. Children work on wages more out of compulsion than out of their own choice. They work under strenuous and unhealthy conditions and without nutritious food and health care facilities, and are susceptible to all kinds of diseases. Acute poverty, coupled with social and educational backwardness, compels the parents to send their children to work. This study suggests that NGOs should be encouraged to take up the cause of child workers.

Being an important part of rural population, the aged are, nevertheless, the most neglected, and their problems with regard to employment need to be particularly investigated. In this direction, the study by Dinesh and Rayappa (1983) examines the data available from census and other sources. A majority of the parents perceive children as their major source of old age support. The study suggests that the skills and experiences of the aged should be utilised and the government should address this issue in a more serious manner. There is a need to focus on the health of the aged. This study also points out that there are considerable differentials in the work participation rates of aged, particularly between rural and urban areas.

Even though there is considerable progress in women's education and employment, it is a fact that there exists a disparity between the proportion of men and women educated and employed. Women's participation in labour force is a matter of great concern. Many studies have examined the employment scenario in the context of women. Based on a sample survey conducted amongst educated unemployed, Satakopan (1983) argues that, on an average, women suffer more unemployment than men even when they possess similar education and other desirable traits required for employment. Women are paid lower wages than men for the same quantum of work done (Samuel and Erappa, 1985). Passing of anti-discriminatory legislation has proved to be insufficient to end sex bias and radical changes in social behaviour are necessary to even up the economic imbalances between males and females. N. Shanta (1982), in her study of

1,465 women employees in public sector and private sector establishments in Bangalore city, probes the socio-economic background of working women and the motives of women in taking up employment. The educational and occupational patterns of the employed women reveal that there is a relationship between the two. More than three-fourths of the women interviewed state that they have taken up jobs for economic reasons. The main reason given by the respondents for taking up employment is either to support the family or to supplement family income.

Based on a survey conducted in 62 villages of two command areas in northern Karnataka, Srikantan *et al.*, (1978) find that mechanisation of agriculture not only leads to the displacement of men by machines but also, the replacement of women by machines. The development projects have to be carefully assessed and selected for their employment potential for women. Female work participation is linked, to a large degree, with the extent of irrigation and the norms regulating the functional and sex division of labour, and only to a much lesser degree to occupational distribution and caste composition. Schooling and work participation make conflicting demands on children so that child earners remain less literate. The study points out that ambitious programmes for the expansion of schools and legislation on compulsory education are not likely to improve school enrolment unless the necessary social conditions and the demand for education of children are created in rural areas.

Weaker Sections and Bonded Labourers

Employment aspects of weaker sections, particularly of scheduled castes and scheduled tribes, have also received attention. Rayappa and Grover (1979, 1980) analyse the attempts made by the government to improve the working and living conditions of scheduled caste and scheduled tribe people. The distinguishing characteristics of the scheduled castes and scheduled tribes are their rurality, illiteracy, economic backwardness and low social status. The study reveals that most of the rural employment schemes neither ensure continuity of employment nor generate income required for a minimum standard of living. Even though the programmes are meant to benefit the weaker sections, they may, in reality, serve the rural elites. They suggest that, in order to improve the working conditions of the poor, it is necessary to modernise the traditional occupations and to make them more productive and remunerative. They conclude by stating that the attempts made so far to ameliorate the living conditions of SCs and STs are of an *ad hoc* nature and have not tackled the problem in its entirety.

P.M. Kulkarni (1988), on the other hand, focusing on bonded labourers in Karnataka examines the rehabilitation schemes implemented by the government. He observes that the process of identification and the release of bonded labourers appears to have been done quite efficiently in Karnataka. Most of the bonded labourers belong to scheduled castes and other backward castes and very few have any schooling. In this study, some strong arguments have been advanced in favour of the provision of employment and assets for the rehabilitation of bonded labourers. The rehabilitation programme needs to be directly linked with employment programmes, so that the rescued labourers are assured of some employment at reasonable wages. This would not only augment their incomes, but would also enable them to make better utilisation of the assets provided to them under the rehabilitation schemes.

Labour Scenario in Different Sectors

Is agriculture more labour intensive? If so, how many does it accommodate? Employment generation in agriculture has received larger attention in comparison with other sectors (Reddy, 1982; Parameshwara, 1983; Grover, 1984; Parthasarathy, 1989; Venkataramanan, 1986; Satyapriya, 1990). All these studies basically examine the labour absorption in agriculture and the factors dertermining the level of human labour in primary sector. The change in labour intensity due to technology and the change in net cropped area are the major factors leading to the growth in employment (Reddy, 1982). V.S. Satyapriya (1990) observes that the growth in employment due to adoption of new technology is considerably higher in unirrigated areas. The hypothesis that smaller holdings adopt a more labour intensive cropping pattern is not conclusive though upheld to some degree in the case of unirrigated crops. L.S. Venkataramanan (1986) specifically deals with the extent to which growth in agriculture output could facilitate absorption of increasing labour force. Increase in irrigated areas and technology inputs like high yielding varieties and fertilizers have led to increased agricultural output and to increased labour utilisation. He maintains that even a successful agricultural production development strategy, however, can only partially absorb the growing agricultural labour force.

R. Parthasarathy (1989) analyses the factors that influence the demand for labour mainly in production. The analysis has been carried out at the farm level, at the individual crop level and at the operational holding level. The study is mainly based on the data drawn from the "cost of cultivation surveys" for Tamil Nadu, conducted by the Central Ministry of Agriculture. The survey covers 400 farm households distributed equally among 40 clusters of villages in six agro-climatically homogeneous zones in the State. The analysis indicates that increase in the intensity of labour use is possible in all the zones of the State through enhancing the use of complementary inputs. The author argues that material inputs, bullock labour, pumpsets and irrigational levels should be enhanced to promote additional labour use in crop production.

N. Parameshwara's (1983) study also assesses the potential of agricultural sector in absorbing the additional labour force. It is found that multiple cropping should have positive and significant impact on total labour use in agricultural households. From the point of view of generating additional productive employment in agriculture, the study recommends extensive cultivation, increasing the rate of adoption of the modern Seed-Water-Fertilizer technology, increasing cropping intensity and changing the cropping pattern, linking agriculture to the allied activities and speedy implementation of land reforms.

Agricultural development and population growth mutually interact and influence each other. Deepak Grover (1984) deals with the impact of agricultural development and demographic change on labour force. He opines that there is a shift away from agriculture and this actually reflects the rural-urban shift rather than any structural change within rural areas. The study finds that mechanisation and migration have weakened traditional employer-employee relations. Employers have used migrant labour as a tool to suppress local labour, weaken their bargaining power and keep their wages low. He concludes by stating that green revolution in Punjab did not fulfil the expectations on the employment front.

M.V. Nadkarni and Johnson Samuel (1984) study the impact of commercialisation of forestry on the pattern of workforce engaged in forestry and forest based activities. They find that in spite of large areas being under forest in Shimoga and Uttara Kannada districts, the employment benefit to the locals appears very marginal. Local people cannot look upon forest development as a source of employment and livelihood. They emphasise the point that unless the people of the region have a stake in forest development and management, it is not going to help afforestation programmes in the region.

The income and employment potentialities in sericulture industry study by Rajapurohit and Govindaraju (1980) is based on two silk producing districts of Karnataka, one growing mulberry under rainfed condition, and the other, under irrigated condition. The hypothesis regarding employment generation in mulberry growing and silkworm rearing being higher than that in the case of substitute crops is proved beyond doubt in respect of both rainfed and irrigated areas. They substantiate the argument that sericulture generates not only higher employment as compared to other crops but it also generates higher incomes.

It is widely believed that the organisation of agricultural labour would go a long way in improving the wages and employment conditions of rural workers. Many recommendations have been put forth in this regard. Particularly, the document containing the recommendations made by the study group on organisation of rural labour under the National Commission of Rural Labour, deserves immediate attention (Nadkarni, 1990). Organising rural labour on class lines, regardless of caste, is undoubtedly the most desirable principle. This is very important because rural labour consists of SCs and STs and various other backward castes. The study group maintains that separate organisation for each economic activity may be impracticable. There is a general consensus that the Kerala Agricultural Workers Act, 1974, has been a very effective legislation which can be adopted as a broad model by other States. This study group recommends that a comprehensive social security legislation is necessary to protect the interests of rural labour. Taking over village CPRs (Common Property Resources) exclusively for the benefit of the poor and the landless, has a more forceful moral justification because households owning lands can meet their bio-mass needs from their own resources, while CPRs are the main source for the landless. Any policy of giving priority to agriculture and improving its status, should address itself to the question of improving the status of rural labour.

The need for organising rural labour has been emphasised by other studies also (Aziz, 1978; Rayappa and Grover, 1980). While recognising the difficulties in organising agricultural labour, Aziz pleads for setting up of Rural Labour Co-operatives (RLCs). Are the RLCs better than the conventional trade unions? The arguments presented by the author in favour of RLCs in a way substantiate this proposition. The trade unions are preoccupied with struggles for better wages but have very little role in generating employment opportunities. But the RLCs can generate employment opportunities as well as bargain with the employer-farmer for higher wages and better working conditions. In general, RLCs can act as welfare organizations to help poor labourers in several ways.

One study examines the role of non-farm employment in rural development, particularly in the case of irrigated command areas (Rao,

1979). Two command areas in Karnataka are taken up for this study. Approximately one-fourth of the rural labour force in most developing countries derive income from non-farm employment. It is believed that rural non-farm activity can increase the flow of benefits from rural development programmes. The author suggests that rural non-farm activities deserve close attention in the formulation of development policies, as they can help the alleviation of poverty in the course of economic growth.

Urban informal sector is playing a significant role in generating income and employment. Two studies conducted at the Institute describe the socio-economic structure of informal sector (Aziz, 1983; Thippaiah, 1985), as well as suggest some measures for improving the health of the sector. A. Aziz states that urban informal sector instead of being a transitory sector has emerged as a permanent sector providing employment and income opportunities to the growing urban population. He argues that the enterprises of the informal sector should be given government help on par with the enterprises of the organised sector. Apart from the reallocation of resources and minimising bureaucratic harassment, there is a need for technology transfer from the formal sector to the informal sector. P. Thippaiah (1985) identifies the factors that can account for the poor conditions of workers in urban informal sector. It is found that a majority of the informal sector workers are migrants to the city. He argues for the extension of minimum wage legislation to this sector so that the wage rates may be regulated in accordance with the social objectives. He is also of the view that denying incentives and concessions to the informal sector is a shortsighted policy.

Studies on Programme Impact on Employment

What have we achieved in terms of providing employment to the needy under various employment generating programmes? Various employment generating programmes specially designed for the rural areas contribute substantially in providing work for the needy and the poor. The performance of these programmes and their evaluation assume greater significance. In this context, two studies—Evaluation of RLEGP by (Vivekananda, 1986) and TRYSEM by (Sangita and Jayalakshmi, 1985) need special mention. M. Vivekananda observes that the project selection and implementation have taken into account the local needs for employment programmes. But, the department officials treat the programme as asset formation programme and this attitude may not fulfil the objective.

S.N. Sangita and K. Jayalakshmi (1985) maintain that no effort has been made to develop managerial skills and entrepreneurial ability of the trainees enlisted for TRYSEM programme. They have pleaded for improving training and post-training facilities. Both studies suggest the need for built-in-mechanisms for the effective implementation of these government programmes. These employment programmes have to be continued till the economy is in a position to provide additional income or full employment to the rural households.

Other Studies

According to Mishra (1978), the unemployment problem in rural areas has assumed serious proportion because of a capitalist class of cultivators with greater access to techniques and credit and monopolistic control of resources. He argues that the flow of productive investment and public spending is not going to generate a meaningful process of employment unless suitable changes in the structure of the rural economy are made. The attempt for employment generation in the rural area has only led to casualisation of employment rather than increase in the employment of a durable nature. He strongly advocates the immediate implementation of land reform programmes to protect the interests of the landless and poor peasants.

M.V. Nadkarni (1981) while reviewing the Tumkur studies states that the emphasis of these studies was to test the suitability of cluster approach for ensuring a faster broad based rural development. Even within the existing economic and political system, the cluster approach can create opportunities for improvement in the living standards and employment of the rural poor.

K.N. Ninan (1977) deals with an entirely different situation in the context of increasing unemployment. The prevalence of wide-spread unemployment and rural poverty has led to the overflow of indigent population to the urban centres which, in turn, has led to rural urban conflicts. The author argues that the prevalence of rural urban conflict is due to the widening disparities between rural and urban areas. The development strategy adopted in our country is heavily biased in favour of urban population and what is needed now is the re-orientation of the existing strategies of socio-economic development.

Mahesh Kumar Sahu (1979), on the other hand, analyses the impact of an irrigation project on labour force and migration. The study was undertaken in the project area of Hirakud dam in Sambalpur district of

Orissa. The study shows that the economic development has some relation with the population attributes, especially labour force and migration. It also indicates that the agricultural development through irrigation can contribute to the increase in labour force participation.

P.H. Rayappa and T.J. Espenshade (1975), in their paper, examine the determinants of unemployment by empirical testing and factor analysis using cross-sectional data for the States of India based on the 1961 census. The paper concentrates on a specific set of indicators of demographic and socio-economic change including the rate of population growth, the degree of urbanisation, educational attainment, levels of living and standards of health and nutrition. The rates of unemployment in developing countries are negatively related to the level of socio-economic development or modernisation. The analysis substantiates the argument that the forces of modernisation have influenced the rates of unemployment (See alao Rayappa, 1977).

P.N. Mari Bhat (1978) analyses the changes that have taken place during the previous fifty years in Tumkur district of Karnataka with a focus on the size and distribution of population, level of literacy and occupational structure of labour force. The analysis is based on census data. He attributes that mechanisation is responsible for the opening up of some new avenues for employment for males but it has also resulted in the net loss of employment for females. The breakdown of traditional rural industries conducted by family enterprises where the women could contribute to the productive work along with child care and other household duties, have resulted in the decline of female labour force participation in the district.

P.H. Rayappa and R. Mutharayappa (1985) look into the development of human resources in the context of employment planning in Karnataka. The study finds that there is no major shift of work-force away from agriculture. But, the productivity per worker in agriculture has declined. The study analyses the wastage of human resources from four angles—educational wastage, unemployment among educated, mismatching of supply and demand for labour, and draining of workers outside the State. Wastage of resources adversely affects the development of the State and remedial measures are warranted. This study also observes that there have been changes in the proportion of population in dependent age (young and old) as well as in the workforce participation rates by age, sex and rural-urban residence.

The above summary though not exhaustive has thrown light on many dimensions of employment situation in the country with a special focus on the State of Karnataka. Each study tackles a particular problem and treats it in a succinct way. By putting them together in one place, the paper has indicated the quantum of work that has been carried out in a premier research organisation in the country. Notwithstanding their limitations, some knowledge has been gained about different dimensions of the problem. However, thre is need for more research studies in the field of employment and related aspects.

REFERENCES

Acharya, J., S. Shashikala, and N.R. Manjula (1992) *Puppets on Silk Strings: Child Workers in the Silk Reeling Industry of Karnataka*. A Beneficiary Assessment Report. Bangalore: ISEC. Mimeo.

Aziz, A. (1978) *Organising Agricultural Labourers in India: A Proposal*. Bangalore: ISEC. Mimeo.

Aziz A. (1983) *Urban Informal Sector: A Study of Waste Recycling in Bangalore*. Bangalore: ISEC. Mimeo.

Aziz, A. and P.H. Rayappa (1980) Estimation of Employment Potential of Plan Schemes: A Methodological Outline. *Indian Journal of Industrial Relations*. 15(3): 433-46.

Bhat, P.N. Mari (1978) *Workshop on Population Planning and Area Development* (Information Data XII, Population Edition and Emp.), Bangalore: ISEC. Mimeo.

Dinesh, B.M. (1988) *Economic Activities of Children: Dimensions, Causes and Consequences*. Delhi: Daya Publishing House.

Dinesh, B. M. and P.H. Rayappa (1983) The Aged and Their Work Status in Rural Areas. *Demography India*, XII(1): 38-51.

Grover, Deepak (1984) Agricultural Development, Demographic Change and Labour Force Dimensions in Punjab. Bangalore: ISEC. Mimeo.

Kamble, N.D. (1973) Absorption of Labour Force in Transport, Storage and Communication Activities: A Spatial Study. Bangalore: ISEC. Mimeo.

Kanbargi, Ramesh and P.M. Kulkarni (1984) Child Labour, Schooling and Fertility in Rural Karnataka, South India. Bangalore: ISEC. Mimeo.

Kulkarni, P.M. (1988) Rehabilitation of Bonded Labour in Karnataka. Bangalore: ISEC. Mimeo.

Mishra, G.P. (1978) Anatomy of Rural Unemployment and Policy Prescriptions: A Macroscopic View. Bangalore: ISEC. Mimeo.

Nadkarni, M.V. (1990) Overview and Recommendations: Organisation of Rural Labour and the Role of Government Unions and Voluntary Agencies. Bangalore: ISEC. Mimeo.

Nadkarni, M.V. (1992) Rural Development and the Cluster Approach: A Review of Tumkur Studies. *Economic and Political Weekly*, XVII(26): 1346-50

Nadkarni, M.V. and M. Johnson Samuel (1984) Population and Workforce Changes in a Forest Region. *Social Science Probings*, I(3): 371-97.

Ninan, K.N. (1977) Unemployment and Rural Urban Conflicts. Economic Affairs, 22(6-7): 257-65.

Parameshwara, N. (1983) *Labour Absorption in Agriculture: A Case Study of*

Karnataka. A Ph.D. Thesis (ISEC), Mysore: University of Mysore.

Parthasarathy, R. (1989) *Labour Utilisation in Agriculture: The Case of Tamilnadu*. A Ph.D. Thesis (ISEC), Mysore: University of Mysore. Rajapurohit, A.R. and K.V. Govindaraju (1980) A Study of Employment and Income in Sericulture. Bangalore: ISEC. Mimeo.

Rao, D. Vasudeva (1979) Role of Non-Farm Employment in Rural Development: An Experience from Command Area. *The Indian Journal of Economics*, LX(237): 231-39.

Rao, N. Baskara, and P.H. Rayappa, (1989) *Child in Karnataka: A Situational Analysis*. Bangalore: ISEC. Mimeo.

Rayappa, P.H. (1977) Determinants of Labour Force in Developing Areas. Bangalore: ISEC. Mimeo.

Rayappa, P.H. and T.J. Espenshade (1975) Demographic and Non-Demographic Determinants of Unemployment Rates in Developing Countries: A Factor Analytic Approach. *Proceedings of the American Statistical Association*, 505-580.

Rayappa, P.H. and Deepak Grover (1979) *Employment Planning for Scheduled Castes and Scheduled Tribes*. Bangalore: ISEC. Mimeo.

Rayappa, P. H. and Deepak Grover (1980) *Employment Planning for the Rural Poor: The Case of Scheduled Castes and Scheduled Tribes*. New Delhi: Sterling Publishers Pvt. Ltd.

Rayappa, P.H. and R. Mutharayappa (1985) Employment Planning and Human Resource Development in Karnataka. (I. Macro Perspectives) Bangalore: ISEC. Mimeo.

Reddy, V. Ratna (1982) Some Aspects of Agricultural Labour in Andhra Pradesh. (Mimeo), Bangalore: ISEC.

Sahu, Mahesh Kumar (1979) *Impact of an Irrigation Project on Labour Force and Migration (A Case Study of Hirakud Project in Sambalpur District)*. Ph.D. Thesis (ISEC). Mysore: University of Mysore.

Samuel, M. Johnson and S. Erappa (1985) Women Workers in Silk Reeling Industry. *Indian Journal of Labour Economics*, XXVIII(3): 221-55.

Sangita, S.N. and K. Jayalakshmi (1985) *Training of Rural Youth for Self-Employment (TRYSEM): An Evaluative Study in Karnataka*. Bangalore: ISEC. Mimeo.

Satakopan, Usha (1983) *Male-Female Differences in Educated Unemployment*. Bangalore: ISEC. Mimeo.

Satyapriya, V.S. (1981) *Labour Utilisation in Agriculture (Tumkur District)*. Bangalore: ISEC. Mimeo.

Satyapriya, V.S. (1990) *Labour Use in Agriculture: The Case of Karnataka, Andhra Pradesh and Tamil Nadu*. Bangalore: ISEC. Mimeo.

Shantha, N. (1976) *A Study of the Profile of Employed Women in the Public Sector in Bangalore City*. A Ph.D. Thesis (ISEC). Mysore: University of Mysore.

Srikantan, K.S., B.K. Narayana, and D. Vasudeva Rao (1978) Population and Employment in Area Planning: Female and Child Work Participation. *Demography India*, VII (1 & 2): 194-210.

Thippaiah, P. (1985) Workers in Urban Informal Sector. *Nagarlok*, XVII(2): 1-9.

Venkataramanan, L.S. (1986) *Agricultural Productivity Growth and Labour Absorption in Agriculture in Karnataka*. Bangalore: ISEC. Mimeo.

Vivekananda, M. (1986) *Rural Landless Employment Guarantee Programme—An Evaluation*. Bangalore: ISEC. Mimeo.

12

POPULATION, HEALTH AND FAMILY PLANNING

N. BASKARA RAO and K.N.M. RAJU

The 1971 Census of India enumerated a population of 548 million, implying an average annual growth rate of 2.2 per cent during 1961-71. During the earlier decades, growth rates were lower, 1.25 during 1941-51, and 1.96 during 1951-61. Married women, effectively protected against conception through the adoption of contraceptive methods, were only 15 per cent in 1973, about 10 years after the extension approach was adopted to educate and motivate couples to accept family planning. It was clear that the family planning programme was not making as much headway as expected and this was causing concern. New strategies to revitalise the maternal and child health programmes and family planning programme were introduced. It was recognised that demographic and socio-economic situation was vastly different among the States in India and also between regions within the States. There was a need for region specific studies to assess the levels as well as the changes in fertility and mortality, the trends and differentials in family planning adoption, the strengths and weaknesses of the health and family planning programmes etc. These research concerns, with special reference to Karnataka, are reflected in the studies undertaken by the Population Research Centre (PRC) (earlier known as Demographic and Communication Action Research Unit) of the Institute.

These studies can be grouped under broad themes: Population Trends and Relationships; Estimation of Vital Rates, Mortality, Fertility, Family Planning, and Health of Women and Children.

Population Trends and Relationships

Professor V.K.R.V. Rao, in his convocation address in the International

Institute for Population Studies in 1973 emphasised the need to study the inter-State variations in demographic characteristics so that population policies can be appropriately adapted to the demographic experiences of individual States. The study, by Bhattacharjee and Shastri (1976), was an attempt in this direction. This study examined the trends in population growth, mortality and fertility among individual States during a fifty-year period, 1921-71. It showed that the disparity among States in population growth observed during the 1940s and 1950s had declined subsequently leading to high growth rates in many States, mainly due to a relatively rapid decline in death rates than in birth rates. Later, a similar study, by Rayappa and Prabhakara (1983) examined the population trends in the southern States of Andhra Pradesh, Karnataka, Kerala, Tamil Nadu and Pondicherry, during a period of 80 years, 1901-1981. The demographic and socio-economic factors contributing to the differences in population growth in these States were identified. While noting the deceleration in growth rates during 1971-81 in Kerala and Tamil Nadu, the authors observed that the decline in population growth rates in the other States could occur even without achieving a high socio-economic threshold level.

For formulating policies and programmes, the planners need to know the current demographic situation and also the likely trends in the future. The studies carried out by the ISEC address themselves to this task. One is the Demographic Profile of Karnataka by Hanumantha Rayappa and Mutharayappa (1990), and the other, Population Projections for Karnataka, 1981-2001, by Kulkarni (1985). The Population projections provide valuable data on population size by age and sex, birth rates, death rates and per cent of couples protected (through family planning), for quinquennial periods up to 2001. It is interesting to note that compared to the projected population (under low fertility, no migration assumption) the 1991 Census Population of the State is lower by about 1.6 per cent. The study, Demographic Profile of Karnataka, examines the demographic trends and characteristics in the context of the social and economic changes that have taken place in the past few decades. This report needs to be updated in the light of the 1991 census data.

A study by Bhattacharjee (1978) examined the changes in agriculture and rural population in Karnataka during 1951-71. Belgaum, Bellary, Mysore, Mandya, Chickmagalur, Dharwad, Uttara Kannada, Hassan, Raichur and Shimoga had shown higher growth in agriculture and the rural areas in most of these districts had gained population through inmigration. The implication is that agricultural development can restrain the urban-ward migration in search of employment.

Demographic experience of neighbouring countries may possibly provide some lessons to India and hence, it is useful to examine the demography of the neighbouring countries. Kulkarni's study examined the demographic situation in China (Kulkarni, 1981). By skilfully collating the scanty data available on China, the author made the point that during the 1970s China had succeeded in reducing the birth and death rates substantially, through a variety of measures. The Chinese success in population control was largely due to strong political commitment, the study pointed out.

Estimation of Vital Rates

For populations of developing countries with deficient data on birth and death rates, indirect estimation procedures have been developed, one of which is through stable population analysis. This procedure, under certain assumptions, helps in the estimation of vital rates based on female age distribution, easily available from the censuses. In a significant paper, Bhat noted a discrepancy between the age distribution constructed by Coale, and the series of birth rate estimates made in Manual IV, for India in 1961 (Bhat, 1977). Tracing the inconsistency to an error in the method of estimating expectation of life at birth at the end of the intercensal period, Bhat proposed an improved method for estimating life expectancy and age distribution of Indian population.

In another study, the same author found some evidence to suggest that the age pattern of mortality decline, implicit in model life tables, was not appropriate for India, since the birth and death rates estimated through reverse-survival method using model life tables tended to be too high (Bhat, 1979). Because of differences in the factors contributing to mortality decline in India and in the western countries, it was probable that, for a given change in adult mortality, the decline in child mortality was relatively less in India.

Fertility

One of the primary goals of population programme is to bring down the birth rate as early as possible, and hence, it is necessary to monitor periodically the levels, trends and differentials in fertility. Measuring fertility, however, poses a number of problems, especially among the illiterate population. Due to recall lapse, all the children born alive are not reported correctly. There could be errors in reporting the timing of births and also, in the ages of women at child birth. Hence, birth rates and fertility rates are periodically estimated through different sources of data. Consistency and comparability of these estimates provide greater credibility to the estimated rates and become useful for policy formulation. There is also the question of the impact of family planning on the birth and fertility rates. Since age-sex-marital status composition of a population influences birth rate, it is necessary to separate out these effects and identify, for example, fertility decline attributable to the family planning programme. Research studies on fertility have examined all these aspects.

In order to examine the impact of family planning on fertility, standard fertility surveys (standardized for methodology and questionnaire) were conducted in selected areas in the country during the 1960s. The main objectives of these standard (longitudinal) fertility surveys were to "study changes in fertility and to test various indices to detect fertility changes". The Committee on Socio-Economic Studies on Fertility, of which Professor V.K.R.V. Rao was the Chairman, in its meeting in late 1973, decided to review the reports of Standard Fertility Surveys. A Review of the Reports on Standard Fertility Surveys in India (Rao and Rao 1974) examined the longitudinal or panel studies of Gandhigram (1964-69), of Shadnagar, (1967-71), of Calcutta (1964-68) and also two cross-section studies of Calcutta and Delhi. This study found that the decline in birth rate in Gandhigram area (Athoor block) was due to family planning adoption, and also to changes in the age-sex-marital status composition. While noting that different indicators of fertility showed different rates of decline, the study suggested that a component analysis of fertility change, taking into account age-sex-marital status composition, family planning adoption, post-partum amenorrhoea, sterility and foetal loss, would be more useful than analysing different indicators of fertility change. It also raised some research issues relating to fertility estimates obtained from panel studies compared to repeated cross-section studies, from questions in the Household Schedules compared to fertility history of individual woman, and also estimates based on *de facto* population, compared to *de jure* population.

Hospitals maintain records which contain data on women who come for deliveries. These records on women and children contain clinical and socio-economic data which have very good research potentialities (e.g., United States National Health Survey, Aberdeen Study). A study was conducted to assess the potentials of such statistics available in some hospitals in Bangalore City (Grover, 1976). This study examined the incidence of stillbirths and associated factors, sex ratio at birth and birth order. Several measures were suggested to improve the system of data recording and maintenance.

Coale, Hill and Trussell developed a procedure for estimating standard fertility measures least affected by errors of age misreporting. The assumption here is that the age pattern of marital fertility is similar to a standard fertility schedule derived from Louis Henry's data on natural fertility. P.N. Mari Bhat (1978) examined the validity of this assumption with respect to the age pattern of marital fertility in India. After a detailed analysis, the author concluded that, compared to the age pattern of natural fertility, the marital fertility of Indian women of 15-19 years was relatively low and that fertility in India declined sharply after age 30. Compared to the differences in fertility (natural fertility and Indian fertility) in 15-19 age group, the differences above age 30 seemed to be "more genuine and less tentative".

As stated earlier, the periodic estimation of the levels and trends in fertility and associated factors is necessary for the purpose of policy formulation. Two major collaborative field-surveys were conducted in this regard, one, during 1979-80, and the other during 1992-93.* The earlier study (Rao, Kulkarni and Rayappa, 1986), undertaken in collaboration with the World Bank and the UNFPA, was part of the World Bank's research project *'Case Studies of the Determinants of Fertility Decline in Sri Lanka and South India'*. This study covered a rural sample of about 3,000 households in Dharwad, Dakshina Kannada and Mandya districts and collected information on the reproductive histories of about 2,600 ever married women of 15 to 49 years of age. According to this study, TFR (Total Fertility Rate) per woman declined from 6.8 births during 1960-69 to 4.1 during 1975-79. One-third of the decline was due to the decline in proportion married (increasing age at marriage) and the remaining due to decline in marital fertility. Roughly, 40-60 per cent of the decline in marital fertility could be attributed to the effect of family planning programme. The mean desired family size was 3.6 children, lower than the TFR of 4.1. Significantly, the study pointed out that fertility could decline even in the absence of high levels of development and literacy. Among the three districts in terms of literacy, per capita income, health infrastructure and infant mortality, Dakshina Kannada had attained the highest level of development; yet it was in Mandya district that the desired family size was

* Apart from fertility, these surveys examined other aspects such as age at marriage, family planning, desired family size, infant mortality, maternal and child health. Findings pertaining to fertility are reported in this section. Findings relating to other aspects are reported in the respective sections.

lower, contraceptive use higher, and marital fertility lower—even when controlled for socio-economic characteristics.

The second major survey was the National Family Health Survey (NFHS), conducted in 25 States of India during 1992-93. The NFHS was a collaborative project of the Union Ministry of Health and Family Welfare, International Institute for Population Sciences (Bombay), Population Research Centres, Consulting Organizations, USAID (New Delhi), East-West Centre (Honolulu) and Macro International (Calvertan). The NFHS was unique in the sense that it provided data on, apart from fertility and related aspects, maternal health, child health, immunization and nutritional status of children for a representative population of each of the States covered (Rao, Rayappa, Raju, and Sinha 1994). In Karnataka, the survey covered 4,269 households in rural and urban areas, and collected information on the reproductive histories of 4,413 ever-married women in 13-49 age group. According to the survey, TFR per woman for the period 1990-92 was 2.85 births, and CBR 26.4 per 1,000 population. Trends in fertility rates showed a decline during the preceding 15 years. Age of woman at first and last child birth indicated that child bearing was concentrated across 15 years, from age 20 to 34. These age groups were, therefore, very important for bringing down fertility levels in the population. The ideal mean number of children preferred by women was 2.5. Roughly, 35 per cent of the births were unplanned in terms of either the number or the timing of births. The wanted fertility rate (excluding the unwanted births) per woman was 2.2, much below the actual fertility rate. All these indicate that there is scope for improving the levels of family planning adoption.

Studies on economic-demographic relationship through models, have also been undertaken. One study examined the pure income effects of redistributive income policies on family size (Narayana 1992). According to the study:

> "Income distribution and fertility can also be positively related due to the non-inflationary nature of financing the redistributive transfers".

It is useful to understand the nature of fertility transition in the neighbouring countries, particularly in a large population like that of China. One such study examined the regional variation in fertility in China (Kulkarni 1989b). Though development variables appeared to depress fertility in some regions, the "bulk of the inter-province variation was attributable to minority population proportion". Controlled for the development, regions with minority population had low contraceptive use and high fertility. This was because the Chinese programme itself had taken a liberal view of the minority fertility factor, in keeping with its overall policy of not imposing rigidly the norms of Han population on non-Han population.

Family Planning

Research on family planning includes studies on the levels, trends and determinants of family planning adoption. The nature of programme implementation and also specific schemes/strategies introduced to promote family planning have received attention. There are studies which have examined the economic aspects of family planning programme. Many of these studies are based on secondary data. Among the studies which have collected primary data, two major field surveys are important. There are also micro studies, combining the questionnaire method and probing techniques, which have enquired into fertility decision making in the context of culture and the type of family.

During 1969-71, family planning adoption rate varied substantially among the districts of Karnataka, from 1-2 per 1,000 population in Bidar, Bijapur, Gulbarga and Raichur, to 4-6 in Mysore, Hassan, Coorg and Chikmagalur. One study tried to examine the reasons for such variations (Rao, 1976). Among the three variables, female literacy, per capita income and per cent urban considered, female literacy was found to be important in explaining inter-district variations. Inter-State comparisons during 1956-71 indicated that Karnataka's performance in family planning, compared to the other States, was not encouraging.

The success of family planning programme depends, to a large extent, on the manner in which the programme is implemented and also on the perception of the people, local leaders, medical and para medical personnel. One study by Jorapur (1976), covering 12 PHCs (Primary Health Centres) and Urban Family Planning Centres in Karnataka, examined various aspects of family planning programme implementation. This study came up with a number of recommendations, and some of them were: local leaders should be officially involved in the programme through local committees; Auxiliary Nurse Midwives and Lady Health Visitors should be authorised to dispense medicines to the people to treat common ailments; top priority should be given to follow-up service to adopters of sterilization and IUD; PHC staff should maintain close and frequent contact with the people by arranging/participating in social functions;

and punitive measures for not achieving targets should be discouraged.

The 1981 census did not indicate the expected decline in population growth rate. On the other hand, the growth rate during 1971-81 was slightly higher than the growth rate of the preceding decade. Absence of decline in growth rate was attributed to the slow progress of family planning adoption. A number of studies have critically examined the various aspects of the family planning programme strategies and the quality of service. Ramesh Kanbargi and Foujdar Ram (1981), after analysing the family planning experience of Indonesia, Republic of Korea, Malaysia, Philippines and Thailand, argued that the Indian family planning programme should give greater importance to spacing methods such as IUD and Oral Pills, rather than relying solely on sterilization. Different strategies have to be followed to motivate newly married couples without children, couples with one child and those with two or more children. Following a similar theme, Foujdar Ram and Veeramatha (1984) observed that the family planning programme of Karnataka had not succeeded in attracting low parity women, mainly because of sterilization oriented programme, and unless spacing methods were adopted by low parity women, the goal of two-child family may be difficult to achieve. In another study, Veeramatha (1987) concluded that the States which had acceptors with low average age and fewer living children seemed to be in an advanced stage of demographic transition.

In Karnataka, Laparoscopic tubectomy was introduced in 1979-80, and the advantage of this method over conventional tubectomy is, that laparoscopic operation can be performed under local anaesthesia and on an out-patient basis. A comparative study of laparoscopic and conventional abdominal sterilisation revealed that the number of laparoscopic sterilisations was declining because of high rate of failure of operation resulting in conception (Veeramatha, 1986).

Another study (Kulkarni, 1989) relating to family planning programme implementation was on target setting for small areas (for districts or PHC area). At the national level, target setting is done in a scientific manner, taking into consideration several demographic parameters. For smaller areas, however, such exercises could become very cumbersome in the absence of required data, and hence, the State level targets are distributed over the smaller areas in proportion to their populations. In this situation, it may so happen that a PHC with high contraceptive prevalence rate could be allotted the same target as a PHC with very low contraceptive prevalence rate. Is this procedure justified? According to the model used in the study, this is justified, since areas with vastly varying prevalence rates, when subjected to identical acceptor targets, soon converge to the common desired goal. Even if an area has reached the desired prevalence level, a large body of fresh acceptors is required to make good the attrition among the past acceptors. P.M. Kulkarni proposed a simple procedure for target setting which can be used as a rule of thumb.

Since women were accepting family planning only after having the desired number of sons, there was concern whether this would result in unbalanced sex ratio. This issue was examined by Kulkarni (1978). In a homogeneous population where the probability of having a son is equal among all couples, stopping child bearing after one or two sons does not alter the sex ratio at birth. On the other hand, in a heterogeneous population where the probability of having a son is unequal among couples, then with family limitation after one or two sons, the resultant sex ratio will be less favourable to males (less males and more females). Based on data from selected districts of Karnataka, the author concluded that heterogeneity in the population studied, was either non-existent or not large enough to be significant, and hence the effect of family planning on sex ratio would not be severe even if there was preference for a son.

After the declaration of emergency in the country, family planning drive was intensified, which resulted in a phenomenal increase in the number of sterilizations conducted in 1976-77. This was followed, after the lifting of emergency, by a decline in performance in the subsequent years. One study examined the effects of this intensification on the programme (Kulkarni, 1984). This study concluded that though there was a setback in the performance after the 1976-77 intensification, this was only for a short period, 3-5 years, and the programme recovered, in all States, to the level prior to the intensification.

Studies which have enquired into the economic aspects of family planning include, family welfare programme expenditure and births averted, and the cost efficiency of family planning clinics versus camps. How much the government should invest in family planning programme was a question that was examined during the 1960s and the early 1970s. However, estimating the benefit-cost ratio of family planning adoption or the cost-effectiveness of a family planning method, poses a number of practical problems. A simpler approach is to estimate how much it will cost the government to prevent one birth. According to one rough estimate, in Karnataka, the cost of preventing one birth varied between Rs. 50 to 100 (1961-62 prices) during 1966-76 (Kulkarni, 1978). Another study on cost efficiency of Clinics *versus* Camps, concluded that camps and clinics catered to different types of clienteles; and that camps could lead to a gain in output (in terms of sterilizations) due to a decline in the overall unit cost through economies of scale. However, this gain in output might involve some loss of quality in terms of pre- and post-operative care (Rayappa, Samuel and Dinesh, 1986). A spatial model for organising routine camps for delivering health and family planning services in sparsely populated rural areas has also been proposed (Samuel, 1992).

According to the study by Rao, Kulkarni and Rayappa (1986), almost 80-90 per cent of women in Mandya, Dakshina Kannada and Dharwad, knew about tubectomy or vasectomy, and 24 per cent of currently married women were using a family planning method at that time. Knowledge about temporary methods was low and their use very negligible. A significant finding is that the programme has succeeded in Mandya district in spite of its being a low literacy district. Mandya's better performance is attributed to the manner in which the programme has been implemented in that district. However, in another study by Raju and his team, the success of family planning programme and the consequent decline in fertility in Mandya district was attributed to factors such as population pressure on land, high dependency on agriculture and exorbitant land value resulting out of long history of irrigation expansion, and atypical characteristics like homogeneous population, predominance of very small farmers, and easy accessibility to health services due to good network of roads and transport facilities connecting large number of villages even with small population size (Raju, Bhat, Umamani and Lingaraju, 1993).

The National Family Health Survey of Karnataka (Rao, Rayappa, Raju and Sinha, 1994) showed that nearly one-half of currently married women were using a family planning method at the time of survey during 1992-93. As observed in the preceding survey (in 1986), adoption of temporary or spacing method was relatively low. This study also examined the socio-economic and demographic differentials in family planning adoption, relative shares of the public and private sectors in providing family planning services, intentions about future use etc. From the point of view of programme implications, the study noted that 18 per cent of currently married women in the State had an unmet demand for family planning, 12 per cent for spacing and 6 per cent for limiting family size. If all such women were to adopt family planning, the current use could go up from 49 to 67 per cent.

While large scale surveys using the questionnaire method can capture the extent and direction of demographic change, micro studies combining questionnaire method and extensive probing techniques can provide insights into the nature of such changes. Changes in the household power structure and in the pattern of decision making are important to understand family planning adoption. Abusaleh Sharief (1987) tried to examine the "*source of such power among the rural population of South India, especially with reference to women, and thus trace a change in the family system and the pattern of decision making*". K.N.M. Raju's study (1992) of a village in coastal Andhra underlines the significance of natal family in influencing fertility decisions of daughters. The natal family provides maternal and child care to daughters during the first and second confinements. Due to some reasons this burden of providing maternal and child care increased in the study area. This increasing burden, in a situation where children ceased to be economic assets, led to limiting the family size of the daughters through family planning adoption.

In addition to these studies, the PRC conducts concurrent evaluation of the family planning programme every year and provides feedback to the Union Ministry of Health and Family Welfare. Every year, one district is covered and surveys are conducted in selected PHC areas in that district. The findings vary according to the PHCs and the year of survey, and however, a few general findings can be presented. The concept of spacing the births has not yet caught on in Karnataka (possibly in the other States as well) except among the better educated and those residing in or around urban centres. Hence, the programme is dependent heavily on sterilization which implies the completion of desired family size with one or two male children. Problems such as inadequate supply of required drugs, poor infrastructure facilities/maintenance, inadequate post-operative care, vacant posts, lack of support from the other departments, from the local leaders etc., are frequently cited in these studies as reasons for low performance of the family planning programme in the study areas.

Mortality among Women and Children

The level of mortality among women and children is an important indicator of the health conditions and hence, it is important to understand the trends and differentials in child and in maternal mortality. P.J. Bhattacharjee's study examined the relationship between sex differentials in mortality and the availability of medical facilities among the States in India (1980). During the early 1970s, female mortality was higher than male mortality in several States up to age 50, and beyond this age male mortality was higher. The author concluded that for lowering the levels of female mortality, substantial improvements in socio-economic conditions were necessary, in addition to the provision of medical facilities. Foujdar Ram, H. Girimaji and K.S. Umamani (1983) examined a variety of sources of data to understand the infant and child mortality situation in Karnataka. According to the authors, the decline in infant mortality in Karnataka was quite rapid during the 1950s and 1960s, but thereafter, the decline was relatively slow. Their study suggested that further decline in infant mortality would be possible only if additional health facilities were provided in interior villages and under-privileged sections of population in urban areas were given easier access to existing facilities.

The sample survey of Dharwad, Dakshina Kannada and Mandya districts showed that infant mortality had declined from 90 per 1,000 live births during 1965-69 to 70 during 1975-78 (Rao, Kulkarni and Rayappa, 1986). The decline in under-five mortality was from 160 to 146 during 1965-74. Infant and child mortality was the lowest in Dakshina Kannada and the highest in Dharwad. Under-five mortality was relatively high among children of illiterates, the scheduled castes and tribes, and the low income households.

The NFHS, based on a representative sample of households in Karnataka, estimated the decline in infant mortality rate from 94 during 1978-82 to 65 during 1988-92 (Rao, Rayappa, Raju and Sinha, 1994). The decline in under-five mortality during the corresponding period was from 141 to 87 per 1,000 live births. Infant and child mortality was higher among children in rural areas, among children of illiterate mothers and in scheduled caste/ tribe families. More significantly, under-five mortality was relatively high among children of mothers who had no ante-natal or delivery care, among children of very young mothers (<20 years), among higher birth order children and also among children born after a short birth interval (<24 months). In other words, children with the above mentioned characteristics had an *elevated risk of mortality*. According to the study, more than one-half of births that occurred during the five years preceding the survey were at elevated risk of mortality. The disadvantages of such high risk pregnancies should be stressed in the health education programme.

Health

Maternal and child health, which constitutes an important component of population control programmes, has been a major area of research. Immunization coverage of children, ante-natal and post-natal care received by mothers, the nature of implementation of certain schemes such as the

Integrated Child Development Scheme (ICDS), Multi Purpose Worker Schemes, Village Health Guide Scheme, and the implementation of the Medical Termination of Pregnancy Act are some of the themes on which research has been carried out.

The earliest study was by Jorapur, on the Integrated Child Development Scheme, which was introduced on an experimental basis in T. Narasipura taluk of Karnataka in 1976 (Jorapur, 1978). According to this study, the coverage of children (under six years) by the ICDS was quite encouraging, but not the coverage of pregnant women and nursing mothers. The distribution of supplementary food was not very regular due to inadequate stock of food stuff and fuel. A number of suggestions made by the author highlighted the need for proper buildings for Anganwadi Centres, the importance of planning and coordination in the distribution of food materials to the Anganwadi Centres, transport facilities for the staff, the need for monitoring morbidity and mortality among children and women in ICDS areas etc.

Two health schemes, Multi-Purpose Health Worker Scheme and the Village Health Guide Scheme, were launched during 1977-80. The idea behind the Multi-Purpose Health Worker Scheme launched in 1977 was that it would be more appropriate to provide a package of health and family planning services through a single administrative set-up, rather than providing such services in a vertical manner through multiple agencies. According to a study which enquired into the working of this scheme, there was no proper integration of work under this scheme at the State and district levels (Rayappa and Rao, 1982). Even at the peripheral or field level, health workers tended to think generally in terms of uni-purpose activities rather than multi-purpose work. Systematic baseline surveys, as recommended in the Manual were not conducted. Health workers faced a number of problems in the field which they were unable to cope with, possibly because of inadequate on-the-job training. Many health workers did not have the Health Worker Manual or the Health kits. Some suggestions had been made to improve the functioning of this scheme.

The Village Health Guide Scheme was launched in Mysore and Dharwad districts in 1980. This scheme aimed to provide some basic health services to the rural people through a cadre of Voluntary Health Guides who would be under the control of the Village Health Committee, but received technical support and guidance from the government. A study of this scheme has identified a number of problems (Rayappa, 1985). Village Health Committees, which were supposed to select the Health Guides, did not exist. Training of Health Guides was found to be inadequate.

The activities carried out by the Health Guides were mainly family planning motivation, treatment of minor ailments and referral of cases to the nearest health centre/hospital. Other activities such as environmental sanitation, immunization and health education did not receive much attention. Supply of drugs to Health Guides was found to be inadequate. Overall, it appeared that this scheme was not well understood by the PHC staff, village leaders and the Health Guides themselves.

The Health Guides Scheme of India was analogous to the Barefoot Doctors Scheme of China. A comparative study of these two schemes made a number of suggestions (Kulkarni, 1987): steps should be taken to ensure greater community involvement through the Village Health Committees; the amount of honorarium to Health Guides should be periodically reviewed; and regular refresher courses for Health Guides and Orientation Programme for doctors should be organized for the effective implementation of the scheme.

The Universal Immunization Programme (UIP) was launched in Karnataka in 1985 with the objective of immunizing the children against six diseases viz., Tuberculosis, Poliomyelitis, Diphtheria, Pertussis, Tetanus and Measles, before they reached one year of age, and also expectant mothers against Tetanus during pregnancy. Following the WHO methodology, an evaluation study was conducted in Hassan district in 1988 (Rayappa and Samuel 1988). According to this study, 51 per cent of the children, 56 among boys and 47 among girls, were fully protected against the six diseases. Another 44 per cent of the children were partially protected and five per cent of the children did not receive even a single dose of any of the vaccines. The study identified certain constraints operating against the programme such as the large number of domiciliary deliveries which made follow-up work difficult, the problem of mobilising enough children to be vaccinated at a specific point in villages with few households, the practice of mothers going to parent's places for deliveries and moving back to husband's place, thereby missing some vaccinations etc. On the other hand, the programme had certain 'spin-off' effects. More and more families from interior areas were brought into contact with the health workers. Such contacts were useful in the sense that the programme became more credible and people gained confidence to seek a variety of health and family welfare services. Recording and reporting of births had also improved to a certain extent.

The Medical Termination of Pregnancy (MTP) Act of 1971 came into force in 1972. This was considered to be essentially a health measure aimed at discouraging and reducing the large number of clandestine abortions conducted in unhygienic conditions, resulting in high maternal mortality. The Union Ministry of Health and Family Planning was eager to obtain information on the impact of this legislation, about the trends in legal abortions, characteristics of women who had abortions, problems relating to the interpretation (by the medical practitioners) of the rules and procedures provided under this Act etc. The PRC undertook quite a few studies on various aspects of legal abortions.

The first study (Kanbargi, 1978) was based on data on nearly 1,000 women who had legal abortions in two approved hospitals in Bangalore city, and examined the short term trends as well as the characteristics of the women. This was followed up by a larger study based on information on about 8,000 women throughout Karnataka (Rao and Kanbargi, 1977 and 1980). These studies examined the trends in legal abortions during 1972-74, socio-economic characteristics of the women, gestation and termination procedures, and post-abortion adoption of contraception. It noted that the under-representation of illiterate women in the sample was probably due to their lack of knowledge about the new legislation and also about the limited number of localities and hospitals where MTP facilities were provided at that time. The study suggested an informal referral system consisting of clinics, dispensaries, family planning workers and *dais*, which can help the illiterate women seeking abortions, with the required particulars, and refer them to the nearest approved hospital. The study, which examined the communication aspects, suggested that the mass media could be effectively used not to encourage abortion but to provide information about the new legislation and the approved hospitals (Kanbargi and Kanbargi 1977). If illegal abortions and the consequent maternal mortality were to be reduced, medical practitioners had to be very considerate and sympathetic to women seeking abortions, particularly to those in a state of mental trauma. At that time, some medical practitioners had a tendency to apply the MTP rules very rigidly and deny abortion facilities. This was highlighted in a small study which pointed out that some women belonging to the lower socio-economic strata were denied abortion facilities on grounds that were inconsistent with the provisions of the MTP Act (Rao, Kanbargi and Kanbargi, 1977).

The NFHS collected a wealth of information from a representative sample on various aspects of MCH such as ante-natal care and assistance at delivery, child morbidity and treatment pattern, vaccination of children and pregnant women, infant feeding and the nutritional status of children (Rao, Rayappa, Raju and Sinha, 1994). Mothers of 84 per cent of children (born during the four years preceding the survey) had received ante-natal care. Similarly, in 70 per cent of births, the mothers had received two doses of Tetanus Toxoid and in 75 per cent of cases, the women had received iron and folic tablets during pregnancy. About 38 per cent of births took place in health institutions, 22 per cent in public or government institutions and 16 per cent in private institutions. Fifty-two per cent of the children, aged 12-23 months at the time of survey, were fully protected against the six immunizable diseases, 42 per cent of them during their infancy. Sixty per cent of the children with diarrhoea were given neither oral rehydration salts, the recommended home solution or increased fluids.

Most of the mothers breast-fed their children, but breast-feeding did not start soon after birth, and two-thirds of mothers followed the undesirable practice of squeezing out the first milk before breast-feeding the babies thereby denying the infants the much needed colostrum which provided immunity against infections. Among children aged less than four years at the time of survey, 48 per cent were under-weight (weight for age), 41 per cent stunted (height for age), and 17 per cent were acutely malnourished (weight for height). The programme implications of these findings are clear. The extension education has to lay adequate stress on the importance of colostrum in providing immunity to children, and on the important role played by Oral Rehydration Therapy (ORT) in preventing deaths due to dehydration. The nutritional status of the children observed in the study highlighted the need to re-examine the nutritional and related policies.

Children and Women

The problems of children are generally examined in a segmented manner, though the health and nutritional status of children are closely related to those of women and the overall development inputs. For example, diseases during early infancy are closely related to the health and nutritional status of mothers. Again, providing supplementary nutrition to children of poor families cannot be effective unless backed by immunization, health education and distribution of subsidised foodgrains. One study, sponsored by the Government of Karnataka and the UNICEF, examined children and women in an integrated manner, in the context of the overall socio-economic situation (Rao and Rayappa, 1990). Using a variety of data including the data available with the government departments and voluntary organizations, this study examined the situation of children and women with respect to physical environment, nutrition and health, literacy and education, child labour, disabilities and destitution. Child development programmes were critically examined and the possible manner in which these programmes could be improved were also indicated. This study was found useful by the Government of Karnataka for preparing the State Plan of Action for the Child.

Conclusions

From the above review of research studies, one can observe that a variety of topics on population, family planning and related aspects have been undertaken. These studies have made use of secondary data or primary data collected through large or small scale sample surveys; while some studies were very technical, others were descriptive in nature.

Family planning has always been the major theme of research. In addition to evaluation of family planning programme on yearly basis to study the changes in the socioeconomic and demographic characteristics of acceptors and non-acceptors, large scale sample surveys have been undertaken to study the correlates and determinants of family planning adoption. Concurrent evaluation of major health programmes have also been undertaken from time to time.

There are, however, some research gaps like linkages between poverty and population, and health facilities rendered by private sector, etc. Recently, some studies have been initiated in this direction. Demographic studies have been commissioned in some communities and groups like various tribes, temporary migrant workers to cities, and various minority communities who live in perpetual poverty. Of late, the scope of primary health care has been enlarged by the State government and also many non-governmental organisations. Therefore, studies relating to the role of indigenous health practitioners and people's attitude to traditional medicine have also been initiated. Further, studies on the role of private organizations and non-governmental agencies in the field of health and family planning have been undertaken.

Although many thrust areas of research importance have been covered and new studies have been commissioned, studies on the demographic change in smaller regions are yet to be initiated on a large scale. Demographic studies pertaining to small regions are important because villages situated in remote corners of the State are being integrated with the main stream of developmental activities due to rapid changes in technology and spread of mass media facilitating efficient and effective communication. People are increasingly exposed to outside world beyond their little village and with that their general perception and attitude are changing. Significantly, with the passing of Constitutional 73 Amendment Act, there is decentralisation of political and financial powers and greater devolution of resources to Panchayats, and more importantly, formulation and implementation of welfare programmes including health and education are delegated to these local self-governing institutions. These changes will have a profound influence on the demographic behaviour of people living in villages and the demographic behaviour may take different pathways in conformation with the cultural and ecological set-up of the region. And hence, there is a need to undertake demographic studies specific to small regions. In future, such studies are likely to be undertaken in keeping with changing political environment and State policies.

REFERENCES

Bhat, Mari P.N. (1977) Estimation of Vital Rates and Age Distribution under Quasi-Stability: Case of India, 1961, Reexamined. *Population Index*, 43(2): 187-205.

Bhat, Mari P.N. (1978) *Age Pattern of Marital Fertility in India*. Bangalore: ISEC. Mimeo.

Bhat, Mari P.N. (1979) *Age Pattern and Estimates of Birth and Death Rates in India*. Bangalore: ISEC. Mimeo.

Bhat, T.N. and B.M. Dinesh (1988) Incentives for Adoption of Family Planning: Views of Acceptors and Motivators. *The Journal of Family Welfare*, XXXIV(4): 23-35.

Bhattacharjee, P.J. (1978) Agricultural Change and Growth of Rural Population in Karnataka, 1951-71. In J.R. Rele and M.K. Jain (eds.), *Population Change and Rural Development in India*. Bombay: IIPS.

Bhattacharjee, P.J. (1980) *Sex Differentials in Mortality and the Availability of Medical Facilities in India*. Bangalore: ISEC. Mimeo.

Bhattacharjee, P.J. and G.N. Shastri (1976) *Population in India, A Study of Interstate Variations*. New Delhi: Vikas.

Grover, Deepak (1976) *An Analysis of Hospital Birth Statistics in Bangalore City*. Bangalore: ISEC. Mimeo.

Jorapur, P.B. (1976) *Problems in implementing Family Planning Programme in Karnataka: A Study of Medical and Para-Medical Personnel and Local Leaders*. Bangalore: ISEC. Mimeo.

Jorapur, P.B. (1978) Health, Nutrition and Family Planning in Karnataka: A Study of the Impact of Integrated Child Development Service Scheme. Bangalore: ISEC. Mimeo.

Kanbargi, Ramesh (1978) *Induced Abortions in Bangalore City 1972-74*. New Delhi: Allied.

Kanbargi, Ramesh and Shanta Kanbargi (1977) Aspects of Communication in Legal Abortions—A Case Study. *The Journal of Family Welfare*, XXXIV(2): 32-40

Kanbargi, Ramesh and Foujdar Ram (1981) *The Need of the Hour: An Innovative Approach to Fertility Control*. Bangalore: ISEC. Mimeo.

Kulkarni, P.M. (1978a) *Homogeneity in Sex Ratio at Birth*. Bangalore: ISEC. Mimeo.

Kulkarni, P.M. (1978b) *Family Welfare Programme in Karnataka, Expenditure and*

Births Averted, 1966-1976. Bangalore: ISEC. Mimeo.

Kulkarni, P.M. (1981) *Demographic Situation in China: What Do We Know?* Bangalore: ISEC. Mimeo.

Kulkarni, P.M. (1984) *An Analysis of the Effects of the 1977 Intensification in Family Planning*. Bangalore: ISEC. Mimeo.

Kulkarni, P.M. (1985) *Population Projections for Karnataka 1981-2001*. Bangalore: ISEC. Mimeo.

Kulkarni, P.M. (1987) The Barefoot Doctors of China and the Health Guides of India. *Social Science Probings*, 4(3).

Kulkarni, P.M. (1989a) *Setting FP Targets for Small Regions*. Bangalore: ISEC. Mimeo.

Kulkarni, P.M. (1989b) *Regional Variations in Fertility in China—The Role of the Minority Population Factor*. Bangalore: ISEC. Mimeo.

Narayana, M.R. (1992) Income Distribution and Endogenous Fertility: An Economic-theoretic Approach. *Asian Economic Review*, XXXIV(1): 131-148.

Raju, K.N.M. (1992) *Family, Family Planning and Fertility*. Bangalore: ISEC. Mimeo.

Raju, K.N.M., T.N. Bhat, K.S. Umamani and M. Lingaraju (1993) *Evaluation of Family Planning and Maternal and Child Health Programmes in Mandya District, Karnataka, 1991-92*. Bangalore: ISEC. Mimeo.

Ram, Foujdar, Jyothi H. Girimaji and K.S. Umamani (1983) *Infant and Childhood Mortality: Levels, Trends and Determinants in Karnataka*. Bangalore: ISEC. Mimeo.

Ram, Foujdar and C.S. Veeramatha (1984) Changing Patterns of Response towards Family Planning programme in Karnataka. *Journal of Institute of Economic Research*, 19(1): 14-29.

Rao, N. Baskara (1976) *Family Planning in India: A Case Study of Karnataka*. New Delhi: Vikas.

Rao, N. Baskara and Ramesh Kanbargi (1977) Legal Abortions in an Indian State. *Studies in Family Planning*, 8(12): 311-15.

Rao, N. Baskara and Ramesh Kanbargi (1980) *Medical Termination of Pregnancy: An Analysis of Trends and Differentials in Legal Abortions in Karnataka*. Bombay: Himalaya.

Rao, N. Baskara, Ramesh Kanbargi and Shantha Kanbargi (1977) Criteria for Denying Medical Termination of Pregnancy. *Economic and Political Weekly*, 12(48): 1985-86.

Rao, N. Baskara, P.M. Kulkarni and P. Hanumantha Rayappa (1986) *Determinants of Fertility Decline; A Study of Rural Karnataka*. New Delhi: South Asian Publishers.

Rao, N. Baskara and P. Hanumantha Rayappa (1991) *Children and Women in Karnataka. A Situation Analysis*. Bangalore: Government of Karnataka and ISEC.

Rao, N. Baskara, P.H. Rayappa, K.N.M. Raju and U.P. Sinha (1994) *National Family Health Survey 1992-93 Karnataka*. Bombay: International Institute for Population Sciences.

Rao, S.L.N. and N. Baskara Rao (1974) A Review of Reports on Standard Fertility Surveys in India. Bangalore: ISEC. Mimeo.

Rayappa, P. Hanumantha (1985) *Village Health Guide Scheme in Karnataka: A Study of Two Primary Health Centres in Kolar District*. Bangalore: ISEC. Mimeo.

Rayappa, P. Hanumantha and R. Mutharayappa (1990) *Demographic Profile of Karnataka.* Bangalore: ISEC. Mimeo.

Rayappa, P. Hanumantha and N.R. Prabhakara (1983) Pattern of Population Growth in Southern States. *Economic and Political Weekly*, XVIII(48): 2018-31.

Rayappa, P. Hanumantha and N. Baskara Rao (1982) Multi Purpose Health Worker Scheme in Karnataka: A Study of Malur and Dibbur Primary Health Centres in Kolar District. Bangalore: ISEC. Mimeo.

Rayappa, P. Hanumantha and M. Johnson Samuel (1989) Universal Immunization Programme in Karnataka: An Evaluation Study in Hassan District of Karnataka, India. *Journal of the Institute of Economic Research*, 24(2): 1-15.

Rayappa, P. Hanumantha, M. Johnson Samuel and B. Manjeshwar Dinesh (1987) Cost Efficiency of Family Welfare Programme: Clinics vs Camps. *Journal of Family Welfare*, XXXIII(3): 56-65.

Samuel, M. Johnson (1992) Taking Health Services to Rural Areas: Neglect of Spatial Dimension. *Indian Geographical Journal*, 67(1): 30-39.

Shariff, Abusaleh (1987) A Micro Investigation of Social Change, Status of Women and Fertility Decisions in Karnataka: Methodology and Some Findings. *Demography India*, XVI(1): 48-69.

Veeramatha, C.S. (1986) A Comparative Study of Laparoscopic and Conventional Abdominal Sterilization in Chikmagalur District of Karnataka. *Health and Population: Perspectives and Issues*, 9(3): 139-45.

Veeramatha, C.S. (1987) Demographic Characteristics of Family Planning Acceptors and Their Implications: State-wise Analysis—India 1979-81. *Demography India*, XVI (1): 33-47.

13

ECONOMIC MODELLING FOR POLICY DECISIONS

M.R. NARAYANA

Introduction

This Chapter provides a coherent review of the research studies in which economic modelling/theorisation has been explicit and has been aimed for policy decisions/purposes in the Institute for Social and Economic Change (ISEC). For the sake of brevity, the review focuses on technical details in regard to formulation of the model and its main analytical results. In addition, the nature and extent of applied/empirical research which have been based on these models are highlighted.

Economic Modelling/Theorisation: An Overview

Nature of Economic Modelling

In general, an economy comprises economic activities such as production, consumption and exchange. The working of these activities is characterised in terms of an economic structure. An economic structure is defined in terms of institutions and behaviours. The institutions may include social institutions (e.g., nature and type of family), economic institutions (e.g., product and factor markets) and political institutions (e.g., governments). On the other hand, behaviours relate to the behaviour of agents in the economy in regard to different economic activities. For example, firms/producers are the agents of production; consumers are the agents of consumption; and buyers, sellers or traders are the agents in exchange. In general, the behaviour may be rational or irrational. For instance, rationality in production (or consumption) implies that producers (or consumers) maximise profits (or utility).

An economic model/theory is a representation of a real economic activity.[1] Its objective is to explain and predict the observed economic phenomenon or phenomena. For the purpose of simplifying the reality, the models make several assumptions/approximations.[2] These assumptions are essentially related to the economic structure in which a phenomenon is aimed to be explained and predicted.

An economic phenomenon may be affected by many factors. These factors may include policy and non-policy factors; or market and non-market factors. And, these factors may be variable or constant. In particular, variables may be endogenous variables (i.e., the variables whose values are determined within the model) and exogenous variables (i.e., variables whose values are determined outside the model). Constants or parameters are those whose values do not change in the model.

An important objective of an economic model is to: (i) identify the relevant economic factors; and (ii) establish/derive and analyse the relationship between economic factors affecting the phenomenon/phenomena. In particular, a model aims at establishing the relationships between endogenous and exogenous variables and parameters, such that the endogenous variables can be expressed as a function of exogenous variables and parameters. In short, an economic model/theory suggests the analytical relationship between economic factors.

Types of Economic Modelling

Economic models can be distinguished by the formulation and expression of the nature and analysis of the underlying analytical relationships between economic factors. Accordingly, there exists a wide variety of economic models which include quantitative models (e.g., mathematical models, statistical models and simulation models), and non-quantitative models (e.g., descriptive models). In recent decades, economic models have been quantitative in all its descriptions.[3]

Empirical Modelling of Economic Relationships

The relationships suggested by the economic model may be estimable, provided the appropriate data are available or collectable. Thus, theory is a guideline for what available data are to be used or what new data are to be collected for measuring the relationships.[4] This is a case for economic measurement with theory. In this way, the theoretical relationships become the testable hypotheses for empirical analysis. From this viewpoint, development of an economic model is a precondition for a systematic empirical study.

Given the relevant data, the search for an appropriate method of estimating the relationships or testing the empirical validity of the hypotheses becomes pertinent. That branch of economics which deals with the methods of estimating the economic relationships with various types of data (e.g., sample/non-sample, cross-section/time series/panel/ longitudinal data) is called econometrics. Thus, econometrics is an essential part of empirical analysis of economic modelling.[5]

In short, economic theory, data and methods of estimation are the essential empirical aspects of economic modelling. A systematic arrangement of these aspects may be called empirical modelling of economic relationships.

Economic Modelling for Policy Decisions

A systematic empirical modelling and estimation of economic relationships is important for: (1) testing the empirical validity of theoretical predictions; and (2) deriving policy implications. The policy implications may be related to the overall study or, in particular, to a policy variable/parameter in question. From this viewpoint, theory and policy are integrated in economics through empirical analysis. And, there is no justification for separating theory, policy and empiric in any economic modelling for policy decisions. Further, in testing the theory-based hypotheses, the empirical results and policy implications have the advantage to be interpreted unambiguously.

Economic Modelling for Policy Decisions in the ISEC

Broadly speaking, five important areas of economic modelling for policy decisions in the ISEC studies may be identified. They are: modelling India's macroeconomic development; modelling India's inter-regional allocation of resources; modelling India's foreign trade; modelling India's economic fertility; and modelling India's economic reforms.

In what follows, a review of only those research studies where economic modelling for policy decisions has been explicit in the areas above will be focused. In order to make this review as wide and recent as possible, all the ISEC studies which are available in the form of research reports (i.e., in published and unpublished forms) and journal articles up to April 1996 have been covered.[6]

Modelling India's Macro-Economic Development

India is an open economy, i.e., there exists mobility of factors of production (e.g., labour and capital) and commodity trade between India and the rest of the world. Secondly, India is a mixed economy, i.e., private and public sectors coexist in different economic activities of production, consumption and exchange. Third, India is a federal economy, i.e., the revenue and expenditure functions of the government are divided at different levels (e.g., between Central and State governments). Thus, India's economic development is influenced by agents and institutions in its underlying economic structure of federal, open and mixed economy.

M.R. Narayana (1995) has captured the importance of the economic structure above while modelling India's macroeconomic development with special reference to the role of fiscal policy. The model divides the national economy into three sectors, viz., private sector, public sector and external sector, and treats the sectors as functionally inter-dependent. Thus, economic growth (i.e., growth of national income) is determined by the combined savings and investments performance of all the three sectors. Using the framework of a three-gap model [e.g., Mills and Nallari 1992], the sectoral performance in national economic development may be defined as follows.

Private (Non-governmental) Sector: This sector may broadly comprise individuals and private and government-supported firms. Let Y be the total national income (GDP); C_P be the total private consumption; I_P be the total private investment which is financed, in part, by borrowed capital; and INT_P be the interest payments by the private sector on external debt. Thus, the total private sector savings (net of direct taxes), S_P, is equal to $[Y - C_P - INT_P]$.

Public (government) Sector: In India's federation, Union and State governments are the major actors in the public sector of the economy. Let TR_u (TR_s) be the total current revenues of the Union (State) government (governments); $C_U (C_S)$ be the Union (State) government's (governments') consumption/revenue expenditure; I_U (I_S) be the Union (State) government's (governments') investment/capital expenditure; INP_G be the total interest payments of the public sector on external debt. Thus,

total public sector savings, $S_G = (S_U + S_S)$ equals to $[\{TR_U + (TR_S)\} — \{C_U + (C_S)\} - INT_G]$.

External Sector: Exports (*X*) and imports (*M*) of goods and services comprise the major activities in the external sector of the economy. In general, imports may be divided into imports of consumer goods (M_C), intermediate inputs (M_I) and capital goods (M_K). The foreign exchange earned in exports is an important source of financing the imports and for interest payments on external borrowing by public and private sectors. Let the foreign exchange used to pay for interest payments on external debt by private and public sector be INT_P and INT_G respectively, and for total imports be $(M_C + M_I + M_K)$. Then, the savings of the external sector (S_F) equals to $[X - \{(M_C + M_I + M_K) + (INT_P + INT_G)\}]$.

From the above analysis, the aggregate relationship between savings and investments in the economy in time t can be expressed as follows:

$$(S_P + S_G + S_F) \equiv S(t) = (I_P + I_G) \equiv I(t) \qquad (1)$$

where I_G (e.g., public investment on social and economic infrastructure) is considered to be complementary to I_P.

The right hand side of equation (1) shows that any shortfall in savings of the private and/or public sector's savings can be accentuated or lessened by savings in the external sector. Thus, the nature and pattern of savings in all the sector is important in explaining the nature and pattern of aggregate investment in the economy.

Determinants of National Income: Assuming that investments are determined by the same conditions as in the static, full employment and fixed-coefficient version of the Harrod-Domar model, the conditions for the growth of real national income (GDP) at full employment (Y*) is given by the following conditions.

$$dY^*/dt = I(t)/\gamma \qquad (2)$$

$$S(t) = I(t) \qquad (3)$$

where $(1/\gamma)$ is the incremental capital-potential output ratio; $\{I(t)$ and $S(t)\}$ are the same as defined in (1) above; and where the rate of inflation needed to arrive at the real GDP growth in (2) is exogenously determined.

Dividing both sides of (2) by Y*, one gets the familiar expression for the proportionate rate of growth of potential national income as given below.

$$(dY^*/dt)/Y^* = (1/\gamma).[I(t)/Y^*] \qquad (4)$$

Equation (4) shows the functional link between the real national economic growth (i.e., potential national income) and the aggregate investment constraint in the economy. This linkage establishes the macro interdependence not only between the revenue and expenditure relationships within the Union and State governments' budgetary process through fiscal gap, but also the impact of changes in budgetary processes in the federation on the savings of private sector and foreign sector.

If the national economic policy, for instance, aims at reducing the fiscal deficit of the Union government without affecting the economic growth, then the fiscal adjustment policy should simultaneously ensure that the current account deficit is reduced or private savings increased, or a combination of both a reduction in current account deficit and an increase in private savings. Thus, the proposed policy framework is useful for co-ordinating the size and growth of fiscal deficit in the Union government which will be consistent with a targeted rate of national economic growth. This policy is called the adjustment policy of national growth with stability.

Modelling India's Inter-regional Allocation of Resources

The presence of inter-regional mobility of resources (or factors of production), such as, labour and capital resources make the regions/ States open in the Indian federation. Thus, the production and consumption activities in different regions are influenced by the regional endowment of fixed resources as well as by the inter-regional allocation of resources due to the mobility of factors of production. In reality, the nature and extent of inter-regional mobility of resources is influenced by various market factors (e.g., market rate of return for mobile factors), policy factors (e.g., taxes and expenditures of the regional and federal governments) and non-market, non-policy factors (e.g., moving costs for labour mobility). In order to focus on the most important and relevant of these factors, a modelling of inter-regional allocation of resources is essential.

Based on the familiar static, neoclassical-general equilibrium theory of inter-regional allocation of labour resources with local public goods, Narayana [1992a] has modelled the inter-regional allocation of labour resource under costly migration in a two-region federal and mixed economy.

The basic model and its analysis are briefly summarised below.

The basic model: Consider a federation with a fixed number of two autarkic regions, *i* and *j*. Each region comprises a total population (or, labour force) of L_i and L_j respectively. The total population in the federation, $L=(L_i+L_j)$ is fixed. Each labourer possesses a given unit of labour which is perfectly mobile with him/her.

On the production side, each region is assumed to produce a homogeneous output, Y^*, under conditions of neoclassical technology with labour and land (Z) as inputs. Land is assumed to be fixed in supply and immobile between regions. The size of land resources is assumed to be different between regions. Thus, $Y_i^*=F(L_i, Z_i)=f_i(L_i)$, and $Y_j^*=F(L_j, Z_j)=f_j(L_j)$, where F is the production function. In particular, F is assumed to be linearly homogeneous and subject to diminishing returns. Secondly, factor markets are assumed to be competitive in each region. Let output prices be fixed and set to unity. Then, given regional wage rates $\{w_i, w_j\}$, regional outputs $\{Y_i^*, Y_j^*\}$ are assumed to be determined under profit maximising conditions by the choice of $\{L_i, L_j\}$ in each region. Thus, labourers are paid wages according to their marginal product in region i (*j*), $[df_i/dL_i\ (df_j/dL_j)]=[f_i'(f_j')]$ and the residual output is defined by: $(f_i-L_if_i')=R_i$, and called total resource rent generated in region *i*. In the same way, the resource rent in region *j* is defined by: $(f_j-L_jf_j')=R_j$. Thirdly, land and other natural resources (e.g., oil and natural gas) are assumed to be owned by the federal government and hence resource rents are collected by the federal government. Assuming that resource rents are redistributed on equal per capita basis all over the federation, per labourer share in resource rent in the federation equals to $R/L=r$, where $R=R_i+R_j$.

Further, each region is assumed to have a regional government whose function is to provide pure public goods (G_i) benefiting only its residents. Let the cost of local public goods supply be uniformly shared in the form of residence-based taxes in each region. Then, the per capita private consumption, say in region *i*, is: $x_i=[(Y_i/L_i)-(T_i/L_i)]$, where $Y_i=(L_if_i'+rL_i)$ is the total expendable income and T_i is the total regional taxes (or public services) in region *i*.

Assuming that all labourers in the federation are rational, identically treated and have identical preferences, the welfare for a representative labourer may be expressed by the standard quasi-concave utility function: $U[x_i, G_i]$, where x_i and G_i are the same as defined above.[7] In the same way, for a representative labourer in region *j*, the utility function is defined by $U[x_j, G_j]$.

In order to decide the allocation of total expendable output within each region, the regional governments are presumed to behave non-strategically and as utility maximisers of their residents. Since all residents are identical, the allocation of output between private and public uses would be such that utility levels of each resident is maximised. The condition for this optimal allocation can be derived by: Max $U_i = U[x_i, G_i]$ with respect to (G_i) subject to the constraint that x_i is the same as defined above. From the first order condition, one gets the result: $L_i.(U_{gi}/U_{xi}) = 1$, which is the familiar Samuelsonian condition which shows the equality between the sum of marginal rate of substitution and the marginal rate of transformation. Hence, G_i denotes the cost of producing the local public good in region *i*.

The conditions for production, income and consumption and for local government's activities above determine the welfare level for labourers in each region separately. In what follows, the economic conditions which determine inter-regional allocation of labour resources are analysed.

Market equilibrium: In order to determine the inter-regional allocation of labour in the federation, it is assumed that there exists inter-regional migration of labourers under perfect information and this migration aims at equalising utility levels between regions. Further, in reality, mobility is constrained by resource costs. For analytical purposes, migration costs are considered to be constant or variable for every migrant and their implications are separately analysed. In what follows, the case of constant migration cost is elaborated.

Consider that the initial conditions in two regions are such that the migration takes place from region *i* to region *j*. Then, the market equilibrium conditions for a labourer who is indifferent to move from region *i* to *j* are given by:

$$U[x_i**, G_i] \geq U[x_j** - d_{ij}, G_j] \quad (5)$$
$$L_i** + L_j** = L \quad (6)$$

where $x_i** = [f_i' + r - (G_i/L_i**)]$; $x_j** = [f_j' + r - (G_j/L_j**)]$ and d_{ij} is the constant resource costs of migration.[8] These conditions show that the inter-regional allocation of labour is determined by the differentials in per capita consumption of private and public goods less moving cost, where differentials in per capita private consumption are determined by inter-regional variations in marginal product of labour and per capita tax price of regional public goods. Thus, for utility levels in region i to be higher than in region j to the extent of moving cost, the marginal product of labour in region i (j) will have to be higher (lower) than in region j (i) in order to offset the fiscal loss (gain), where fiscal loss (gain) refers to the positive (negative) difference in per capita tax price of local public goods between regions.

Interestingly, in market equilibrium in (5) and (6), three groups of labourers may be identified by their levels of utility. First, non-movers in region i, whose level of utility equal to: $U^{NM} = U[x_i^{**})^*, G_i]$. Second, movers from region i, whose level of utility equal to: $U^M = [U\{x_j^{**})^* - d_{ij}, G_j\}]$. Third, the stayers in region j, whose level of utility equals to: $U^S = U[x_j^{**})^*, G_j]$. Since the level of utility of these groups of labourers is different, there is an inherent inequality of welfare levels in the federation not only between regions but also within a region (e.g., between migrants and stayers in region j) due to moving cost. Thus, market equilibrium under costly migration is essentially characterised by unequal utility levels.

Policy Intervention: Assuming that there exists no institutional arrangement for voluntary redistributive economic policies between regions, the inequity in market equilibrium calls for federal policy intervention in the model's economy. For instance, consider a federal policy of inter-regional fiscal transfers in order to improve the welfare levels in the region that experiences out-migration. Let the federal government tax the total disposable income of labourers in region j at the rate ß in order to subsidise the population in region i. Then, the total tax collections in region j is $S = \beta . x_j$, which are assumed to be distributed on equal per capita basis as subsidies in region i. The implications of this policy intervention on market equilibrium is analysed below.

Market equilibrium under policy intervention: If the initial economic conditions in the two regions with federal inter-regional transfers are such that migration would go from region i to j, then the market equilibrium is given by:

$$U[x_i^*, G_i] \geq U[x_j^* - d_{ij}, G_j] \quad (7)$$

$$L_i^* + L_j^* = L \quad (8)$$

where $x_i^* = [f_i' + r - (G_i L_i^* + (S/L_i^*)]$; $x_j^* = [f_j' + r - (G_j L_j^*) - (S/L_j^*)]$ and other notations are the same as before.

The market equilibrium above implies several alternative resource allocative effects of federal fiscal transfers. For instance, if federal transfers were to offset the entire moving cost between regions, then the market allocation in (7) and (8) would be equitable in terms of equalising per capita welfare levels between regions. Or, if federal transfers were to offset only the per capita fiscal gain or loss, then per capita welfare levels would not be equalised between regions (in terms of wage differentials) to the extent of inter-regional moving cost.

Comparative statics: The impact of changes in federal transfers on market allocation of labour is determined by the technique of comparative statics. In determining the unambiguous sign of the comparative static derivatives, the condition for dynamic stability for the market equilibrium is explicitly used.

First of all, by totally differentiating (7) and (8) with respect to S, we get:

$$L_i{*}'(S) = [(U_{xi*}L_j + U_{xj*}L_i)/g(L_i{*})] < 0, \qquad (9)$$

where

$$g(L_i{*}) = \{\{U_{xi*}x_i{*}'(L_i{*}) + U_{xj*}x_j{*}'(L_j{*})\}.(L_i{*}.L_j{*}) + S.\{U_{xi*}(L_j{*})^2 - U_{xj*}(L_i{*})^2\}/(L_i{*}L_j{*})] < 0,$$

is the condition for dynamic stability of the equilibrium. This result shows that an increase in taxes on labour supply in region *i* is negative, provided that the equilibrium is dynamically stable.

On the other hand, the impact of an increase in subsidies on the labour supply in region 2 is given by

$$L_j{*}'(S) = -[(U_{xi*}L_j + U_{xj*}L_i)/g(L_i{*})] > 0 \qquad (10)$$

which indicates the labour supply is positive to federal subsidies in region *j*.

Next, using the results in (9) or (10) above, the impact of an increase in taxes-subsidies on the utility level of labourers in region *i* (i.e., non-movers) and in region *j* (i.e., stayers in region *j* and movers from region *i*) can be determined. These comparative static results show that as marginal labourers moving from region *i* to region *j* in response to taxes-subsidies, the post-migration welfare levels depend on the per capita total taxes (local plus federal) between regions, provided that the labourers are paid according to their marginal products in each region and resource rents are distributed uniformly all over the federation.

An important implication of the comparative static results above is that a common federal inter-regional transfers policy would lead to varying utility levels among labourers grouped under non-movers, movers and stayers, and hence, the aggregation of labourers between groups is neither possible nor practicable.

The market equilibrium and comparative static analyses under constant moving cost above can be undertaken if the moving cost is a variable, i.e., different labourers have different moving cost. In this case, when migration takes place, labourers with less moving cost move first, and are followed by labourers with high moving cost. Thus, per capita moving cost can be considered to rise with the number of migrants or migration. For instance, if migration takes place from region 1 to region 2, the variable migration cost can be expressed as: $D_{ij}=D(L_i)$, where $D'(L_i)<0$. Accordingly, the market equilibrium, under variable moving cost, may be derived and analysed with the introduction of federal taxes-subsidies by the technique of comparative statics. Such an analysis shows that welfare changes for different group of labourers is not independent of moving cost. Since moving cost is different not only between migrant groups but also within the group, aggregation of labourers at the individual level (as compared to between groups under constant moving cost) is neither possible nor practicable.

Efficient/optimal allocation: Consider the problem of determining a necessary condition for optimum/Pareto efficient allocation of resources. That is, for a given level of optimally chosen local public goods in two regions, there can be no alternative feasible bundle of private goods and no alternative distribution of labourers between regions such that someone is made better-off and no one worse-off. For this purpose, consider the following two standard frameworks for the formulation of efficient allocation problem where inter-regional migration is constrained by constant moving cost.

First, the Rawlsian framework which can be formulated, given the optimising behaviour of local government, is as follows:

$$\max_{\{L_i^*, L_j^*, S\}} U[x_i^*, G_i] \qquad (11)$$

subject to the constraints:

$$U[x_i^*, G_i] = U[x_j^* - d_{ij}, G_z] \quad (12)$$
$$L_i^* + L_j^* = L. \quad (13)$$

These constraints are the same as the market equilibrium conditions in (7) and (8). However, the constraint in (12) equalises only the utility levels between non-movers in and movers from region *i*. That is, the above allocation problem completely ignores the utility levels of labourers who stayed in region *j*.

Second, in the Benthamite framework, the allocative objective is to maximise the sum of utilities of all labourers in the federation. In formal terms, the problem is to:

$$\underset{\{L_i^*, L_z^*, S\}}{Max}\; nm.U[x_i^*, G_i] + m.U[x_j^* - D_{ij}, G_j] + s.U[x_j^*, G_j] \quad (14)$$

subject to the constraint:

$$L_i^* + L_j^* = L \quad (15)$$

where

nm is the total number of non-movers in region *i*;
m is the total number of movers in region *i*; and
s is the total number of stayers in region *j*.

This formulation assumes that the federal government has perfect information to distinguish those different groups of labourers in equilibrium. In the absence of perfect information, however, a federal planner would end up in having broadly two groups of labourers in equilibrium: (i) residents in region *i* who can be considered as non-movers in region *i*, and (ii) residents in region *j* who are a pool of stayers in region *j* and movers from region *i*.

Thus, under costly migration, neither the formulation in (11)-(13) nor in (14) and (15) strictly holds. Nevertheless, assuming that the per capita utility levels of movers in region *i* and stayers in region *j* are the same, the allocation problem in (14)-(15) may hold, and a restrictive condition for efficient allocation can be obtained as given below.

$$[G_i + S]/L_i^* = [G_j - S]/L_j^* \quad (16)$$

which shows that if labourers are paid according to their marginal product in each region, and resource rents are distributed over the entire federation on an equal per caoita basis, then the labourers will allocate themselves optimally only if total (local plus federal) taxes paid per labourer are identical between the two regions. In this situation, the per capita private consumption or utility of labourers will remain unchanged if a labourer is relocated since the marginal product of labour less moving cost in the region of arrival will be the same as the marginal product of labour in the region of departure. Hence, whenever (16) holds, the resulting allocation is Pareto efficient since any reallocation of labourers would not alter the utility levels.

Extensions/modifications: The theoretical model of inter-regional allocation of labour resource has been theoretically extended/modified in several directions. These extensions/modifications are summarised below.

The problem of aggregation: M.R.Narayana (1993a) demonstrates that the problem of aggregation in not concomitant with moving cost as shown in Narayana (1992a). Rather, it depends on specifying the utility function with moving cost. For the demonstration of this point, he considers a specification where the determinants of utility levels are additively separable between moving costs and other factors. It is shown that the additively separable specification of moving cost solves the aggregation problem and makes the Benthamite social welfare maximisation compatible with moving costs assumptions. Secondly, the Benthamite posture of treating each individual as an equal results in each individual attaining the same utility level at the welfare optimum as in Narayana (1992a), provided the welfare maximisation is constrained by the market equilibrium conditions. These results generalise the conditions for social optimum under costly migration and underline the need for different theoretical restrictions while designing an inter-regional transfer policy on efficiency grounds.

Welfare effects: Using the basic model and market equilibrium conditions as in Narayana (1992a), the paper by the same author (1996a) derives an estimable equation for welfare effects of federal fiscal transfers by assuming a linear specification of the utility levels of different groups of labourers in region *i* and *j* as follows:

$$U^{NM} = U[x_i^*), G_i] = [G_i + \alpha_i x_i^*] \qquad (17)$$

$$U^M = [U\{x_j^*), G_j\}] + d_{ij} = [(G_j + d_{ij}) + \alpha_j.x_i^*] \quad (18)$$
$$U^S = U[x_j^*), G_j] = [G_j + \alpha_j x_i^*] \quad (19)$$

where $\{G_i, G_j\}$ are services from an arbitrary and fixed number of pure local public goods in region i and j. The formulation above is different from Narayana (1992a) in two respects. First, $\{G_i, G_j\}$ are not determined by Samuelsonian conditions. Second, moving cost is addictively separated from the utility function.

For the purpose of actual estimations using grouped data, utility functions of non-movers, movers and stayers are assumed to be parallel, i.e., the slope of the utility function of all the three group of labourers is the same and set to unity. Next, aggregating the utility level of non-movers, movers and stayers in the federation according to the Benthamite social welfare function, and the total welfare levels in the federation (W) may be expressed as:

$$W = L_i^*.[G_i + x_i^*] + M_{ij}.[(G_j + d_{ij}) + x_j^*] + L_j.[G_j + x_j^*], \quad (20)$$
$$= L_i^*.[G_i + x_i^*] + L_j^*.[G_j + x_j^*] + M_{ij}.d_{ij},$$

where $M_{ij} = (L_j^* - L_j)$ is the number of migrants from region i to j with L_j as the number of stayers (or, initial population) in j.

Totally differentiating (20), and remembering that $dL_i^* = -dL_j^*$, and treating the aggregate resource rents as endogenous, the following equation is obtained:

$$dW/dS = [(f_i' + G_i) - (f_j' + G_j) - d_{ij}].(dL_i^*/dS) \quad (21)$$

Equation (21) is an expression of marginal social welfare gain/loss from the resource allocative effects of federal transfers. Since resource rents are nationally distributed on equal per capita basis, the inter-regional difference is the sum of equilibrium wage rates and per capita services of local public goods less moving cost represents the differences in resource available for per capita private consumption out of wage income between regions. Thus, the marginal social welfare change in (21) is the product of changes in private consumption out of wage income and resource allocative effects of federal transfers.

Note that in (21), $dL_i^* = dM_{ij}$, the model allows for changes in regional population only due to inter-regional migration. Thus, $(dL_i^*/dS) = (dM_{ij}/dS)$, where M_{ij} is influenced by the economic factors in (7) and (8). This general migration function can be expressed as follows.

$$M_{ij} = f[w_i^*, w_j^*, t_i^*, t_j^*, s_i^*, s_j^*, L_i^*, L_j^*, d_{ij}] \qquad (22)$$

or,

$$M_{ij} = f[w_i^*, w_j^*, G_i, G_j, s_i^*, s_j^*, L_i^*, L_j^*, d_{ij}] \qquad (22)$$

where $w_i^* \equiv f_i'(L_i^*)$; $w_j^* f_j'(L_j^*)$; $s_i^* \equiv (S_i/L_i^*)$; $s_j^* \equiv (S_j/L_i^*)$; $t_i^* \equiv (T_i/L_i^*)$; $t_j^* \equiv (T_j/L_i^*)$ and the other notations are the same as defined earlier. These functions serve as alternative general empirical bases for estimation of federal transfers and other determinants of inter-regional mobility of labourers/workers in a federal economy.

In order to extend the welfare analysis in (21) for a multi-regional economy, let us consider that there exists a set of N number of origin regions and M $(=N-1)$ destination regions. Then, the marginal social welfare change for the nation (ΔW), arising from the resource allocative effects of federal transfers between region i and the rest of regions in the federation, is given by:

$$\Delta W = \sum_{i=1}^{N} [\sum_{j=1}^{N} \{(f_i' + G_i) - (f_j' + G_j) - d_{ij}\}.(dM_{ij}^*/dS)] \qquad (23)$$

where all migration flows are presumed to be bi-directional.

The expression above is a plausible analytical basis for the estimation of welfare consequences of resource allocative effects of federal fiscal transfers in the Indian federation.

Empirical Applications and Policy Implications

Based on the theoretical modelling of inter-regional allocation of labour resources above, empirical modelling of economic migration (i.e., inter-regional or inter-State migration) in India has been attempted. These models include pure simulation modelling [Narayana, 1992b], and empirical modelling with econometric estimations and/or simulation analysis [Narayana (1991), Narayana (1993b), Narayana (1993c), and Narayana (1994)]. In these papers, the basic macro migration function is of the form in equation (22) with varying empirical specification of variables, data bases and hypotheses. In general, in these studies the estimated coefficients have predicted signs and are statistically significant at conventional levels of significance. And, other things being equal:

(i) workers move from regions of low wage income to regions of high wage income. Hence, accentuation of inter-regional wage differentials, encourages migration;

(ii) worker migrants in India move from regions of low per capita transfers to regions of high per capita transfers. This finding underlines that federal fiscal transfers in India have resource allocation effects rather than pure income redistribution effects;

(iii) worker migrants move from high tax regions to low tax regions. This offers indirect evidence for the familiar "Tiebout hypothesis" (i.e., "consumer-voter moves to that community whose local government best satisfies his preference patterns for public goods" [Tiebout 1956: 418)], perhaps for the first time in the case of a developing country;

(iv) distance elasticity is largest but gradually declining (or labour is becoming more mobile) which may be a recognition for the improvements in transportation and communication in the country; and

(v) the greater the population of region *i*, the greater the number of persons who are likely to migrate from *i*, or the greater the population of region *j*, the greater the number of persons who are likely to migrate to *j*.

The empirical results above offer new evidence in regard to the resource (labour) allocative effects of fiscal variables. Accordingly, the results provide with empirical bases for factors to be incorporated in an inter-regional migration policy, which is yet to be formulated in India.

Further, the empirical application of equation (23) for India by Narayana (1996a) shows that the resource allocative effects of federal transfers are welfare-improving in terms of its positive contribution to changes in total private consumption for all regions in the federation. These welfare estimates provide unambiguous welfare basis for the extent and the direction in which the federal transfer can be used as one of the instruments of spatial allocation of labour resources for national welfare.

Modelling India's Foreign Trade

Economic modelling of India's foreign trade is focused on the impact of export subsidies and export competitiveness.

Modelling India's export subsidies: The case for direct and indirect export subsidies for promotion of exports needs no emphasis in India.

These subsidies include Duty Drawback Scheme; Cash Compensatory Support; Replishment Licences for imported Inputs; Import-Export Pass Book Scheme; and Duty Free Imports against REP Licences.

Following Brander and Spencer (1985), the impact of export subsidies on export performance and domestic welfare in the framework of Cournot Duopoly is modelled for India by Narayana (1992c). The basic model and analytical results may be summarised as follows: first, let X and Y denote respectively the domestic and foreign firms sales to the home market; X^* and Y^* denote respectively the domestic and foreign firms sales to the foreign market; $p(X+Y)$ be the inverse demand function in the home market; $p^*(X^* + Y^*)$ be the inverse demand function in the foreign market; C (C^*) be the home (foreign) firm's constant marginal cost; F (F^*) be the home (foreign) firm's fixed cost of production; t is the tariff per unit imposed on imports (Y) into the domestic market; and s is the export subsidy per unit of home country exports to the foreign market (X^*).

It is straightforward to formulate the profit function of the domestic and foreign firms as follows.

$$\pi = X.P(X+Y) + X^*.P^*(X^*+Y^*) - [CX+CX^*] + sX^* - F, \quad (24)$$
$$\pi^* = Y.P(X+Y) + Y^*.P^*(X^*+Y^*) - [CY+CY^*] - tY - F^* \quad (25)$$

Assuming Cournot-Nash behaviour and with constant marginal costs, it is possible to solve the profit maximising problem for each market in isolation. Hence, the domestic firm chooses X and X^* to maximise π, and the foreign firm chooses Y and Y^* to maximise π^*. And, for the home firm in the home market, or foreign firm in the foreign market, the equilibrium condition shows the equality between the firm's price and marginal cost. For later purposes, let:

$$\delta\pi/\delta X \equiv N(X,Y);\ \delta\pi/\delta Y \equiv M(X,Y);\ \delta\pi^*/\delta X^* \equiv N(X^*,Y^*);\ \text{and}$$
$$\delta\pi^*/\delta Y^* \equiv M(X^*,Y^*);$$

Next, in order to evaluate the impact of export subsidies on increasing the market share of subsidised export firm in foreign market, the following comparative static analysis is undertaken

Totally differentiating the first order conditions with respect to s, we get:

$$N'(X^*).X^{*\prime}(s).ds + N'(Y^*).Y^{*\prime}(s).ds - ds = 0 \quad (26)$$
$$N^{*\prime}(X^*).X^{*\prime}(s).ds + N^{*\prime}(Y^*).Y^{*\prime}(s).ds = 0 \quad (27)$$

where $N'(X^*)]$ represents the partial derivative of N(X*,Y*) with respect to X^*, $X^{*\prime}(s)$ represents the derivative of X^* with respect to s and so on.

For deriving unambiguous signs for the comparative static derivatives, we obtain the following three results. First, from the assumption that an increase in one firm's sales to a particular market reduces both profits and the marginal revenue of its rival in the market, we have: $M'(Y) < 0$; $N'(Y^*) < 0$; $M^*(X^*) < 0$; and $N^{*\prime}(X^*) < 0$. Second, from the second order conditions for the maximum profits in home and foreign markets, we have: $M'(X) < 0$; $N'(X^*) < 0$; $M^*(Y^*) < 0$; and $N^{*\prime}(Y^*) < 0$. Third, a sufficient condition for the stability of the Cournot-Nash equilibrium in the foreign market is: $[N'(X^*).N^{*\prime}(Y^*) - N^{*\prime}(X^*).\ N'(Y^*)] \equiv Z > 0$. Using these results, the unambiguous signs for the comparative static derivatives of $X^{*\prime}(s)$ and $Y^{*\prime}(s)$ are as follows.

$$X^{*\prime}(s) = -\ [\{N^{*\prime}(Y^*)\}/[Z] > 0 \tag{28}$$
$$Y^{*\prime}(s) = [\{N^{*\prime}(X^*)\}/[Z] < 0 \tag{29}$$

These results imply that export subsidy will have positive (negative) impact on home exports (foreign imports). In other words, export subsidy is justifiable as a means of increasing the market share, or profits, of the home firm [since, using envelope theorem, $\pi'(s)=\{\pi'(Y^*).Y^{*\prime}(s)\}>0$, and $\pi^{*\prime}(s)=\{\pi^{*\prime}\ (X^*).\ X^{*\prime}(s)\}<0$].

The above analytical results have several important implications. For instance, if policy makers are committed to giving subsidies to domestic exporting firms, then the policy is justifiable on economic grounds if the underlying market structure can be described by the strategic behaviour of its production agents. In this way, the governmental subsidisation policy may have a strategic implications. Second, this sort of subsidisation may be one possible way of integrating strategic market behaviour with non-strategic policy intervention such that the very policy is strategic.

Modelling India's export competitiveness: M.R. Narayana (1993d) has developed a static model which captures the general equilibrium impact of competitive export trade on domestic welfare through optimal allocation of resources. The model considers a world with a fixed number of independent nations (sellers) where nation i denotes the home country and j denotes the rest of the world. The total population (or, labour force) in i is L_i and in j is L_j. The total population in the world is $L= (L_i+L_j)$ and is fixed. Each labourer possesses a given unit of labour which is immobile between nations.

The domestic economy is assumed to produce a homogeneous output, Y, under conditions of neoclassical technology with labour and fixed land/natural resource (Z) as domestic inputs and with fixed amount of non-competitive imports from the rest of the world as non-domestic input. That is, $Y_i=F(L_i,Z_i, M_i)$, where F is the well-behaved production function. Second, the domestic factor market is assumed competitive. Let output price be fixed and set to unity. Then, given domestic wage rate $\{w_i\}$, the national output $\{Y_i\}$ is assumed to be determined under profit maximising conditions by the choice of $\{L_i\}$. Thus, labourers are paid wages according to their marginal product, $[dF_i/dL_i]=[F_i']$, and the residual output is defined by: $(F_i\ L_iF_i')=R_i$. Third, assuming public ownership of land/natural resource, resource rents are captured by the national government. The residual output is assumed to be used, in part, to financing imports and the balance is equally shared by every labourer within the nation as per capita resource rent which equals to: $r_i=[(R_i-M_i)/L_i]$.

Further, the domestic economy is assumed to have a government whose functions are twofold. First, redistribution of resource rents on equal per capita basis within the nation as described above. Second, determination of the allocation of total output between uses such that the welfare of its population is maximised. This assumes that all labourers in the nation are rational, identically treated, and have identical preferences as given by the standard quasi-concave utility function of a representative labourer, $U[.,.]$. Throughout, the utility function is being treated as a proxy for the welfare function of a representative labourer.

Domestic resource allocation effects: The resource allocation problem is modelled in two stages. In the first stage, the government determines the allocation of total output between domestic use and exports. That is,

$$\underset{\{X_i,E_i\}}{Max}\ W = U[X_i, E_i]; \tag{30}$$

subject to the constraint:

$$Y_i=X_i+X_i^* = P_i.X_i+ P_i^*.E_i \tag{31}$$

where X_i is the domestic use of Y_i; E_i is the export use of Y_i; P_i is the domestic price of X_i; and $P_i^* = \{P_i^{**}-(P_i+K_i)\}$ is the export price for i in the world market where K_i is the cost of transportation and other expenses to be incurred in shipping the goods to the world market, and P_i^{**} is the world market price which does not equal to P_i^*. The national economy is assumed to be a small economy, i.e., it takes P_i^{**} as given. It is to be noted that if P_i^* is constrained to be non-negative, it will also ensure that exports are competitive or profitable.

In stage two, the government determines the allocation of optimal total domestic resources (X_i) between private consumption (C_i) and public use (G_i). Implicitly, G_i is considered to be a pure public good whose benefits are restricted to residents within the nation. Let the cost of public goods supply (G_i) be financed by domestic as well as by export taxes. The domestic taxes are considered to be uniformly shared in the form of residence-based taxes. Let the domestic tax rate be t. Then, the total domestic tax collection is: $T=(t.X_i)$. In the same way, let the tax rate on profitable export earnings be: t^*. Then, the total export tax collection equals to: $T^*=(t^*.X_i^*)$. Hence, $G_i=(T_i+T_i^*)$ and per capita private consumption is: $c_i= [(X_i/L_i)-(T_i/L_i)]$. In this post-export stage, the government's allocation problem can be formulated as follows.

$$\underset{(c_i, G_i)}{Max}\ W^* = U[c_i, G_i]; \tag{32}$$

subject to the constraints:

$$c_i= [(X_i/L_i)-(T_i/L_i)] \tag{33}$$
$$G_i=(T_i+T_i^*) \tag{34}$$

The formulation in (34) is intended to capture the benefits of export tax revenue for the economy as a whole and to link the export sector with the domestic economy. In this formulation, profitable exports may improve (or worsen) domestic welfare through reduction in domestic tax burden (or private consumption). Alternatively, export taxes may be interpreted as a way of partly financing the public sector investments which are conducive to exporting industries.

From the necessary conditions for the maximisation in (32)–(34), the following result is obtained:

$$[L_i.(U_{Gi})/(U_{ci})]=1 \tag{35}$$

where the marginal utilities of c_i and G_i, {U_{ci} and U_{Gi} respectively) are assumed to be positive. This is the familiar Samuelsonian condition in the welfare-economic theory of public goods. This condition tells that, for the supply of pure public goods to be Pareto-optimal, the sum of marginal rate of substitutions must equal to the marginal rate of transformation.

Domestic welfare effects: Consider a situation where the government may want to increase the tax revenue from the export earnings. For this purpose, it will have to change the tax rate on profitable exports earnings. The consequence of this change in export tax rate (t^*) on domestic welfare can be determined as follows:

Assume that the government has a Benthamite social welfare function (W^{**}) which represents the aggregate domestic welfare as a function of total domestic private consumption, public consumption, and tax revenue from exports as defined below:

$$W^{**} = L_i.U[c_i, G_i, T_i^*/L_i] \tag{36}$$

Totally differentiating (36) with respect to t^*,

$$dW^{**}/dt^* = L_i.U_{ci}.(\delta c_i/\delta G_i).(\delta G_i/\delta t^*) + L_i.U_{Gi}.(\delta G_i/\delta t^*) + U_{Ti^*}(\delta T_i^*/\delta t^*), \tag{37}$$

where U_{Ti^*} (i.e., marginal utility of T_i^*) is assumed positive. In fact, equation (37) is an expression for a marginal social welfare change in the economy due to changes in t^*. The first term on the right hand side (R.H.S.) of (37) is the private consumption effect and the second term is public consumption effect of changes in t^*. These two consumption effects may account for the resource allocative effects. The last term on the R.H.S. of (37) is the effect of changes in export taxes on export tax revenue of the government. This effect may be called revenue effect. Thus, when the export sector is integrated with the domestic sector, changes in export tax will affect domestic welfare through resource allocative effects and revenue effect.

Since $[\delta c_i/\delta G_i] = -(1/L_i)$, and $[\delta G_i/\delta t^*]=[\delta T_i^*/\delta t^*]=(X_i^*)$, equation (37) can be rewritten as follows:

$$dW^{**}/dt^* = [L_i.\{U_{Gi} - U_{ci}/L_i\} + U_{Ti^*}].(X_i^*), \tag{38}$$

Substituting (35) into (38),

$$dW^{**}/dt^* = U_{Ti^*}(X_i^*) \tag{39}$$

That is, if the domestic resources are optimally allocated between private and public consumption uses as given by the Samuelsonian condition in (35) and if the marginal utility of T_i* is positive, then the changes in national welfare due to changes in export taxes depend only on the nature of profitable earnings or export competitiveness.

Empirical applications: Equation (39) is used as the basis for empirical estimation of welfare consequences of changes in export taxes in India. The empirical estimates show the positive welfare impact of net export tax revenues in India for most of the years during 1970-90, and especially increasing for all the years during 1970-77 and 1986-90. These results offer both analytical and empirical justifications for export taxes as a policy instrument for national welfare in India. Accordingly, the results reject the general belief that export taxes as such may have deterrent effect on export performance and, ultimately, on domestic welfare.

Modelling India's Economic Fertility

In a developing country like India, the presence of unequal (or skewed) and non-optimal income distribution calls for policy intervention in terms of redistributive income policies (RIP). And, the determination of income effects of RIPs on family size through changes in fertility (assuming mortality is constant) is a policy imperative from the viewpoint of fertility regulation.

M.R. Narayana (1992d) has developed a simple economic model of fertility with nonlinear budget constraints to incorporate the role of redistributive income, and its nature of financing, for the purpose of explaining and predicting the nature of economic relationships between redistributive income and fertility.

The basic model considers a representative family comprising a pair of rational parents, and N number of children. All children are assumed identical in the sense that they are symmetrically treated by their parents. Hence, the expenditure incurred on each child's quality (e.g., expenditure on health/education) is the same and will be denoted by Q. Thus, the total child services, $S = NQ$.

Parents have mainly two sources of income. (1) Income from labour resources (Y); and (2) income from non-labour resources (X). The non-labour income comprises two sources. First, non-distributive, non-labour income (V). Second, redistributive, non-labour income (T), e.g., governmental subsidies, transfer payments etc. In particular, T is treated to be a control (or policy) variable in the hands of the government through costless redistributive income policies. One possible way of specifying variable T is to define it as a function of N, i.e., $T = T(N)$, where $T_N = (dT/dN)$, may be positive or negative. Assuming that Y as constant, the aggregate income changes only due to changes in T through N.

Parents are assumed to derive utility from their child services and from their own standard of living. Let the parental standard of living be represented by the Hicksian composite good, Z. Then, the parental welfare can be expressed in the form of $U = U[N, Q, Z]$, following standard utility function.

Next, let P_S represents the market, or observed price for child services, and P_Z represents the observed price of parental standard of living. Thus, the parental budget constraint, under the usual assumption of local nonsatiation, can be written as: $I = P_S S + P_Z Z$. If redistributive income for families are financed by non-inflationary ways, then $dP_S/dT = dP_Z/dT = 0$.

Maximisation of parental utility with respect to N, Q, and Z, and subject to the budget constraint, yields the following Marshallian demand functions:

$$N = N[P_S, P_Z, I^*]; \; Q = Q[P_S, P_Z, I^*]; \; Z = Z[P_S, P_Z, I^*].$$

In order to derive the impact of T on N, Q and Z, the following comparative static derivatives are obtained:

$$dN/dT = [(1/|\Delta|).\{(\Delta_{ii} \cdot \mu \cdot dPn^*/dT) + (\Delta_{zi})dPq^*/dT\}], \quad (40)$$
$$dQ/dT = [(1/|\Delta|).\{(\Delta_{iz} \cdot \mu \cdot dPn^*/dT) + (\Delta_{zz})dPq^*/dT\}] \quad (41)$$

where $|\Delta|$ is the determinant of the bordered Hessian matrix, Δ_{ij} and so on are the co-factors of elements on the principal diagonal; μ is the marginal utility of money which is assumed to be positive; and $\{Pn^*, Pq^*\}$ are the shadow prices or marginal costs of N and Q. Thus, from the second order conditions defined above, the sign of these comparative static derivatives cannot be determined unambiguously. Hence, several alternative cases are considered. For instance, consider the following simple case.

Given that T is financed by noninflationary measures, let us further consider a situation where $Pn^*=Pn^{**}$ and $Pq^*=Pq^{**}$, and Pn^{**} and Pq^{**} can be varied independently or changes in Pn^{**} (e.g., price of contraceptives which affect child quantity) does not affect Pq^{**} (e.g., expenditure on education of children). In this case, the implied budget constraint is convex or a linear function of prices and the following results are obtained as a form of compensated own-substitution effect of price changes.

$$dN/dPn^{**} = [(1/|\Delta|).\{\Delta_{ii} \bullet \mu\}] < 0; \quad (42)$$
$$dQ/dPq^{**} = [(1/|\Delta|).\{\Delta_{zz} \bullet \mu\}] < 0, \quad (43)$$

where the signs are clearly determined by the second order conditions and by the assumed positive μ. Thus, the redistributive income will have only pure income effect on child quantity due to its incentive for expansion of family size in terms of reduced marginal cost of child quantity, provided that the redistributive transfers are financed by noninflationary measures and the budget constraint is linear in prices.

The above analyses of pure income effects of redistributive transfers on fertility provide with an understanding of the nature of empirical restrictions on the nature and financing of redistributive transfers, underlying budget constraints, assumed direction of influence between redistributive income and marginal costs of child quantity, nature of child quality etc. These restrictions also offer analytical support for those empirical findings that are consistent with the qualified theoretical predictions and underline the limitations in drawing policy implications from a restricted empirical study.

Modelling India's Economic Reforms

India has initiated a set of economic reforms since July 1991. These reforms include two parts. First, the stabilisation part which aims at reducing the level of aggregate demand. Second, the structural adjustment part which aims at increasing the level of supply/rate of growth of output. These reforms are undertaken in different sectors of the economy.

Coffee is one of the sectors in which structural adjustment programme is introduced under economic liberalisation and globalisation measures. These measures include the recent introduction of Free Sale Quota (FSQ), under which the large (or small) coffee growers in India are entitled to sell 70 per cent (100 per cent) of their production within the country and/or anywhere in the world.

M.R. Narayana (1996b) develops an economic model with domestic marketing, production, consumption of coffee in India. The model explains the observed market structure of coffee before 1993 and the changing market structure since 1993 as a consequence of economic liberalisation measures. Further, the welfare implications of recent liberalisation measures are derived and an empirical framework for implementing a welfare economic policy, as they are related to coffee sector in India, is suggested for the consideration of applied economists and policy makers. The model is briefly discussed below:

Pre-liberalisation Scenario

Domestic production: The total production of coffee by the i-th grower is denoted by x_i. The production function is neo-classical with land (N), labour (L) and capital (K) as inputs: $F[N_i, L_i, K_i]$. Land is assumed to be owned and capital is invested by producers/growers of coffee, and labour is hired from the local labour market. Assuming competitive factor markets and profit maximising behaviour of coffee growers, the rewards for different factors of production are expressible in terms of the value of its marginal product, where w = wages for labour; k = interest on capital; r = residual payment as rent for the fixed land input; and p^P is the uniform output price of x_i.

Domestic marketing: Before 1993, the domestic coffee marketing in India was characterised by a single buyer, viz., the Coffee Board. Thus, the theory of monopsony in the product market is employed for characterising the observed market structure of coffee before 1993. On the other hand, since the entire coffee is pooled only by the Board, it is obviously vested with monopoly powers in selling the coffee to domestic consumption. Accordingly, profit maximisation for the Board requires that pooling from individual growers is to be done up to the point at which the marginal revenue from selling equals to the marginal cost of pooling of coffee for the Board.

Domestic consumption: For a representative consumer in the economy, the strictly quasi-concave utility function is defined by: $U = U[y_i, z_i]$ where y_i is the amount of coffee consumed and z_i is the consumption of all other commodities (or the Hicksian composite good). The linear budget constraint for the consumer is: $I = p_i.y_i + p_Z.z_i$ where I is the total wage and non-wage income; and $\{p_i, p_Z\}$ are the retail prices of coffee and other commodities. Maximisation of utility with respect to y_i and z_i and subject to budget constraint yields the familiar Marshallian demand functions $[y_i^M, z_i^M]$ in terms of all prices and income.

Macroeconomic equilibrium: In the economy described above, the decentralised production and consumption decisions are made for achieving rational allocation of resources by producers and consumers in accordance with the producer and consumer prices set by the Coffee Board. This implies that, for the economy as a whole, a macroeconomic equilibrium is attained such that

$$\sum_{i=1}^{N} (p^C.x_i) = \sum_{i=1}^{N} (y_i^M); \tag{44}$$

$$\sum_{i=1}^{N} (p^E.x_i) = y; \tag{45}$$

$$\sum_{i=1}^{N} (x_i) = \sum_{i=1}^{N} \{F[N_i, L_i, K_i]\}; \tag{46}$$

$$\sum_{i=1}^{N} (p^C + p^E).x_i = \sum_{i=1}^{N} (y_i^M) + y; \tag{47}$$

where y is the exogenously given external demand (or export quota) for coffee at fixed export price, p^E. In essence, the equilibrium shows the equality between the total quantity of coffee supplied by producers and pooled by the Board on the one hand and, on the other hand, between the total quantity of coffee sold by the Board and total quantity demanded by both internal and external consumers.

Post-liberalisation scenario: In essence, the FSQ has introduced a greater competition, or reduced monopsony and monopoly powers of the Coffee Board, in the domestic and export marketing of coffee in India. Consequently, the market demand, supply and price of coffee in India is now guided by the competitive conditions of supply, demand and prices in the world as well as in the domestic markets. Thus, the analytical characterisation of coffee sector under liberalisation measures in India needs an alternative framework than for the pre-liberalisation period.

Production: Since sudden demand changes cannot bring sudden long term changes in supply of a commodity like coffee, in the short run, a given total output has to be divided between domestic sales and exports, depending on market prices. Let current domestic producer price be p^D; current world market price received by the producer be p^W. Thus, the supply $[s(x_i)]$ decision of a producer (in value terms) is formulated in following terms.

$$s(x_i;\, p^E, p^W) = \{p^D + (p^W - p^E)\}.x_i \qquad (48)$$

where p^E is the export price of domestic coffee. For reasons which are exogenous to the analysis, it is assumed that: $p^D \leq p^E \leq p^W$. This contains alternative cases. For instance, consider the following cases. First, $(p^E = p^W)$. Second, $(p^W > p^E)$. It can be clearly shown that, from the viewpoint of producers' income, case 2 is superior to case 1. Hence, the impact of globalisation measures seem to be unambiguously positive for the producers of coffee.

Consumption: As there are exports with total restrictions on imports, and other things being the same, domestic price of coffee is increased as a consequence of the reduction in domestic supply of coffee. And, the Marshallian demand for coffee $[y_i^{M*}]$ and other commodities $[z_i^{M*}]$ can be derived by incorporating changes in consumer income and commodity prices.

Market equilibrium: Under the mechanism of voluntary exchange, the market equilibrium is defined by the equality between the aggregate domestic supply of and demand (domestic and world) for coffee.

$$\sum_{i=1}^{N} (p^D.x_i) = \sum_{i=1}^{N} (y_i^{M*}) \qquad (49)$$

$$\sum_{i=1}^{N} (p^W - p^E).x_i = y^* \qquad (50)$$

$$\sum_{i=1}^{N} (x_i) = \sum_{i=1}^{N} \{F[N_i, L_i, K_i]\} \qquad (51)$$

$$\sum_{i=1}^{N} (p^D + (p^W - p^E).x_i = \sum_{i=1}^{N} (y_i^{M*}) + y^* \qquad (52)$$

where $y^* = y^*(p^E, p^W)$, is the world market demand for domestic coffee. Other notations are the same as defined earlier.

As compared to the equilibrium in (44)-(47), the equilibrium in (49)-(52) is different in regard to the supply of and demand for coffee in the domestic and world markets. These differences are the combined consequences of: (i) the liberalisation and globalisation measures which have been undertaken in the coffee sector in India since 1993; and (ii) changes in the world coffee production and market conditions, especially in the 1990s.

Welfare implications: The welfare change for the consumer between pre-liberalisation period and post-liberalisation period can be determined by the method of compensating variation (CV). For the i-th consumer: $CV_i = I^* - E\{p_i^{**}, p_z, u\}$

where E is the familiar expenditure function, p_i^{**} is the equilibrium price of coffee in the post-liberalisation period; p_z is the price of composite good which is presumed to be invariant between pre-liberalisation and post-liberalisation periods; u is the given level of utility; and I^* is the income of the consumer in the post-liberalisation period. If $CV_i > 0$ (or, $CV_i < 0$), the consumer experiences welfare improving (or worsening) situation due to the change. Or, if $CV_i = 0$, the consumer faces a welfare neutral situation due to the change.

In case the compensating variation is negative, an equivalent amount of consumption subsidy is required to make the consumer to be welfare-neutral between periods. The subsidy is totally self-financing, and the net impact of liberalisation is unambiguously positive, if the amount of total tax collectable is greater than the total amount of subsidy in the coffee sector.

An empirical implementation of the analytical framework above will: (i) resolve several current policy debates, such as, the continuation of economic liberalisation in coffee sector and the existence of a Coffee Board in future in India; and (ii) test whether or not the consensus in favour of new orthodoxy of economic liberalisation, as it is related to coffee sector, is sound on both theoretical and empirical grounds. Thus, the analytical framework is useful to the policy analysis.

Conclusion

This review has provided with an overview of economic modelling for policy decisions in the ISEC studies. The areas covered for modelling are wide and diversified, such as, macroeconomic growth, inter-regional allocation of resources, foreign trade, economic fertility and economic reforms. This diversity implies the vast scope of the models for different

empirical applications and policy uses. In fact, there exists a vast potential for empirical and policy studies in future based on economic modelling for policy decisions in the ISEC.

It should be emphasised that, above all, ISEC is an applied social science research institution. Thus, a judicious combination of theory and application is essential for all systematic research.

NOTES

1. Two points deserve mention here. First, in this paper, the term model and theory are used interchangeably. However, for a purist, a model/theory distinction may be essential. For a detailed discussion on this distinction, see Walsh (1987). Second, it is important to note the relationship between economic theory and methodology. Following Mark Blaug [as quoted in Hoover (1995: 716)], "methodology is that branch of economics where we examine the ways in which economists justify their theories and the reasons they offer for preferring one theory over another". For a recent discussion on methodological issues in economics, see Hoover (1995).
2. For a discussion on the role of assumptions in economic theory, see the classic paper by Nagel (1963).
3. For a simple exposition of model building and types of models in economics, see Chapter 2, in Intriligator (1978).
4. The relationship between economists and data is well articulated recently by Brian (1992).
5. For the latest discussion on the role of econometrics in economic theory, see Eichenbaum (1995). And, for an excellent introduction to basic econometrics, see Gujarathi (1995).
6. An important theoretical contribution from the viewpoint of non-modelling is by Thimmaiah (1982). This paper provides a discussion on the meaning of macroeconomics, and highlights the inadequacy of the textbook approach to macroeconomics for explaining and predicting economic phenomenon. In addition, a useful discussion between microeconomics and macroeconomics is made in terms of core determinants and analytical frameworks. For instance, in microeconomics (or macroeconomics), the core-determinant is price (or income of producers, consumers and factors of production). In terms of analytical framework, microeconomics deals with equilibrium (in particular, neo-classical) economics and macroeconomics deals with disequilibrium (in particular, Keynesian) economics. The major conclusions of the paper are as follows: "Any attempt to provide microeconomic foundations for macroeconomic analysis is only an attempt to convert the macroeconomic analysis into neoclassical microeconomics. Such an attempt, to say the least, is probably the result of the failure to appreciate (let alone accept) the distinct paradigms and core determinants of micro- and macroeconomic analysis." Indeed, "the search for microeconomic foundations for macroeconomic analysis is futile because both of them have independent determinants and analytical frameworks"

(1982: 105).

7. For a recent critique on the models of representative individuals, see Kirman (1992).

8. For a good exposition to the techniques of equilibrium analysis, optimisation and other mathematical methods used in this paper, see Silberberg (1978).

REFERENCES

Brander, J.A. and B.J. Spencer (1985) Export Subsidies and International Market Share Rivalry. *Journal of International Economics*, 18: 83-100.

Brian, D.P. (1992) Economists and Data. *British Journal of Industrial Relations*, 30: 253-85.

Eichenbaum, Martin (1995) Some Comments on the Role of Econometrics in Economic Theory. *The Economic Journal*, 105: 1609-21.

Gujarathi, Damodar N. (1995) *Basic Econometrics*. New York: McGraw Hill International.

Hoover, Kevein D. (1995) Why does Methodology Matter for Economics. *The Economic Journal*, 105: 715-34.

Intriligator, Michael D. (1978) *Econometric Models, Techniques and Applications*. New Jersey: Prentice-Hall Inc.

Kirman, Alan P. (1992) Whom and What does the Representative Individual Represent. *Journal of Economic Perspectives*, 6: 117-36.

Mills, Cadman Atta and Raj Nallari (1992) *Analytical Approaches to Stabilisation and Adjustment Programs*, EDI Seminar Paper No. 44, Economic Development Institute. Washington: The World Bank.

Nagel, Ernest (1963) Assumptions in Economic Theory. *American Economic Review*, 53: 211-19.

Narayana, M.R. (1991) Federal Inter-regional Fiscal Transfers Policies and Population Redistribution in Space: An Econometric Policy Simulation Analysis for India. *Manpower Journal*, XXVII: 1-24.

Narayana, M.R. (1992a) Market Equilibrium and Social Optimum in a Multi-regional Economy: The Role of Moving Cost. *The Indian Economic Review*, XXVII: 73-89.

Narayana, M.R. (1992b) Criteria for Federal Inter-regional Fiscal Transfers in India: A New Base for Population Factor in the 10th Finance Commission. *Margin*, 25: 104-15.

Narayana M.R. (1992c) Export Subsidies in India: Need for a Strategic Approach. *Foreign Trade Review*, XXVII: 35-50.

Narayana, M.R. (1992d) Income Distribution and Endogenous Fertility: An Economic-Theoretic Approach. *Asian Economic Review*, XXIV: 131-48.

Narayana, M.R. (1993a) Social Optimum under Moving Cost: Some Further Results. *The Indian Economics Review*, XXVIII: 229-34.

Narayana, M.R. (1993b) *Determinants of Inter-temporal Distribution of Migrants: An Inter-regional Study for India*. Bangalore: ISEC. Mimeo.

Narayana, M.R. (1993c) Fiscally-induced Inter-regional Migration in India: Some New Empirical Evidence. *Indian Journal of Regional Science*, 25: 1-11.

Narayana, M.R. (1993d). Export Competitiveness, Taxes, and Domestic Welfare in India: Some Empirical Evidence. *Productivity*, 34: 390-98.

Narayana, M.R. (1994) Continuity of Inter-regional Migration of Workers in India: A Spatio-temporal Analysis. *Demography India*, 23: 183-202.

Narayana, M.R. (1995) Strategy for Deficit-reduction in the Union Budget of India: Recent Trends and Implications. *Finance India*, IX: 909-32.

Narayana, M.R. (1996a) Welfare Effects of Inter-regional Allocation of Resources: A New Evidence for Labour Resource in India. *The 32nd Annual Conference of the Indian Econometric Society*, March 21-23. Bangalore: Indian Social Institute.

Narayana, M.R. (1996b) Economic Liberalisation of Coffee Sector in India: Analytical Characterisation and Welfare Implications. Unpublished.

Silberberg, Eugene (1978) *The Structure of Economics: A Mathematical Analysis*. New York: McGraw Hill.

Thimmaiah, G. (1982) What is Macroeconomics? A Critique of Textbook Version. *The Indian Economic Journal*, 30: 87-107.

Tiebout, Charles M. (1956) A Pure Theory of Local Expenditure. *Journal of Political Economy*, 64: 416-24.

Walsh, Vivian (1987) Models and Theory. In John Eatwell, Murry Milgall and Peter Newman (eds.), *The New Palgrave: A Dictionary of Economics*, London: The McMillan Press.

14

VOLUNTARY ORGANISATIONS AND SOCIAL SCIENCE RESEARCH

G.S. AURORA and T.V. SEKHER

I

This Chapter highlights the processes whereby applied social science research attempts to, assess the role and potential of the voluntary organisations in socio-economic development. By and large, the studies conducted by the members of the faculty in ISEC, have been used to illustrate this process. But, before we delve into the core theme, some brief recounting of the dominant patterns of organisation and articulation of concerns of the voluntary sector institutions must be mentioned so that the context of the emerging discourse between research and grass-roots action is clearly presented.

While there are thousands of voluntary organisations (henceforth VOs) registered with various State governments in India, we are mainly concerned with only those voluntary organisations which engage in 'developmental' work. In the context of our particular concern with the role of the voluntary sector in development, we need to clearly bring out the basic difference between charitable activity and the "developmental activities". Need for charity is recognised by all societies and communities. Practically all religions tend to glorify the expression of compassion for the suffering members of the humanity, nay, all living beings. 'Developmental' impulse, on the other hand, is associated with the desire to see improvement in the living conditions by bettering the social organisation as well as its material base. Most of the voluntary organisations working in the developmental field combine the concern born of compassion and the desire to see an improvement in the status of the underprivileged and the suffering at the level of the individuals and their communities.

Probably the best integral articulation of the two concerns may be found in Gandhiji who advocated the empowerment of the rural masses through constructive work, moral and cultural rejuvenation and appropriate improvements in the rural crafts and rural markets. His idea was that improvements in rural crafts would enhance rural self-sufficiency and thus reduce, if not abolish, large pockets of rural poverty. Improved "rural economy" would also tend to strengthen the village communities. At the same time, he was also conscious of the need to fight against the institution of untouchability in the Hindu society and the need for establishing decentralised governance by the local communities through their own traditional institutions of self-governance. The unjust elements in these institutions needed to be eliminated. But this was to be accomplished through non-violent struggles of the oppressed for equality. He was of the firm view that only decentralised systems of management would be able to bring about and sustain such a society. In contradistinction to Gandhi, Nehru's vision of the "just and egalitarian society", emphasised the role of the State in development through sponsoring science and technology institutions, as well as creating an industrial base within the country. Such an approach tended to emphasise centralised modes of development and led to an increased role for the State. However, in the first-two decades after independence the inefficiencies of the State were forcing many to rethink. The growth of the voluntary sector, which in India occurred mainly during the 70s and 80s, was partly a response to the growing disenchantment with the State. The process of disenchantment with the State and the polity began in, in fact, the 60s, when a large number of young people took to the path of radical protest, but, by the end of the 60s, there was a realisation that the way of the "revolution" was not only difficult but could also be counter-productive. The state of the affairs in the communist countries, had already begun to show the hollowness of the claim that State, in the hands of the 'parties of the proletariate' could indeed bring about an end to inequity and oppression. May be the true alternative was in constructive work? In the 70s, a number of funding agencies began to look for channelling their funds through non-governmental organisations, since the funds allocated to the State were not reaching the beneficiaries, but were getting 'eaten-up' by the State itself. Thirdly, even within the political system itself there was an increasing awareness that the State run systems were not as effective as some of the voluntary groups, which used innovative ways to motivate the beneficiaries, and got maximum benefits from the developmental funds. In fact, the establishment of CAPART in the early 70s was itself a recognition of the effectiveness of the voluntary sector.

Most of the 'development experts' had begun to accept that while the State was necessary to provide financial assistance to development agencies, an alternative system was required because of the 'relative failure' of the State's development agencies. The major points of criticism of the State were:

1. The government departments tended to have a top-down-approach, dominated by the bureaucratic tendency towards centralized management, and were insufficiently sensitive to the wide variety of problems of the local levels;
2. State agencies tended to be subject to political manipulation and were, therefore, an easy prey to corrupt practices; and
3. Powerful people in the villages tended to view, 'all that comes from the State' as essentially meant for themselves. The real, intended beneficiaries—the weaker sections—did not realise that what was being 'stolen' from the State resources was in fact "their" resources. The alienation of the common masses from the State was complete.

As opposed to the "State based" developmental work, the voluntary agencies had the following advantages that:

1. most of the voluntary organisations were infused with an idealistic spirit. This was seen firstly in the Christian and some non-Christian (i.e., Ramakrishna Mission) missionary workers and secondly, in the Gandhian and neo-Gandhian workers (e.g., Satish Das Gupta, Anna Saheb Hazare and Bunker Roy);
2. the commitment to the cause of the welfare of the people was personal and direct, at least as far as the leaders were concerned. This was communicated to the middle level whole-time and part-time grass-roots voluntary workers;
3. most of the voluntary organisations started with limited number of problem areas which they felt to be within their competence to tackle. They could, thus, evolve strategies of most effective interventions and in turn, gather enough funds to carry out their programmes. In due course, they extended their operations in other areas. However, their successes in the new areas were not

always as spectacular; and

4. the major advantage with the voluntary sector organisations was their flexibility. The hiring and firing of people could be done by leaders, depending on their control over their own organisations. The red-tape of the bureaucracy did not cripple the dynamism of the leadership. Thus, effectiveness could be much greater.

While we recount the advantages of the voluntary sector, we would also not like to over-emphasise their achievements. To some extent, their achievements were there also because of the higher levels of resources invested in their programmes, as compared to the resources invested by the States in their programmes. This apart, a large number of VO based programmes also became gigantic, over a period of time, resulting in the creation of VO bureaucracies. This, in turn, increased the distance between the top leadership and the grass-roots workers. The voluntary sector, has, since recent times, become acutely conscious of the growing ills of gigantism. Ways are being evolved to create new smaller organisations, which can call upon the help of their larger sister organisations. Another important development in the VO sector is the realisation, that, in the ultimate analysis these organisations are rarely able to mobilise their own funds and have to, therefore, depend mostly on either government funds or solicit funds from the richer funding organisations in the western countries. Thus, there is a danger that some VOs may become ends in themselves rather than the instruments of people's well-being.

Fortunately, for the VO sector, the level of idealism has remained fairly high; and this, in turn, has made most organisations to seek policy level reflections from the academic community. These interactions often take place at the instance of the research institutes as well as foreign funding organisations. Gradually, the networking between different VOs and policy level discussions have become a regular part of the life of most of the active developmental agencies. What is of special interest to us is the fact of an increasing involvement of NGOs in some research activity. Some of the organisations such as Participatory Research in Asia (PRIA), and SEARCH (Bangalore) as well as ICRA (Bangalore) regularly conduct research. The funding organisations such as HIVOS, Action Aid, NOVIB, Oxfam and SDC also sponsor policy level surveys and research. The research programmes help them to be more effectively involved in policy levels.

Since 1980s, participatory research methods have become a regular tool kit with many of the VOs to identify problem areas and mobilise village level support for developmental activities. These methods are now being disseminated by some of the VOs to the applied research Institutes.

II

Way back in 1973, Dr. V.K.R.V. Rao, the founder of ISEC, delivered a key-note address at the Silver Jubilee celebrations of the Indian Council of Social Welfare. In this he highlighted the importance of the voluntary agencies. To quote here: "voluntary agencies have a vital role to play in making social development programmes and agencies function in the desired directions" (1973:6). He felt that the voluntary organisations should be involved in restoring 'values in Indian society'. He identified education, adult literacy, health, family planning, social welfare and housing as areas where the voluntary agencies could effectively collaborate with the State agencies. Dr. V.K.R.V. Rao ridiculed many of the developmental programmes which appeared good on paper but were, in effect, a waste of precious national resources. He said that "the whole process of rural development we have embarked upon may well be described as a 'rural do gooder movement' planned by government and run by its army of bureaucratic personnel, with all the accompanying ills of political patronage, leakages in flows, influence of local vested interests and passivity of the beneficiaries" (1984:2). The rural poor, according to Rao, were developing a 'Bakshish-mentality' and continued dependence on '*ma-bap sarkar*' rather than a feeling of pride and dignity which could have been born of their own quest for self-reliance. For him, participative rural development had to be ultimately based upon the "organisation of the rural poor as well as their direct participation in the development activities". He also felt that to achieve this "we have to bring in voluntary organisations and dedicated and socially motivated workers and institutions into the picture". He was very conscious of the fact that the village community was no longer an emotionally united whole. However, he was also aware that there were some aspects of life which could bring the village communities together. These, basically, were—children and cultural activities. Thus, dramas, theatres, music and games, as well as primary and secondary educational institutions, should be the focal points to bring the village communities together. Their presence in the village could help to increase the consciousness of positive secularism, social harmony and regard for human dignity within the local communities.

The leadership of the Institute had continued to show considerable interest in the broader policy aspects of the voluntary sector. A more recent paper of Srinivas and Aurora (1994) has brought out the role of non-governmental organisations in the context of the on-going structural adjustment policies. After reviewing the centralising tendencies of the States, which had encouraged large scale bureaucratization and criminalisation of politics, the paper has highlighted the capacities of voluntary organisations in mobilising the women and natural resources of the village communities through decentralised grass-roots action. A reference has also been made to the importance of credit associations or '*Sanghas*' which had been playing a significant role in mobilising the village folk, in general, and village women, in particular. Through these *Sanghas* the credit mobilisation had generally led to the establishment of group discussions amongst women on various problems faced by them, identification of their felt needs and the emergence of action programmes to solve group and village level problems. The authors state that "these models of organisation by-pass the bureaucratic procedures of government in performing developmental and welfare functions. Because of the flexibility of these organisations, they are able to respond to local people's needs as well as the manner in which they are to be met" (Srinivas and Aurora 1994: 21).

In another study (Aurora *et al.*, 1994), the role of voluntary organisations in rural development has been discussed in the context of theory, history and practice of voluntary organisations. The two substantive chapters of this monograph deal with the theory of voluntarism and its praxis as displayed in the case studies of five innovative voluntary organisations in South India. Historically, voluntarism is shown to be linked with two kinds of broader social concerns, namely, the concern for the sufferings of the humanity and the concern for struggle against oppressive social order. The voluntary movement has tended to integrate these two concerns. By their very nature, voluntary societies, dealing with development, tend to critically view the role of the State and act as the instruments of the civil society. In India, the VOs, despite their scepticism about the State, have had to work with the agencies of the State. State too seems to have realised their importance, particularly for demonstrating innovative 'models of development programmes'. A kind of symbiotic relationship is thus evolving between the State system and the 'voluntary sector'. This trend has found its advocates both amongst those who espouse reduction in the State's involvement in the 'social sectors', as well as those who clamour for greater social responsibility of the State in tackling the problems of social development (i.e., in education, health, food security etc.,).

III

A number of scholars in ISEC have studied the role of voluntary organisations from the point of view of their own discipline and problem foci. These include such areas as environment, health, rural credit, employment, decentralisation, welfare of women and weaker sections, and sericulture development.

M.V. Nadkarni (1994) examines in detail the role of VOs in 'greening' India. Environment movements try to generate awareness of environmental issues and eco-development. In India, they have played a far more vigorous role as protest movements, such as the Narmada Bachao Andolan and the Chipko and Appiko movements. M.V. Nadkarni also refers to some of the movements which have been involved in constructive activities such as social forestry, and joint forest management. These movements have invariably achieved their momentum through the participation of a very large number of voluntary organisations. The NGO involvement has generated a more critical evaluation of the development process itself and a search for sustainable alternatives. The struggles carried out by NGOs in India was instrumental in reversing the unsustainable use of natural resources for commercial purposes at least in some areas and also in improving the access of the local people to natural resources. "The flexibility, eagerness to be responsive to and work with people, environment-friendliness etc., as well as instances of their own success have aroused high expectations about VOs". He has stated that "ultimately the test of success of a VO consists in whether it enables the people to be self-reliant through their own organisation and efforts, so that even if the VOs leave the area, people's efforts can go on unaffected" (1994:40). M.V. Nadkarni cautions the VOs to make sure that their influence is not needlessly lost due to an obscurantist and purely negative attitude towards the development programmes of the government.

Another study (Mallik 1994) compares the role of VOs with that of two other types of local organisations namely, government-engineered local organisations (GONGOs) and traditional people's organisations in the context of the management of common property resources in the State of Orissa. The study shows that the VOs alone cannot be effective in bringing about much rural development unless there is the mobilisation of the local community as well. She suggests that within the village communities, there have been and still are traditional committees (*Samiti*) with specific role of regulating the use of forest resources. The NGOs can be successful in extending the role of these *samitis* by mobilising them for further developing the forest resources.

D. Rajasekhar's (1996) study deals with the problems and prospects of group lending in NGO credit programmes. Based on field level data from nine NGOs spread across the country, he argues that although pre-conditions for successful group lending did not exist, these groups survived because of certain strategies such as placing the responsibility of identifying the beneficiaries upon the local groups. Thus placing the moral authority of the group behind the process. The analysis suggests that if NGOs can positively influence savings mobilisation, scale up their programmes and provide support to the poor in their income generation activities, they can promote the objectives of equity and participation irrespective of their size and heterogeneity.

S.N. Sangita (1990) examines the role of VOs in self-employment programme for rural youth. He has taken up TRYSEM for special attention. The study is based on a survey conducted in 1985 in the four districts of Karnataka. The districts selected were Dakshina Kannada, Dharwad, Gulbarga and Kolar. Altogether three blocks were selected from each one of these districts for identifying a final sample of 178 respondents representing government, voluntary organisations, co-operative societies and a few private organisations. Some of the critical aspects of the report are as follows: firstly, in many cases no systematic attempt was made to identify the beneficiaries through well planned household surveys; secondly, often no effort "was made to ascertain the attitude and interest of the beneficiaries during selection". At the same time, the schemes that were given over to the voluntary organisations were found to be "quite innovative and effective". Before inviting applications from eligible candidates, the voluntary organisation usually conducted motivation camps. On the whole the study finds that the voluntary organisations had many advantages over the government and private organisations in implementing this programme.

In the Population Research Centre of the Institute, a study has been recently conducted on the role of non-governmental organisations in promoting reproductive health in Karnataka (Veeramatha 1996). The study reviews the activities of four voluntary organisations working in Karnataka in the field of reproductive health care and counselling. These organisations are Family Planning Association of India, Parivara Seva Samstha, HOPE World-wide and SAMUHA. The study indicates that VOs have the potential to complement government efforts towards the achievement of demographic goals and improvement of the health status of the poor people. The study attributes the success of the programme conducted through the NGOs to the following: (a) adoption of 'beyond family planning' approach; (b) integrated package of MCH and family planning with general health and educational programmes; and (c) ensuring health service facilities at the doorstep of the people through various channels.

In a collection of essays edited by Rajasekhar, Bhat and Webster (1995), based on a workshop conducted at ISEC, the role of NGDOs in decentralised governance have been examined. Below we present brief comments on each one of the papers presented in this volume. The conceptual approach of the workshop has been elaborated in the paper by Webster. Webster proposes that the VOs should adopt a dual track approach, one facilitating the target group to participate in the developmental projects and the other to lobby with the State to change its policy environment. Kirsten Westergaard, in her paper on NGDOs and the Decentralised Government in Bangladesh, brings out the important role which the NGOs are playing in Bangladesh. They facilitate the rural development far more successfully than the States development agencies which suffer from excessive bureaucratization and centralised decision-making. However, the NGDOs are totally dependent on foreign funding and are, therefore, finding problems of dependency on resources which cannot be considered sustainable in the long run. In the paper on "NGDOs, Panchayat Raj Institutions (PRIs) and People's Empowerment", Bhat discusses the possibility of a symbiotic relationship between the voluntary sector and the grass-roots panchayat organisations. In order to facilitate the link-up between the two, Bhat specially emphasises, increased space in policy making processes for the NGDOs. He feels that the sensitivity to the problems of the poor is reflected in the policies if the NGDOs are involved at the policy levels as well. He does not rule out the possibility of tension and conflict in the development process, particularly where the grass-roots organisations face the governmental bureaucracies as equal participants in decision-making. The NGDOs should avoid total cooption within the politico-bureaucratic system and constantly remember that the interests of the poor need to be protected through struggles, dialogues as well as constructive work. The paper by Rajasekhar "NGDOs, People and Decentralised Government in Karnataka" raises the question of sustainability of PRIs in Karnataka. While the leadership of the PRIs comes and goes, the continuity of the development has to be maintained. Unless there is a heightened awareness and participation of the local people in the total process such a continuity cannot be expected merely through the establishment of the PRIs. The paper by Anitha and Gayathri, 'Training Initiatives for Gram Panchayat Members in Karnataka: Some

Issues' has gone into some of the factors that necessitated the provision of training to members. Another paper by Rajasekhar and Nair 'Networks amongst NGDOs in Karnataka' examines the role of networking among NGDOs. The authors conclude that some of the active networks in the State have democratic set-ups and have established good rapport with the government officials.

There are a few studies on the role of VOs in the empowerment of women and weaker sections. A study by Shantha Mohan and Usha Ramkumar (1993) has dealt with the problems of education and social change amongst rural women. The authors have chosen to focus on Mahila Samakhya programme launched by the Department of Education, Ministry of Human Resource Development. This micro-study, conducted in Ullahalli village in Nanjangud taluk of Mysore District, Karnataka, investigates the organisational structure of the Mahila Sanghas and their effectiveness in promoting women's welfare and empowerment. These people's organisations have been organised by the government department itself, (hence the term—GONGO). The organisations have a high degree of flexibility of operation and at the same time maintains close contact with the implementing agencies. The key functionaries in the organisation are the *Sahayakis* (animators) and *Sahayoginis* (facilitators). These two functionaries are identified by the group of women beneficiaries and therefore, have the status of natural leaders. The study finds the GONGO strategy an effective tool for empowering women. G.K. Karanth (1995) identifies the importance of NGOs for providing adequate support to the depressed communities. He finds that the NGO support to the weaker sections in the rural areas has been activated through saving-groups. While some of these groups are involved in agriculture, others have been organised to provide the weaker sections with market support structures.

One of the major involvements of the Sociology Unit of the Institute has been in the area of beneficiary assessment of the National Sericulture Project (NSP), funded by the World Bank. This programme covers three traditional sericulture States, namely, Karnataka, Andhra Pradesh and Tamil Nadu. In the organisation of the beneficiary assessment programme, ISEC has also been given a coordinating role whereby the other research institutions involved throughout India meet annually at Bangalore to review the researches done by them. A large number of studies have emerged out of the beneficiary assessment of the Sericulture Project. Out of these, there are five studies which have specially focused on the role of voluntary organisations in the sericulture development. The first of the studies (Acharya *et al.*, 1992) is based on an intensive village survey of Vijilapuram, a multi-caste village in Ramakuppam mandal of Andhra Pradesh. The study brings out a number of problems faced by the farmers in Sericulture such as disease of mulberry leaves and silk worms. The study focuses on the part played by some of the NGOs e.g. GRASS in organising the weaker sections. This NGO has taken up programmes to organise Mahila Savings and Credit Cooperatives. Other voluntary organisations have helped in the development of groundwater resources by introducing borewell technology, organising community irrigation for weaker sections and have motivated the farmers to take up mulberry and silk worm rearing. The provision of credit at lower rates is a crucial strategy of the NGOs. Women's Sanghas are preferred because they show better results than men's Sanghas.

Another paper (Gregory, Parthasarathy and Aurora) on "NGOs, Sericulture and Development" was presented at the International Conference on Sericulture in 1994. The paper discusses the criteria for the selection of the NGOs for the sericulture programme. Implementation of criteria for selection is a crucial step in the whole process of involvement of NGOs in the NSP. While one cannot find fault with the criteria itself, its implementation leaves much to be desired. For example, according to the criteria, the selected NGO should be a registered body; that it should be working within the project area; it should have a good reputation, and it should particularly promote the participation of women and weaker sections and possess the infrastructure—or the ability to establish one—for the sericulture promotion programme in the villages. The paper brings out that many of the failures of the NGOs have been due to the inadequate infrastructure and technical expertise with the NGOs. The NGOs often do not have regular interaction with the DOS (Department of Sericulture). Some of the NGOs are big and successful, but since 'sericulture development' is only one of their programmes they cannot afford to give high priority to the sericulture project especially when they realise that they do not have much in the project for themselves. The bureaucratic handling of funds is particularly galling for many of the NGOs.

The three studies conducted in Andhra Pradesh, Karnataka and Tamil Nadu (Parthasarathy and Sundaravalli, 1994; Parthasarathy and Gregory, 1994; and, Parthasarathy and Krishnappa, 1994) also present similar results. In all the three States, the NGOs are relatively ineffective in either developing the sericulture activities or in improving the economic conditions of women through sericulture. Often, this failure is in spite of the fact that they are comparatively successful in non-sericulture activities.

It is this success in other areas which had earlier influenced the Department of Sericulture (DOS) to involve these NGOs in sericulture. But, the conditions in sericulture are such that a larger measure of expertise (which the NGOs do not possess) and motivation are required to carry out sericulture; and they also have to face several conditions which the DOS stipulate. Such conditions include the fact that NGOs are expected to raise their own funds for administrative purposes, and present frequent project reports before the release of funds. This makes them spend considerable time on report writing, resulting in delays in the release of funds. As of now, most NGOs do not want to be associated in sericulture activities, nor are the DOS interested in including them either. The mutual disillusionment appears to have been a consequence of inadequate planning on the part of DOS, and heightened expectations, particularly financial, from the NGOs.

IV

Until 1993, the focus of ISEC's involvement with the NGOs was restricted to the role of 'outside observers' of the NGO movement and their programmes. This academic interest was taken a step further in 1993 when a project was taken up by a team of ISEC faculty—Policy Research and Voluntary Action. This project initiated direct collaboration between the research Institute and the NGOs. The major focus of the study was to assess the impact of structural adjustment policies, particularly on the rural poor (Aurora *et al.*, 1996). The project itself was funded by HIVOS, a well-known Dutch humanitarian funding organisation. The strategy of research, on the one hand, and action, on the other hand, was finalised through a series of workshops held at ISEC between the NGOs, the NGO funding organisations, and, the academic institutions including ISEC faculty. On the research side an inter-disciplinary team was built-up to conduct surveys of 30 villages spread across 15 districts in the four southern States. Two surveys were conducted. The first one in 1994 covered a total of 4,300 households and the second survey was conducted in 1995 covering 1,500 sample households from the same villages. All the surveys were done with the active participation and collaboration of fifteen (15) voluntary organisations from the fifteen selected districts. The training of the NGO workers was one of the major tasks of the research team. Besides training the NGO workers in the survey methodology, the ISEC team also conducted their training in participatory rural appraisal (PRA) methods. The PRA exercises were, in addition, useful for the research purposes. Besides PRA and field surveys, eleven grass-root level workshops were also conducted in collaboration with the NGO partners. These grass-roots workshops provided an opportunity to the NGOs for not only discussing the problems of the structural adjustment policies at the grass-root level but also gave them an occasion to extend their networks within their own districts. The draft reports of the project have been presented in a national seminar. As part of this project, a detailed analysis of the activities of the 15 NGO partners and their role in evolving safety-nets to safeguard the interest of the rural poor has been studied (Sekher, 1996).

Another collaborative study (Reddy and Rajasekhar, 1996) provides information on various programmes and government funds to NGOs by the central government. It also provides information on objectives, activities, eligibility criteria, financial assistance and procedural details of various government programmes, for which the NGOs could get government assistance. The study overcomes the weak interface between the government and the NGOs due to lack of sufficient information on the various programmes of the government.

V

There is an evolving pattern of the Institute's involvement in the applied areas of social concern. This is reflected in not only in the large number of applied research projects undertaken with very close linkages with the action agencies but also Institute's emergence as a focal point for policy level thinking as well as training of grass-root functionaries. For example, an on-going training programme of the Zilla Panchayat members of Karnataka is one of the responsibilities entrusted by the State government to ISEC. Again, the interest in the NGOs is reflected by a large number of Ph.D. students choosing to work on the broad area of NGOs and development.

REFERENCES

Acharya J., E.N. Ashok Kumar and D.V. Gopalappa (1992) *NGOs, Development and Sericulture: A Study of a Backward Cluster in Ramakuppam Mandal of A.P.* A Beneficiary Assessment Report. Bangalore: ISEC. Mimeo.

Aurora, G.S, V.S. Parthasarathy and V. Ramaswamy (1994) *Voluntary Organisations and Rural Development*. Bangalore: ISEC. Mimeo.

Aurora, G.S. *et al.* (1996) *Structural Adjustment and the Rural Poor.* A draft report of the PRAVA Project. Bangalore: ISEC. Mimeo.

Gregory, S., V.S. Parthasarathy and G.S. Aurora (1996) NGOs, Sericulture and Development. In *Global Silk Scenario-2001*, Proceedings of the International Conference on Sericulture-94, Central Silk Board and Swiss Development Co-operation. New Delhi: Oxford and IBH Publishing Co. Pvt. Ltd.

Karanth, G.K. (1995) Scheduled Castes and Social Mobility: An Agenda for NGOs. A paper presented at the *Third National Seminar on SAP, NGOs and the Rural Poor*, organised by the ISEC, February 28-March 1,

Mallik, Madhushree (1994) *Local Organisation and Common Property Land Resources with reference to Social Forestry in Orissa*. A Ph.D. Thesis (ISEC). Bangalore: Bangalore University.

Mohan, Shantha and Usha Ramkumar (1995) *Education and Social Change among Rural Women: A Micro Study*. Bangalore: ISEC. Mimeo.

Nadkarni, M.V. (1994) Voluntary Organizations in Greening India. *Studies in Third World Societies*, Publication No. 51.

Parthasarathy, V.S. and S. Gregory (1994) *NGOs and Sericulture Development: A Case Study of Tamil Nadu*. A Beneficiary Assessment Report. Bangalore: ISEC. Mimeo.

Parthasarathy, V.S. and B.L. Krishnappa (1994) *NGOs and Sericulture Development: A Case Study of Karnataka*. A Beneficiary Assessment Report. Bangalore: ISEC. Mimeo.

Parthasarathy, V.S. and Sundaravalli (1994) *NGOs and Sericulture Development: A Case Study of Andhra Pradesh*. A Beneficiary Assessment Report. Bangalore: ISEC. Mimeo.

Rajasekhar, D. (1996) Problems and Prospects of Group Lending in NGO Credit Programmes in India, *Savings and Development*, 1.

Rajasekhar, D., M.K. Bhat and Neil Webster (eds.) (1995) *People Centered Rural Development—NGDOs and Decentralised Government*. Bangalore: Bangalore Consultancy Office.

Rao, V.K.R.V. (1973) Social Development during the Seventies and the Role of Voluntary Agencies. A Key-note address delivered at the *ICSW Silver Jubilee Celebrations Workshop on Social Development*, Indian Council of Social Welfare, held in collaboration with Canadian Council on Social Development, at Madras, January 27-31. Mimeo.

Rao, V.K.R.V. (1984) Role of Voluntary Agencies in Rural Development. *Pigmy Economic Review*, 29(12).

Reddy, Narasimha N.L. and D. Rajasekhar (1996) *Development Programmes and NGOs—A Guide on Central Government Programmes for NGOs in India*. Bangalore: Bangalore Consultancy Office, and The Hague: NOVIB.

Sangita, S.N (1990) Self-employment Programme for Rural Youth: The Role of Non-governmental Organisations (NGOs). *Management Review (IIMB)*, 5(2).

Sekher, T.V. (1996) Voluntary Organisations and "Safety Nets": Experiences of 15 NGO Partners. A paper presented at the *Fourth National Seminar on SAP, NGOs and Rural Poor*, ISEC, Bangalore, Feb. 22-24.

Srinivas, M.N. and G.S. Aurora (1994) From Structural Adjustment to Structural Change. A paper presented at the *Round Table on Economic Liberalisation: Challenge and Response*, ISEC, Bangalore, September 10-12.

Veeramatha, C.S. (1996) *Role of Non-governmental Organisations in promoting Reproductive Health in Karnataka*. Bangalore: ISEC. Mimeo.

INDEX